MYSTERIES OF THE UNKNOWN

INSIDE THE WORLD OF THE STRANGE AND UNEXPLAINED

TIME LIFE BOOKS

NEW YORK

1

22

46

130

112

138

188

196

202

CONTENTS

INTRODUCTION iv

1 **PSYCHICS AND MEDIUMS** 1

2 **TELEKINESIS AND ESP** 22

3 **FUTURE FORETOLD** 46

4 **CURSES** 70

5 **MYSTIC GEOGRAPHY** 84

6 **MYSTERIOUS VANISHINGS** 112

7 **SECRETIVE SOCIETIES** 130

8 **VAMPIRES AND ZOMBIES** 138

9 **GHOSTS AND HAUNTINGS** 154

10 **MORE OR LESS THAN HUMAN** 178

11 **NEAR DEATH EXPERIENCES** 188

12 **WITCHERY** 196

13 **CRYPTOZOOLOGY AND BOTANY** 202

14 **UNNATURAL SCIENCE** 226

15 **ALIENS AND UFOS** 244

INDEX 260

PHOTO CREDITS 264

INTRODUCTION

Humans are nothing if not curious. Ever since we became aware of our surroundings, we have searched the sky, the world around us, and our own minds to understand both nature and its countless contradictions.

This investigation has involved imagination and ingenuity in equal measure. Over the millennia, we have developed sophisticated science and technology to make sense of the cosmos and its inhabitants.

But even with the tools and brainpower at our disposal, some things continue to defy explanation—or at least a single explanation. Certain abilities, events, and creatures just don't fit into the set of rules we've come to rely on. Can people read minds? Is there life after death? What could cause thousands of fish to rain from the sky, ships to vanish without a trace, multiton rocks to move across the desert? Are vampires real? How do we explain the inexplicable?

In *Mysteries of the Unknown*, the editors of Time-Life Books explore some of the universe's strangest phenomena, probing their origins, history, plausibility, and influence on our culture. Certainly these pages contain unsettling real-life stories and incredible facts. They also shed light on the lively debate among believers, scientists, and mystics. But *Mysteries of the Unknown* does not attempt to settle arguments or draw definitive conclusions. Instead, it seeks to spark the imagination and to open the mind. It takes aim at the most essential question of all: Are we alone in the universe?

Some readers have already begun this journey. Almost half of Americans say ghosts exist and 22 percent say they have actually seen or felt the presence of one, according to a recent poll. More than three-quarters of us said we believe in the afterlife. When researchers from the University of Oxford recently analyzed the genetic material of the creatures we know as Sasquatch or Bigfoot, they found the beasts were related to dogs and bears, not humanoids. But they were not discouraged. "Absence of proof is never proof of absence," said Bryan Sykes, the human genetics professor who led the study.

Whether you believe in the supernatural, in life on other planes or planets—or in Bigfoot—there are wondrous things to ponder in *Mysteries of the Unknown*. It is filled with amazing tales and images that at the very least challenge rational explanation. Now, turn the page. Come along and explore with us.

Crystals are said to have a special energy that connects them to the spiritual realm.

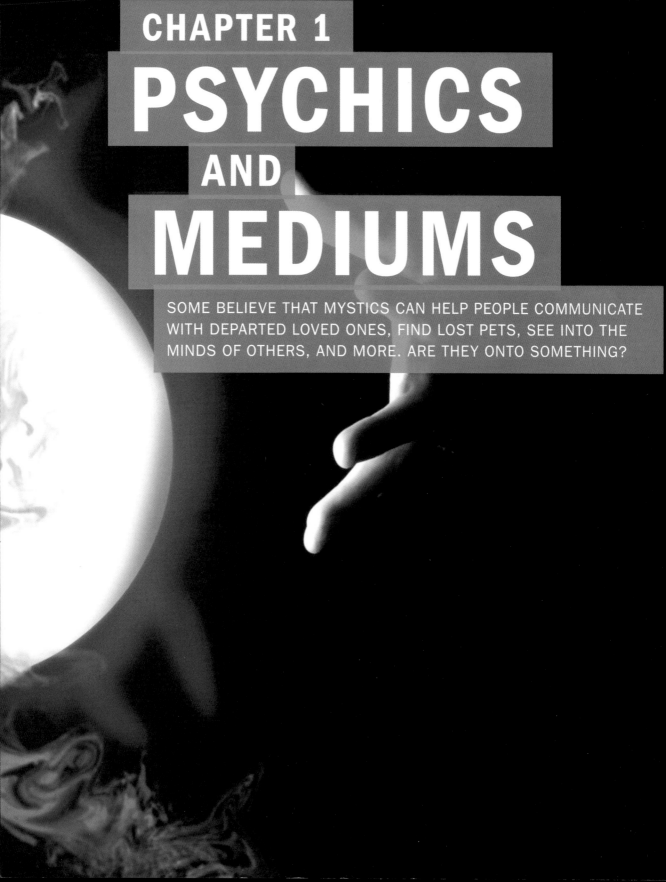

CHAPTER 1

PSYCHICS AND MEDIUMS

SOME BELIEVE THAT MYSTICS CAN HELP PEOPLE COMMUNICATE WITH DEPARTED LOVED ONES, FIND LOST PETS, SEE INTO THE MINDS OF OTHERS, AND MORE. ARE THEY ONTO SOMETHING?

SEERS OF
THE BIBLE

THE OLD AND NEW TESTAMENTS ARE RIFE WITH PROPHETS, THOUGH BELIEVERS ARE WARNED TO BE WARY OF FALSE ONES.

A painting of the Prophet Isaiah, c. 1525.

Seers, psychics, and prophets make regular appearances in the Bible, and when the characters in question are legitimate, the Good Book embraces them. Yet the text is quite clear about the dangers of consulting false prophets. In the Old Testament, for example, Moses warns against divination, interpreting omens, and contacting the dead "for all that do these things are an abomination unto the Lord." The problem with such actions, believers say, is that false prophets cannot speak for the Lord, even if they pretend to. Instead, they seek their information from human spirits and other lesser entities who might even be Satan in disguise. From a strictly practical perspective, these false prophets also threaten a religion's authority and can erode its power.

The Perils of False Prophets

The case of Saul, the first King of Israel, provides an excellent example of the woe that can befall someone who

MESSAGES FROM THE MAJORS

The books referred to as the Major Prophets of the Old Testament are those of Isaiah, Jeremiah, Ezekiel, and Daniel—not because they are more important than the other sections, but because they're so long. Each of them includes numerous prophesies.

PROPHET	Isaiah	Jeremiah	Ezekiel	Daniel
WHO WAS HE?	Son of an elite Jewish family	Son of a Jewish priest	Descendant of the prophet Aaron	Either a pseudonym for later scholars, or a Jewish noble exiled in Babylon, depending on interpretation
PREDICTED	Birth of Jesus	Fall of Jerusalem	The Jews' return to Israel	Continuing miseries in Israel for 70 more weeks
BOOK/VERSE	Isaiah 7:14	Jeremiah 21:10	Ezekiel 36:24	Daniel 9:24
THE MESSAGE FROM GOD	"Behold, a virgin shall conceive and bear a son, and shall call his name Immanuel."	"[This city] shall be given into the hand of the king of Babylon, and he shall burn it with fire."	"For I will take you from among the heathen, and gather you out of all countries, and will bring you into your own land."	"Seventy weeks are determined upon thy…holy city, to finish the transgression, and to make an end of sins."
NOTES	Only the first part of the Book of Isaiah is believed to have been written by Isaiah himself.	Jeremiah sternly warned against false prophets with more optimistic predictions.	Ezekiel and Jeremiah were contemporaries.	The "70 weeks" is interpreted to mean 490 years.

Ghost of Samuel Called Before Saul by the Witch of Endor (1668), by Salvator Rosa.

No one has been raptured up to heaven yet, but some believers continue to hope.

WILL THERE BE A RAPTURE?

Christian believers say it's not a question of "if" the rapture will come, but "when."

In the first book of Thessalonians in the New Testament, the apostle Paul writes a letter in which he describes a profound forthcoming event. The Lord, he writes, will descend from heaven and His followers "shall be caught up...in the clouds, to meet the Lord in the air: and so shall we ever be with the Lord." According to some branches of Christianity, this literal departure of the chosen from Earth to Heaven, known as the Rapture, is certain to take place. But when? The exact date has lately been predicted to be in 1992, 1994, and twice in 2011. So far, no Rapture. But apparently these errors, too, are prophesied in the Bible. "But of that day and hour knoweth no man, no, not the angels of heaven, but my Father only": Matthew 24:36.

consults a psychic. Saul tries to decide what to do about the encroaching Philistine army, but his mentor, the prophet Samuel, has died and Saul no longer has a trusted counselor. Desperate for advice, Saul disguises himself and visits a medium known as the Witch of Endor, instructing her to summon Samuel's ghost. Samuel appears but is angry that Saul has disobeyed God and spoken with a witch. He predicts that the King and his sons will die the next day—which they do, in a battle with the Philistines.

The Word of the Lord

At the same time, the Bible is rife with true prophets who receive and spread the word of God. Depending on who is counting, there are close to 50 of them, including a few women, such as Miriam, sister of Moses, who prophesied while still a child that her as yet unborn brother would lead the Jews to freedom from Egypt. According to believers, the ultimate test for a true prophet is that the things he or she foretells actually come to pass.

A true prophet also acts in the best interest of the Lord, not out of self-interest. So the prophesies of the Bible tend to be similar in message. Most convey some version of the following messages:

- Stop sinning and worshiping false idols
- The Messiah is coming
- The Messiah is returning
- The End Times are on their way.

As for those who argue that certain Biblical prophesies have not come to pass, believers have only one word to add: *yet.*

THE POETIC PROPHET

NOSTRADAMUS IS SAID TO HAVE PREDICTED EVERYTHING FROM THE GREAT FIRE OF LONDON TO THE KILLING OF JFK.

French royal coat of arms.

Who could have predicted that unassuming Michel de Nostredame, born in 1503 in a small village in southern France, would become one of the most famous seers to ever live?

Better known by the Latinized name Nostradamus, this Frenchman, influential to this day, began his career as a learned man of letters who studied medicine at several universities. He first applied his education to healing the sick and established himself as an apothecary. As the deadly bubonic plague swept through Europe, Nostradamus gained notoriety for

BREAKING THE CODE

Here are some of the prophesies made by Nostradamus and the major world events they are said to have predicted.

	The Prophecy	The Historic Event
1696	Long before such events, Those of the East, by virtue of the (Crescent) moon, In the 17th century will make great conquests. They will nearly subjugate a corner of Russia.	Some believe "East" could refer to the Ottoman Turks, "conquests" to the Balkans, and "Russia" to the land between the Caspian and Black seas. The reference would correlate with Peter the Great wresting control of the Russian port of Azov from the Ottoman Turks.
1789	Before the war comes, The great wall will fall, The King will be executed, his death coming too soon will be lamented. (The guards) will swim in blood, Near the River Seine the soil will be bloodied.	Here, "great wall" could refer to the famous French prison, the Bastille, the "king" to Louis XVI, and the "River Seine" to Paris. Some believe this poem foreshadowed the French Revolution, which was notoriously bloody.
1856	The lost thing is discovered, hidden for many centuries. Pasteur will be celebrated almost as a God-like figure. This is when the moon completes her great cycle, But by others' slanders he shall be dishonored.	What could be hidden for many centuries? Some believe the reference is to bacteria, discovered by French microbiologist Louis Pasteur. His significant contributions to science and medicine included pasteurization and vaccination, but jealous colleagues ridiculed his work.
1940s	Beasts ferocious with hunger will swim across the rivers, greater part of the army will be against Hister. The great one will cause him to be dragged in a cage of iron, when the German infant observes no law.	Is this a reference to Adolph Hitler and World War II? Some have understood "Hister" to mean Hitler and the "German Infant" as the Third Reich. During the war, Germany fought on two fronts, losing both.

his novel approach to treating the disease. Instead of advising popular but dangerous treatments such as bloodletting, he encouraged patients to practice good hygiene, to avoid infected cadavers, and to take a vitamin C–rich pill he made from rosehips. Eventually, Nostradamus moved beyond medicine and began publishing books that offered general advice and forecasts for the coming year. He became known for writing mostly in four-line verses called quatrains, and won a devoted following, even though many of his predictions proved false.

Royal Pain

When Nostradamus suggested in one prophesy that harm might come to the royal family, he caught the attention of the queen, Catherine de' Medici. He was called to join her court in 1555, and asked to draw up horoscopes for her children and to provide advice and counsel based on his special insights. At least one of Nostradamus's early predictions proved startlingly true for Catherine's husband, Henry II.

Nostradamus wrote:

The young lion will overcome the older one,

On the field of combat in a single battle;

He will pierce his eyes through a golden cage,

Two wounds made one, then he dies a cruel death.

In July 1559, King Henry II was killed after a jousting tournament. His opponent, Gabriel Comte de Montgomery, was the young captain of the Scottish Guard regiment in Henry's armed forces. During the fight, Montgomery's lance struck Henry's face shield with such force that a shard of the lance penetrated his head. A second shard bore through his eye. The wound became infected, and Henry suffered for ten days before he died.

Nostradamus

A Rhyme Every Time

Today, Nostradamus is best known for the prophecies he made about what would happen long after his own death, in 1566. Many of the predictions were based on classical Roman and Greek works and medieval writings about the end of the world, as well as on obscure works of Nostradamus's own era, according to historians and literary experts. Some believe his verses foretold the Great Fire of London in 1666, the fall of Napoleon at Waterloo in 1815, the dropping of the atomic bomb in 1945, the assassination of John F. Kennedy in 1963, and many other seismic events. Others dismiss such notions, pointing out that the wording of many of the quatrains are too general and vague to link them to such specific developments.

MOVED BY THE SPIRITS

OOZING ECTOPLASM, RAPPING GHOSTS, AND PSYCHIC FORCES. WELCOME TO 19TH-CENTURY AMERICA.

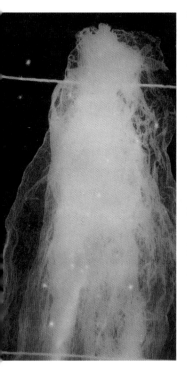

It was conveniently claimed that ectoplasm could be produced only under low light conditions or else the substance would disintegrate.

The mid-19th century was an intellectually fertile yet emotionally trying time in the United States. While new religions, utopian experiments, and strong abolitionist and feminist movements flourished, infant mortality was high. The average lifespan was a brief 50 years, and staggering casualties from the Civil War had plunged the nation into deep, shared grief.

Spiritualism, the belief that spirits of the dead were able to communicate with the living, seemed to offer some hope. For many Americans, the movement appeared to meld aspects of religion with hard evidence of a life beyond. Just as Charles Darwin's theory of evolution had sparked an almost religious faith in science, the spiritualist movement energized a population looking for answers.

Psychic mediums "proved" their abilities to communicate with spirits through levitation—a table seeming to rise on its own, for example—or the phenomenon of *apports*— objects appearing out of thin air. Some mediums reportedly expressed "ectoplasm" from their bodies—a light-colored substance that could take on the physical features of humans in the form of ghostly faces.

The Fox Sisters

The term *spiritualism* was first used in 1848, when Maggie and Kate Fox, two young sisters, claimed to hear rapping noises inside their family's farmhouse in Hydesville, New York.

The girls insisted that the sounds were made by the spirit of a man who had been murdered there before the family moved in. Soon, other spirits began making themselves heard and crowds gathered to watch Maggie and Kate perform. The two became a sensation, touring the world and charging enormous sums to perform in theatres and to privately assist people in communicating with their dearly departed. The Fox sisters fanned the flames that ignited the powerful Spiritualist Movement, which lasted through the early decades of the 20th century.

The Fox sisters.

Mary Todd Lincoln, in a photo by William H. Mumier

MRS. LINCOLN: GRIEVING SPIRITUALIST

Mary Todd Lincoln, wife of President Abraham Lincoln, was an avowed spiritualist who often invited mediums to the White House to try to reach her two deceased sons, Willie and Eddie. Though her husband was skeptical, he also attended the séances.

"Willie lives," Mary wrote in 1863. "He comes to me every night and stands at the foot of the bed with the same sweet adorable smile he always had.... Little Eddie is sometimes with him.... You cannot dream of the comfort this gives me."

After the president's death, Mary Lincoln posed for a photograph in her mourning clothes, hiding her identity from the photographer, William H. Mumler. In the resulting photo, the ghostly presence of a figure resembling Lincoln is seen standing behind her. Coincidentally, Mumler's wife was a medium.

"Spirit photography" was extremely popular and lucrative in the 19th century. However, every spirit photographer who was investigated was revealed to be a fraud, including Mumler — though Mary held on to her belief in the photo.

Scottish medium Daniel Dunglas Home was a 19th-century superstar, famous for levitating and speaking with the dead.

Spiritualist Henry Slade frequently appeared throughout Europe and North America; he was regularly exposed as a fraud. By his death in 1905, he had been thoroughly discredited.

In 1888, Maggie confessed before a live audience that the sisters themselves had produced the raps. She demonstrated by cracking her toe joints to reproduce the sounds.

Ardent spiritualists refused to accept Maggie's confession and she later recanted.

In 1904, a human skeleton was revealed behind a basement wall in the farmhouse where more than 50 years earlier, the young Fox sisters had claimed the spirit of a murdered peddler created mysterious rapping sounds.

Epidemic Delusion

By the late 1880s the spiritualist movement's credibility flagged. Many set about debunking the mediums' claims, including William Benjamin Carpenter, an invertebrate zoologist and physiologist, who described spiritualism as an "epidemic delusion."

Not all of the "ghostbusters" pointed to trickery, however. The well-known chemist and physicist William Crookes postulated that mediums unconsciously stored up psychic forces that were released during trances.

THEY SEE!

MODERN PSYCHICS

PSYCHICS AND MEDIUMS CLAIM TO PEER INTO THE FUTURE AND GRASP REALMS MOST OF US CAN HARDLY IMAGINE.

WHO KNEW?
According to a 2005 Gallup poll, 31 percent of Americans believe in psychic communication and 26 percent believe in clairvoyance.

The words *psychic* and *medium* can call up images of costumed fortune-tellers with crystal balls, tea leaves, and levitating tables. Yet many different types of psychics exist, and believers feel certain that such mystics can help them communicate with departed loved ones, find lost pets, see into the minds of others, and more, while skeptics dismiss psychics as mere entertainers or scam artists.

Psychic techniques and specialties range from séances to dream interpretation, which are used to read the present, probe the past, or predict the future.

IN RECENT MEMORY

Some contemporary psychics have been accused of exploiting followers for their own gain; others have focused on revealing hoaxes; while many say they truly believe they are in contact with supernatural entities. Here's a look.

1985 American ESTHER HICKS starts channeling a being called Abraham. She also translates Abraham's philosophy, which she refers to as the "law of attraction." This is the concept that thoughts attract related actions and events: good thoughts attract beneficial events, and vice versa.

1987 THE NEW AGE MOVEMENT reaches a high point at the Harmonic Convergence, a synchronized worldwide meditation session centered in Sedona, Arizona.

1991 Launch of the PSYCHIC FRIENDS NETWORK, a U.S. company that connects the viewers of its television infomercials with psychics via a 1-900 telephone number. The rate: $3.99 a minute.

1992 THE SKEPTICS SOCIETY publishes the first edition of *Skeptic*, a quarterly academic journal that prints scientific research debunking psychic and paranormal phenomena.

Some clairvoyants say they can use crystal balls to obtain meaningful information.

1998 American television medium **JOHN EDWARD** rises to prominence with the publication of his first book, *One Last Time*. This led to the premiere of his popular Sci-Fi Channel television show, *Crossing Over with John Edward*, in 1999.

1999 Americans **TERRY AND LINDA JAMISON,** "the Psychic Twins," predict there will be terrorist attacks on the World Trade Center and U.S. federal buildings in 2002. (They are off by one year.)

2000 **JAMES UNDERDOWN,** executive director of the anti-paranormal Center for Inquiry, founds the Independent Investigations Group. Its purpose is to investigate psychic and pseudoscientific claims through scientific tests that reveal psychic power to be a sham.

2002 Animal Planet's television show *THE PET PSYCHIC* premieres, starring British intuitive Sonya Fitzpatrick. She facilitates communication between audience members and their living or deceased dogs, cats, and other animals.

2005 The television series *MEDIUM* premieres on NBC, based on the life of Allison Dubois. She claims to be a psychic detective who works in tandem with law enforcement agencies on cases, including that of the so-called Baseline Rapist in Phoenix, Arizona.

2013 Colombian astrologer **RODRIGO RODRIGUEZ ARDILA** predicts the death of Lady Gaga will come soon. He had previously correctly predicted the deaths of Whitney Houston, Amy Winehouse, and Michael Jackson.

Harry Houdini was a master of magic and illusion. He was born Ehrich Weiss, in 1874.

HARRY HOUDINI

VICTORIAN GHOSTBUSTER

IN THE EARLY 1900S, THE FAMOUS ESCAPE ARTIST BEGAN TO DEBUNK SPIRITUALISTS WHO SAID THEY COULD COMMUNICATE WITH THE DEAD.

Harry Houdini was a Hungarian-American magician and illusionist, known during his life—and perhaps even now—as the world's greatest escape artist. He was also deeply interested in spiritualism, demonstrating both profound ambivalence and intense fascination toward it. As an illusionist, he performed all over the world, freeing himself from straitjackets while under water or dangling from buildings and squirming out of handcuffs while inside locked caskets. For decades, the question of whether or not spiritualism was as much of an illusion as his feats compelled him to investigate the phenomenon.

Houdini's boyhood fascination with magic and his curiosity about the afterlife and the belief that the dead could communicate with the living led him to spiritualism. "I am not a skeptic," he said during a 1926 radio address. "I am willing to believe and my mind is wide open." He amassed a large and unique library on spiritualism and wrote his own book entitled *A Magician Among the Spirits.*

Séance Busting!

It was after World War I when Houdini did an about-face, becoming a hardcore skeptic. He'd attended thousands of séances and could duplicate the activities he'd experienced in the darkened parlors: tables floating on their own, objects appearing from nowhere, ghostly faces emerging from darkness.

It enraged him that mediums took advantage of grief-stricken families who had lost loved ones during World War I by claiming to carry messages from the other side. He made it his mission to go after the fakes, referring to it as his "adventure."

Houdini began attending séances in disguise, accompanied by reporters and police officers. At key moments he would leap up from his chair, reveal his identity, and expose the fraud. He began to debunk psychics and mediums during touring shows, offering $10,000 to anyone who could demonstrate spiritualist powers that he was unable to re-create.

Elegant séances attracted wealthy patrons—and sometimes, predatory mediums.

11

The writer Sir Arthur Conan Doyle feuded with Houdini.

THE FINAL WORD

The story of Houdini and spiritualism continued after his death, but perhaps not the way either he or spiritualists imagined.

→ Following Houdini's death in 1926, Sir Arthur Conan Doyle published an article claiming that Houdini had used supernatural powers to achieve many of his stunts. He accused Houdini of intentionally blocking the powers of mediums he was debunking.

→ According to Houdini's obituary in the *New York Times*, the master illusionist asserted that "there is and can be no such thing as suspension of natural laws; that everything done by fakir, medium, clairvoyant, horologist, palmist can be explained in terms of physics, chemistry, and psychology manipulated with agility."

→ Houdini was not a believer, yet he told his wife that if there was an afterlife, he would contact her from beyond the grave. He never did.

Houdini sits at a Margery box, which he designed to reveal fraudulent mediums by limiting their range of motion.

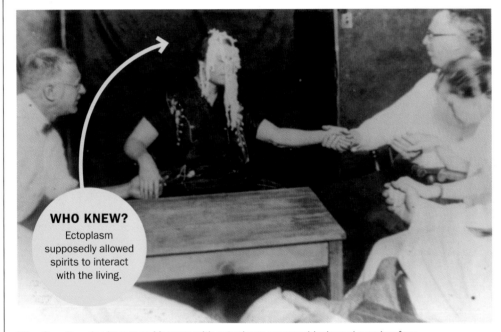

WHO KNEW?
Ectoplasm supposedly allowed spirits to interact with the living.

Mina Crandon, also known as Margery, with ectoplasm presumably draped over her face.

It Takes a Flimflammer

Perhaps Houdini's best-known effort at debunking involved the medium Mina Crandon, known as Margery. In the 1920s, *Scientific American* magazine offered a $2,500 prize to any medium who could produce a verifiable psychic event. Mina nearly won, until Houdini himself journeyed to her home in Boston, where he observed her and denounced her as a fraud. Houdini described mediums as "vultures who prey on the bereaved."

For Houdini, exposing trickery became a personal crusade, and it was one to which he was well suited. As he told a *Los Angeles Times* interviewer, "It takes a flimflammer to catch a flimflammer."

OUIJA
ADVICE FROM
THE OTHER SIDE

THE BOARD IS MARKETED AS A HARMLESS PASTTIME, BUT MANY
BELIEVE IT ALLOWS PLAYERS TO COMMUNICATE WITH SPIRITS.

Marie Louise de la Ramée

THE NAME GAME

According to one tale, the board itself generated the term *Ouija* when asked its name. However, others say Helen Peters, sister-in-law of the Ouija board's designer, wore a locket with a woman's image and the name "Ouija" above it. Peters admired a popular author and feminist called Ouida, the pen name of Marie Louise de la Ramée (1839–1908); "Ouija" may have been a misreading of Ouida.

In addition to providing a healthy income for thousands of mediums who claimed to communicate with the dead, 19th-century spiritualism offered merchandising opportunities. In 1891, a Pittsburgh shop placed the first newspaper ad for a unique item that would catch on like wildfire, "a mysterious device that answers questions about the past, present, and future with marvelous accuracy": the Ouija board.

Marketed by the Kennard Novelty Company as a game, the Ouija board brought the medium's tool of automatic writing into the comfort and privacy of people's homes. The board is still popular today and is one of the best-selling novelties ever created—outperforming even Monopoly—with tens of millions produced since its introduction.

How to Play

The design of the Ouija board, now produced by Parker Brothers, remains unchanged, featuring the letters of the alphabet and the words *yes, no,* and *good-bye*. A teardrop-shaped device known as a planchette is used to navigate the board. Just ask a question and the planchette will guide you—on its own—to the answer.

An Investigative Tool

While advertised as amusement and recreation, the board was taken seriously by those who hoped to verify links between the known and unknown, the material with the immaterial.

Others, like British physiologist William Benjamin Carpenter, sought to poke holes in such theories. In 1852, Carpenter published a report on the "ideomotor effect"—the body's reflexive subconscious reaction to an idea. In other words, people could be moving the planchette toward the answer they want. Carpenter suggested this principle might be at work in other spiritualist phenomena as well, including table-tilting during séances.

The Ouija board has been a spooky part of American adolescence for more than a century.

OUIJA ON THE SCREEN

The Ouija board has figured in everything from low-budget horror movies to Hollywood blockbusters—and even cartoons.

→ *The Uninvited* (1944) Ray Milland's character buys an old English house where a makeshift Ouija board is used in an impromptu séance.

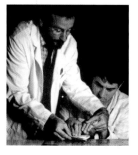

→ *Awakenings* (1990) Robin Williams, as the physician Oliver Sacks, uses a Ouija board to communicate with a catatonic patient played by Robert DeNiro.

→ *What Lies Beneath* (2000) Michelle Pfeiffer and Diana Scarwid wield a KMart Ouija board in a bathroom séance; otherworldly havoc ensues.

WHO IS ON THE OTHER SIDE?

Zozo, Ouija's evil spirit, might not be who you were looking for.

Of all the anecdotal experiences reported by Ouija users, none conjures more fear than encounters with a dark entity named Zozo. Thousands have reported similar details since the board debuted in the late 19th century: Once conjured, Zozo rages with profanity and makes death threats.

Cautionary tales about this so-called demon are shared between Ouija practitioners on paranormal websites. Psychic investigator John Zaffis has been investigating firsthand Zozo accounts for more than 40 years and has said he does not believe Zozo is a demon. Instead, Zaffis sees him as a negative deity such as those found in prebiblical mythologies.

Many feel that the most logical explanation of the Ouija phenomenon—and of encounters with Zozo—is the power of suggestion. Those who are exposed to the stories are more likely to "encounter" Zozo via their own involuntary manipulations of the board.

NEW AGE HEALER

EDGAR CAYCE, WHO HELPED DEVELOP MODERN HOLISTIC MEDICINE, SAID HE COULD PREDICT WORLD EVENTS.

The original Cayce medical facility, the Hospital of Enlightenment in Virginia Beach, Virginia

THE HEALING DIET

The "Father of Holistic Medicine" recommended alternative diets and remedies combined with mental and spiritual work.

The Basic Cayce Diet still has enthusiastic adherents today. Mandating an 80/20 balance between acid and alkaline foods (the distinction is Cayce's), the diet recommends avoiding combining certain foods at meals and excludes lentils, asparagus tips, buttermilk, yogurt, plums, olives, cranberries, and several other items.

A Cayce prescription: "Maintaining an attitude of desiring and expecting to be healed is essential."

Edgar Cayce (1877–1945) was one of the best-known, controversial, and written-about psychics of the 20th century. He gave thousands of private readings to individuals, claimed to see spirits, diagnosed and healed illnesses, and predicted future events—often successfully. Cayce never took payment for his services, considering his powers to be gifts from God that he should use to serve humanity.

Raised on a farm in Kentucky, Cayce began to exhibit psychic abilities during childhood. He claimed to be able to memorize a book by sleeping on top of it, and in his early twenties he discovered that he could put himself into a trance by lying on his back and folding his hands over his chest. This trick earned him the nickname "The Sleeping Prophet."

Cayce the Healer

Cayce gained renown in the early 20th century for diagnosing and treating debilitating physical conditions. He is said to have rid his wife of a potentially fatal case of tuberculosis and to have once treated President Woodrow Wilson for a heart murmur. In 1928, Cayce opened the Hospital of Enlightenment, a healing center in Virginia

Beach, Virginia, where he utilized many of the tools now common in New Age movement, including astrology and healing crystals. In 1910, the *New York Times* wrote about Cayce's remarkable medical knowledge and his skill as a diagnostician, while emphasizing that he'd had no training whatsoever in the field of medicine. Other skeptics pointed out there was no data documenting how successful—or not—Cayce's treatments were.

Predicting World Events

Cayce is believed to have predicted significant world events, including the stock market crash of 1929, the assassination of President John F. Kennedy, and the social upheavals of the 1960s. Not all of his predictions have come to pass, but enough of them have to impress believers and skeptics alike.

Cayce undermined his credibility with public commentary about the Lost Continent of Atlantis, a mythical island that he believed once floated in the Atlantic Ocean. Supposedly inhabited by an advanced race, Atlantis was first conceived of by Plato, the Ancient Greek philosopher. Cayce insisted that many subjects of his psychic readings

Edgar Cayce in 1943

"Clarify your personal spiritual ideal ('core value'). Identify your four or five most prominent talents, abilities, and strengths. Choose how to word your mission statement: This describes the special gift you have to offer the world around you." —Edgar Cayce

A cosmic compendium of all human knowledge.

For believers, the Akashic Records include everything that has ever been done, said, felt, or thought by everyone that has ever lived or will live. They do not exist in the physical universe, but can be "read" by those who can mystically perceive them.

Cayce claimed that he psychically tapped into the Akashic records as a primary source of information. He credited the records with providing his information about the lost continent of Atlantis as well as mysteries in the present and future.

Today, the Akashic records are frequently referenced by many types of psychic practitioners in a number of different schools of New Age thought.

WHO KNEW?
The term *Akashic* derives from the Sanskrit word meaning "sky" or "space."

were reincarnations of ancient Atlanteans and that Atlantis was destroyed in a cataclysmic event 10,000 years ago. He predicted that it would rise from beneath the ocean during the 1960s.

All of Edgar Cayce's psychic readings were captured by a stenographer and are cataloged at the Association for Research and Enlightenment (A.R.E.) in Virginia Beach, the organization Cayce founded in 1931.

Cayce sits on the couch where many of his readings took place.

PSYCHIC DETECTIVES

NEW AGE GUESSWORK MEETS OLD-FASHIONED POLICE WORK AND THE RESULTS ARE INCONCLUSIVE.

Jack the Ripper etching.

IN SEARCH OF
JACK THE RIPPER

In 1888, London was panicked by a series of brutal slayings, which were attributed to a killer dubbed Jack the Ripper. The perpetrator left no evidence at the scenes, and Scotland Yard had nothing to go on in its investigation of as many as 17 victims.

In the 125-plus years since, psychic detectives have offered insight into the case. Channeler Pamela Ball published a book entitled *Jack the Ripper: A Psychic Investigation* in 1998, in which she described "seeing" several men in connection with the murders. Ball reported that the spirits, asked if Jack the Ripper would ever be identified, answered "no." The case of Jack the Ripper remains open.

In 1997, when Fordham University student Patrick McNeill disappeared and a search by New York City police came up empty, McNeill's family asked the NYPD to consult psychic detective Dorothy Allison. She delivered a hodgepodge of clues, including "White's Restaurant," "laundromat," and "he's in the river." Detectives did find a white restaurant in McNeill's neighborhood, but were unimpressed by the laundromat tip, since the area had dozens of laundries. Even after McNeill's body was found in the East River, police were

John List, who was accused of murdering his family.

dismissive. "She did predict that he was in the river. But that was my guess, too," said the chief detective on the case.

Psychic detectives claim to be able to solve crimes using their alleged gifts as clairvoyants, mediums, telepaths, and diviners. Sometimes they turn to psychometry—handling a missing person's possessions—or visit locations related to the case. Solicited or not, these investigators often declare their predictions to the media, to anguished loved ones, and to law enforcement agencies.

Peter Hurkos, for example, a Dutch clairvoyant, was called on by friends of Roman Polanski in 1969 when Polanski's wife and four others were brutally murdered in the filmmaker's Los Angeles home. Hurkos walked through the house touching things and later told police that three men had committed the crime while tripping on LSD. He described a Satanic ritual and a string of debauched parties. After cult leader Charles Manson was arrested for ordering the murders, Hurkos' theories were proved wrong. The victims had been asleep when the killers broke in, and there had been no wild parties. The murderers were three women and a man, not three men as Hurkos insisted.

Typically, psychic detectives make vague statements such as, "I see a shallow

Clairvoyant Peter Hurkos studying the bloodstained living room where Sharon Tate and others were found murdered.

grave" or "the perpetrator is male," both likely, since murderers seldom bury bodies properly and most homicides are committed by men.

Such predictions simply reflect a basic understanding of human behavior, say crime experts. Take the case of John List, a New Jersey accountant who disappeared after allegedly murdering his family in 1971. Psychic detective Elizabeth Lerner posited that List was alive and that Baltimore or Virginia figured into the picture. It turned out List had remarried in Baltimore and was living with his new wife in Virginia. But those could have been good guesses: It would make sense for a murderer to move far from the crime and start a new life.

Today, a handful of police departments officially permit the use of such advisors. The FBI and the National Center for Missing and Exploited Children maintain that psychic detectives have never actually cracked a case.

MEET THE SLEUTHS

DOROTHY ALLISON (1924-1999). Allison claimed to have worked with police on over 5,000 cases, locating 250 bodies and solving hundreds of crimes. In 1974, she took credit for pinpointing the California location where kidnapped newspaper heiress Patty Hearst was being held captive.

SYLVIA BROWNE (1936-2013). One of the most notorious psychic detectives of recent times, Browne made several false predictions in sensational cases. In 2004, she announced that kidnapping victim Amanda Berry was dead. Berry was found alive in 2013.

ALLISON DUBOIS (B. 1972). DuBois, a self-identified medium, telepath, and "psychic profiler," says she has put people on death row, although no evidence supports her claim. The TV drama *Medium* was based on her disputed stories of working closely with police, attorneys, and the Texas Rangers.

PET POWER

CAN HUMANS AND ANIMALS BYPASS LANGUAGE BARRIERS WITH TELEPATHIC COMMUNICATION?

The Boeing 747 where Tabitha hid out.

THE CASE OF THE FLYING CAT

In 1994, a cat named Tabitha made headlines when she disappeared while flying from New York to Los Angeles with her companion, Carol Ann Timmel. Tabitha was lost for 12 days as a squad of searchers combed the plane to no avail. Finally, Timmel turned to pet psychic Christa Carl, who asked the *New York Post* to print a photograph of Tabitha's sister Pandora. If readers gazed into Pandora's eyes, Tabitha would be located, Carl claimed. Timmel soon found her cat exactly where the psychic said she was: in the drop ceiling of the 747. Carl claimed she had helped Tabitha address an issue from a past life and used visualization to "show her how to come out." Or maybe Tabitha's loud meowing that day revealed her whereabouts.

Humans have long been amazed by tales of lost dogs who travel hundreds of miles to return to their families, and cats who somehow know when their human companions are about to fall ill. Some pets seem to intuit when their humans are in distress, and have summoned neighbors or yowled for aid. Both domesticated and wild animals have warned people away from accidents and disasters. Are man's best friend and other creatures psychic?

Many people believe they are, and claim that animals have a number of special powers: precognition, or knowing the future; clairvoyance, or the ability to sense remote events; telepathy, or the power to send or receive mental messages; mediumship, or the ability to contact the dead and to see ghosts; and psi trailing, or the talent of finding someone who is lost.

Paging Dr. Doolittle

Pet psychics, who say they are able to communicate with beasts, from parakeets to racehorses, attribute pets' special powers to animal superiority. In their view, animals understand existence more deeply than humans, and as a result have more fully developed psychic powers. Skeptics attribute the so-called paranormal gifts

> **Humans want to feel they have a bond with their pets that goes beyond playing fetch and snuggling up.**

to coincidence or yet-to-be-understood biological attributes.

Pet psychics, also known as animal intuitives, claim to have extrasensory powers that they use in communicating with various critters. When a pet owner wants to converse with Fido or Kitty, the intuitive acts as an interpreter. Some say they "speak" with the creatures via telepathy and clairvoyance, while others claim to connect with an animal's electromagnetic energy. Pet psychics maintain that any animal, domesticated or exotic, can connect with human beings, including birds, rabbits, mice, snakes, turtles, and even komodo dragons.

Bad Kitty

When a pet is naughty, withdrawn, aggressive, or has other behavioral issues, a pet psychic is sometimes called in to penetrate the animal's thoughts and feelings and share them with the human companion. In the case of a lost pet, a psychic can be brought in to advise a family where to search.

Some are asked to diagnose health problems and transmit healing energy to sick or injured pets. On occasion, pet psychics are consulted by owners who want to know if a gravely ill pet wishes to be euthanized, or are hired to help contact a dead pet.

For centuries, cats' uncanny abilities have made some humans uneasy. Black cats have long been associated with witches.

BELIEVING CATS AND DOGS

Supernatural, or superhuman? Most scientists assert that animals' remarkable sensitivity to humans and the world around them can be explained by biology, physics, and psychology.

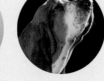

A cat's ear can hear five times as much as a human's.

A cat's nose has nine to 16 times as many odor-detecting cells as a human's.

A dog's nose has 30 to 60 times as many odor-detecting cells as a human's.

A dog's ear can hear four times as much as a human's.

Cats' and dogs' eyes have stronger night vision, a greater ability to see motion, and a broader field of vision than humans'.

Animals' senses allow them to detect things that humans can't. When they "predict" a storm, they may be using their sensitivity to barometric pressure. When they detect illness or imminent death, they may be picking up on distinctive scents. When they "foresee" an earthquake, they may be sensing subtle vibrations or subterranean gases.

When a lost pet finds its way home from hundreds of miles away, it may simply be using the same homing abilities common in birds, salmon, and sea turtles. For some animal species, this skill is based on a sensitivity to the earth's magnetic field. For others, it comes from an awareness of the positioning of the stars and sun.

Sonya Fitzpatrick

READING ROVER

One of the world's most famous pet psychics is Sonya Fitzpatrick, an author, the star of the short-lived Animal Planet television show *Pet Psychic*, and host of *Animal Intuition*, a popular call-in radio program. Fitzpatrick claims to help people contact pets who have "crossed the rainbow bridge to heaven" and to read the minds of their living pets. Believers say she has helped them find out everything from why their parrot has stopped speaking to how their poodle prefers to be groomed.

A woman practices qigong, an ancient Chinese discipline that combines medicine, philosophy, and martial arts.

CHAPTER 2

TELEKENISIS AND ESP

THE MIND CAN BE AS MYSTERIOUS AS IT IS POWERFUL. BUT WHAT CAN YOUR THOUGHTS REALLY DO?

Near-death experiences can't be
explained by traditional science.

PARAPSYCHOLOGY
BEYOND THE
FIVE SENSES

AN EXPLORATION OF UNCONVENTIONAL
HUMAN POWERS.

Parapsychology is the study of psi, the mysterious, unquantifiable factor in psychic phenomena. It can include everything from extrasensory perception and mind-matter interaction to brushes with mortality like near-death experiences and reincarnation. These phenomena can't be explained by—and tend to conflict with—the principles of biology, physics, statistics, and general science. In fact, most scientists consider parapsychology a pseudoscience and say that parapsychologists have yet to prove the existence of psi.

The history of parapsychology studies includes debate both for and against the existence of parapsychological phenomena. Here is an overview.

CLAIRVOYANCE, ALSO REFERRED TO AS REMOTE VIEWING: Awareness of distant people, places, or events that can't be seen, heard, or detected through the five physical senses.

ESP (EXTRA-SENSORY PERCEPTION): Encompasses the various ways of "seeing" things outside the range of the five senses, such as telepathy, clairvoyance, and precognition.

HAUNTINGS: Ongoing presence of apparitions and unexplained sounds and moving objects at a given location.

MEDIUMSHIP: Opening a path of communication between the living and the dead.

NEAR-DEATH EXPERIENCES: Mysterious sensations, such as visions of lights and tunnels, experienced by people who are revived after they die.

OUT-OF-BODY EXPERIENCES: When the body separates from the mind or spirit and is able to observe the body and its surroundings from nearby.

PRECOGNITION OR PREMONITION: Sensing or foreseeing future events, but not through normal channels such as the news media or conversation.

REINCARNATION: The after-death survival of the spirit, which is transferred from a human or animal to other bodies over multiple lifetimes.

TELEKINESIS, ALSO KNOWN AS PSYCHO-KINESIS OR MIND-MATTER INTERAC-TION: Mental control of physical objects, time, space, energy, or another person's body or mind. Includes pyrokinesis and brainwashing.

TELEPATHY: Mental communication of thoughts or feelings between people.

THE FATHER OF ESP

J.B. RHINE EXPLORED TELEPATHY, CLAIRVOYANCE, AND OTHER PHENOMENA AT DUKE UNIVERSITY.

Hubert Pearce (left) with J.B. Rhine (right) at Duke University in the 1930s.

STUDYING PSI

The Duke Parapsychology Laboratory studied four separate psychic phenomena, which its researchers referred to as *psi*. Rhine is thought to have invented the term, along with *parapsychology* and *extrasensory perception*. The first three were collectively known as ESP:

Telepathy
Reading another person's mind.

Clairvoyance
Obtaining extrasensory information from a non-human source.

Precognition
Predicting future events.

Psychokinesis
Moving objects with the mind.

In 1932, a young divinity student named Hubert Pearce fidgeted nervously as he listened to a lecture by J.B. Rhine, the director of the Duke Parapsychology Laboratory in Durham, North Carolina. Rhine had been searching for scientific evidence of what he called extrasensory perception (ESP), the ability of the mind to gain information from something other than the five senses.

When Rhine finished speaking, Pearce approached Rhine and told him that his mother had had psychic abilities. Pearce suspected that he had inherited her talents and the thought frightened him.

Rhine convinced Pearce to undergo an impromptu experiment. He pulled out a pack of 25 cards, each of which was marked with one of five symbols. One by one, Rhine placed the cards facedown on a table and asked Pearce to guess the symbols on them. Pearce got ten right—double the number predicted by pure chance.

Rhine repeated the test on Pearce thousands of times under different conditions. Sometimes, Pearce's performance was average, but on many trials, he scored ten or higher.

It's Scientific—and It Sells

Pearce became the star subject in Rhine's *Extrasensory Perception* (1934), a book detailing and analyzing his experiments.

Rhine claimed he had scientifically proven that some people possessed ESP. *Extrasensory Perception* became an immediate bestseller, and magazines from *Reader's Digest* to *The New Yorker* offered glowing accounts of Rhine's work. Pearce's celebrity status was sealed when some of the best-known personalities of the era—including Helen Keller, Aldous Huxley, Richard Nixon, and Carl Jung—visited his laboratory

Rhine conducted ESP studies on dogs.

WHAT ARE ZENER CARDS?

J.B. Rhine used these colorful cards to prove that ESP exists.

When J.B. Rhine wanted to create a special deck of cards for ESP testing, he turned to Karl Zener, a Duke psychology professor. The result was a 25-card deck that featured five simple symbols—a square, a circle, a star, a cross, and a trio of wavy lines.

Stores began selling Zener Cards that customers could use to test their own psychic abilities—but many of them were printed on stock so flimsy that, in the proper light, people could see through the card and cheat their way to astounding displays of ESP prowess.

Using a commercial pack of Zener Cards, famed behavior psychologist B.F. Skinner tried to discredit Rhine by making 100 consecutive correct "guesses." The cards soon became so controversial that Zener disowned them, though they bear his name to this day.

at Duke University. The workshop received tens of thousands of letters from people recounting their own experiences with ESP and other unexplained phenomena.

Attack of the Skeptics

Rhine's discoveries were hailed as great scientific advances, but soon his work drew the attention of skeptics who insisted that parapsychology was a pseudoscience, similar to fortune-telling or faith-healing.

Mathematicians criticized Rhine's statistical analysis and scientists attacked his methodology. Researchers who tried to duplicate his experiments found no evidence to support his conclusions, accusing Rhine of fixing his results. When Rhine retired in 1965, his research had fallen into such disrepute that Duke ended its affiliation with the lab. He died in 1980.

In recent years, there has been increased interest in parapsychology as part of the study of consciousness. At facilities in Europe and the United States, including the privately funded Rhine Research Center in Durham, researchers are reexamining Rhine's experiments and reassessing what they might reveal about the human mind.

RUSSIAN SUPERPOWERS

FROM COURT INTRIGUE TO COLD WAR TELEKINESIS, SPIRITUALISM FASCINATES AN EMPIRE.

The Russian obsession with the unknowable is reflected not only in the writings of the country's great novelists, but also in the influence of a mystical monk and in the legacy of a man of letters who popularized séances.

A Monk's Strange Powers

To the world he is known as Rasputin, a master of court intrigue, and often he is credited with directing the fate of Imperial Russia. Yet this mysterious Siberian monk, Grigori Yefimov-ich Rasputin (1869–1916), was not a doctor, priest, or learned man. How did he wield such control? By gaining favor in the court of Czar Nicholas II and convincing the czar's wife, Alexandra, of his super-natural powers.

The granddaughter of Queen Victoria, Alexandra, like many royals of the era, carried the gene for hemophilia, or "bleeder's disease." While Alexandra herself showed no signs of illness, she passed the gene on to her son, Alexei, heir to the Romanov throne. When Alexei was diagnosed with the illness, Alexandra feared for his life and turned to prayers—which Rasputin seemed to answer. She deeply believed the monk's spiritual and hypnotic powers had saved Alexei. "The Little One will not die," Rasputin pronounced during an excruciating attack the child suffered when he was eight. "Do not allow the doctors to bother him too much." The next day, the bleeding stopped. To a desperate and grateful mother, Rasputin had worked a miracle and gained her complete confidence.

When Czar Nicholas left to fight in World War I in 1915, Alexandra turned to Rasputin as her domestic advisor. He made many enemies in the Romanov court and sought to protect himself, warning his rivals that if they killed him, the family would perish within two years.

Rasputin survived multiple assassination attempts, including one by poisoning, a shooting, and a stabbing. Finally, he was attacked and thrown into in a freezing river, where he drowned in 1916.

On July 17, 1918, the Czar and his family were executed.

Magnetic Attraction

Russian interest in spiritualism wasn't limited to religious figures, as evidenced by the success of Alexander Aksakov (1832–1903). A so-called scientific spiritualist, Aksakov studied animal magnetism, also known as hypnosis, and wrote of it in his book, *Animizm i spiritizm.*

Aksakov came from an educated, elite background. At the University of Moscow he studied sciences and was fascinated by the idea of mind over matter, and by the apparent power of mediums. Aksakov coined the term "telekinesis" for the ability to move objects with thoughts alone. He popularized séances in Russia, and although many of the mediums he studied turned out to be frauds, he remained a believer.

Czar Nicholas II, with his family: Duchess Olga, Duchess Marie, the Grand Duchess Anastasia, the Czarevitch Alexis, the Grand Duchess Tatiana, and the Czarina.

Alexander Aksakov.

RUSSIAN DRAMA

Examples of Soviet deep interest in life's mystical side appear in the country's literature, science, and history books.

→ **Live souls:** Many Russian writers have explored the nation's spiritual side, including Fyodor Dostoevsky, who attended a séance conducted by scientific spiritualist Alexander Aksakov in 1876 and later described the experience in *Diary of a Writer*.

→ **A strong hand:** In one experiment, the telekinetic Nina Kulagina reportedly was able to stop a frog's heartbeat with only the electromagnetic energy from her hands. Her work is said to have been studied by Russian scientists.

→ **An iron constitution:** Enemies of Rasputin, advisor to the Russian royal family, attempted to kill him by lacing his wine and food with deadly cyanide. Rasputin ate and drank—but nothing happened.

WHO KNEW?
Often called the Mad Monk, Rasputin was widely known as a mystic and faith healer—and a formidable foe.

NINA KULAGINA: A MOVING EXPERIENCE
This one-time radio operator in the Red Army is said to have mastered mind over matter.

During the Soviet era, Nina Kulagina (1926–1990) was celebrated for her telekinetic powers. Kulagina served as a radio operator in the Red Army in World War II and also fought at the front. As the years passed, Kulagina developed a sharp pain in her back—an ache she said became a signal that her telekinetic powers were about to take over. During demonstrations, Kulagina was seen to make a compass needle spin around and to inch a matchbox across a table. Detractors dismissed her feats, maintaining that she was moving the objects with the help of nearly invisible threads. It's been said that Soviet officials, determined to keep her powers secret, insisted that she use a false name. But the West discovered Kulagina in 1968, in film clips shown at the First Moscow Conference on Parapsychology. In one experiment, Kulagina was seen using her telekinetic powers to separate the white of a raw egg from the yolk.

THE PSYCHIC COLD WAR

IN AN INTERNATIONAL BATTLE OF THE MINDS, WHO WOULD EMERGE THE WINNER?

"The discovery of the energy behind telepathy will be as important as the discovery of atomic energy!" exclaimed Leonid Vasilev, the Soviet Union's leading telepathy expert, to his parapsychologist comrades in 1960. A decade later, a zealous U.S. congressman, Charles Rose, declared that psychic powers "[are] a low-cost radar system. And if the Russians have them, then we should have them too!" In the Cold War era, the psychic arms race was on.

Defense Mechanisms

Since ancient times, military commanders have sought the advice of soothsayers, fortune-tellers, and even genies when scoping out enemies and planning battle strategy. The Roman emperors Maxentius and Constantine I, Greek king Alexander the Great, and Napoleon Bonaparte are believed to have been among them.

More recently, during the Cold War tensions between the United States and the USSR, both countries conducted research into psi phenomena, hoping to develop new weapons and ways of spying. The efforts intensified in the late 1950s, as the CIA experimented with gathering information by mind-reading, aka ESP; remote viewing, aka clairvoyance; and paranormally planting disinformation in the minds of enemies, via telepathy. Both the Americans and the Soviets were interested in trying to communicate secret reports and orders directly from mind to mind, to control soldiers through hypnosis and brainwashing. They also wanted to mentally sabotage equipment and facilities—or even kill enemies—from a distance with telekinesis.

Racing Minds

The Soviets gave the field of parapsychology a new name: psychotronics. Governments on both sides funded laboratories staffed with physicists, engineers, and biologists who approached paranormal potential as a question of applied technology. They used strictly controlled experimental techniques aimed at discovering the scientific basis of psychic phenomena. For the most part, the Americans and the Soviets came at the challenge in the same way, but by the early 1970s, the Soviets were leading in the mind race; the American effort eventually fizzled out, while the Russians have reportedly picked up psychic research where the Soviets left off.

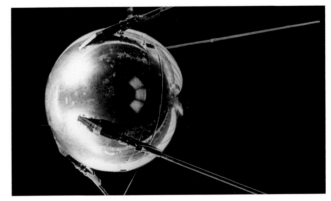

Sputnik, launched by the Soviet Union.

"Happy," a computer storage device at CIA headquarters that holds 1.2 million megabytes of information.

WHO KNEW?
Along with physical barriers such as the Berlin Wall, built in 1961, the Cold War generated new interest in psychic warfare.

THE STARGATE PROJECT

From 1972 to 1995, the federal government spent $20 million investigating psi phenomena like clairvoyance.

In 1972, worried about the Russians gaining the psychic edge in the Cold War, the U.S. government authorized The Stargate Project. Run by the CIA, the U.S. Army, and other government entities, Stargate investigated clairvoyance, which they thought could allow spies to "see" enemy locations, activities, and material, even from far away. Stargate details:

→ **Mission:** Develop the human mind to reach out, locate, and describe remote targets.

→ **Subjects:** 22-plus military personnel and civilian psychics.

→ **Accomplishments:** Identified and described landscapes and buildings at specified geographical coordinates, detected nuclear material, explored building interiors.

→ **Outcome:** Scrapped after an independent audit concluded that Stargate failed to adequately prove the existence of remote viewing.

THE REAL MANCHURIAN CANDIDATES

Hypnotized assassins sound like science fiction, but in the psychic Cold War, both sides tried to produce such secret operatives.

The 1962 political thriller *The Manchurian Candidate* depicted the terrifying potential of psychic warfare in the Cold War years. The story followed U.S. Army Sergeant Raymond Shaw, who was brainwashed during the Korean War and turned into a Communist-controlled assassin.

In reality, both the U.S. and the USSR experimented with mind control, hoping to train operatives to execute certain orders and to forget their actions afterward.

In a 1966 experiment, Russian telepathy expert V.L. Raykov reportedly hypnotized a group of subjects and put them in a Faraday Cage, an enclosure that simulated the electromagnetic signal-blocking properties of a submarine hull. While the participants were sequestered, Raykov, from outside the cage, commanded them to wake up at specific times. Odds that the group members would have woken up at those times on their own were considered one in a million, but the results are unknown, as details of the experiment remain classified.

Similarly, the CIA, in one instance, allegedly tried to hypnotize a double agent so he would kill a Soviet KGB operative. It is also said that a CIA hypnotist attempted to send three Cuban exiles back to assassinate Fidel Castro. None of the purported experiments succeeded.

A scene from *The Manchurian Candidate*.

COMMUNICATING WITH THE
NAUTILUS

THE SUB COULDN'T COMMUNICATE WITH SHIPS ON THE SURFACE. COULD TELEPATHY BE THE SOLUTION?

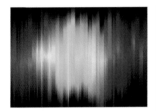

Electromagnetic waves.

NEW WAVES

Might the human brain be wired for biological radio communication?

Soviet scientists, including Ukrainian electrical engineer Bernard Kazhinsky, were fascinated by possible telepathic communication aboard the *Nautilus*.

In his 1962 book, Kazhinsky proposed that the human brain could emit "cerebral radiation" in the form of electromagnetic waves, allowing the "broadcast" of thoughts to others. Unlike conventional radio waves, organic human waves could travel through deep oceanic waters and a submarine's hull, said Kazhinsky.

While no hard evidence of such waves has ever been established, Kazhinsky's theories continue to be explored today.

The U.S.S. *Nautilus* SSN571, launched in 1954, was the world's first nuclear-fueled submarine. Unlike conventional diesel-powered subs, which needed periodic fill-ups, the *Nautilus* could cruise for months or even years without surfacing. This made her ideal for Operation Sunshine, the U.S. Navy's program to send a submarine to the North Pole. On August 3, 1958, the *Nautilus* became the first ship in history to reach the top of the world. It was a great achievement not only navigationally but militarily: While under the polar ice cap, the sub was invisible to enemy surveillance. The problem was, it also couldn't communicate with American ships on the surface. Some suggested that mental telepathy was the only answer. Perhaps the U.S. military was desperate enough to look into the possibility.

As soon as the navy released news of its success—and problem—with the *Nautilus*, the press began discussing possible extrasensory solutions. Magazines printed sensational reports that President Dwight D. Eisenhower had authorized thought-transmission experiments aboard the *Nautilus*. Major corporations such as Westinghouse Electric, General Electric, and Bell Laboratories were said to have provided ESP intelligence to the military. When government officials and company executives denied the existence of such psychic experiments, the statements were treated as evidence of a coverup.

Sixteen Days with Smith and Jones

The navy's probe of telepathy's military potential reportedly began in 1959, when a mysterious passenger, identified only as Jones, secluded himself in a cabin on the *Nautilus*. For 16 days, no one saw Jones except the ship's commander, Captain William R. Anderson, and the sailor who delivered Jones' meals. Meanwhile, a man identified as Smith—allegedly a student at Duke University's famous parapsychology laboratory—was isolated in a room at Westinghouse in Maryland, with Air Force Colonel William H. Bowers.

Using a deck of cards printed with various symbols, called Zener cards, a standard tool in ESP testing at the time, Smith was reportedly asked to concentrate twice a day on five cards pulled at random from a deck of 25. As Smith tried to transmit the images to Jones telepathically, Jones concentrated on receiving them. Both men wrote down the symbols they saw, sealed the session's notes in an envelope, and gave them to Bowers or

WHO KNEW?
Reports of parapsychological experiments aboard the *Nautilus* led the USSR to conduct similar research.

The first atomic submarine, U.S.S. *Nautilus*, being launched at Groton, Connecticut, January 21, 1954.

Anderson, who locked the information away.

At the end of the experiment, Jones and his envelopes were reportedly flown under military guard to Westinghouse in Maryland. Smith's notes were compared to Jones's, and were found to match 70 percent of the time. Bowers was quoted as saying, "For the first time ever, under conditions that precluded trickery, and with a precision great enough to open the way to its practical application, human thought has been transmitted through space, without any intermediary, from one brain to another."

Con or Conspiracy?

As reports of the *Nautilus* project appeared, the navy denied the experiments. "Although the *Nautilus* engaged in a very wide variety of activities, certainly these did not include experiments in telepathy," said Captain Anderson. Colonel Bowers did an about-face as well, stating, "The experiment in which I was alleged to have participated never took place."

Under pressure, two media sources said they had relied on unverified reports. Some observers declared the story a hoax; others insisted it was a CIA deception to distract the Soviets from actual U.S. tactics in the Cold War. Believers still swear that the U.S. military was willing to try anything to communicate with the *Nautilus*—even ESP.

STIRRING SOVIET WATERS

When news of Operation Sunshine spread, the KGB and Soviet military intelligence started building a network of institutes tasked with developing deadly psychic tools and weapons.

Site	Institute	Research Topics
Alma-Ata	Kazakh State University	bioenergetics
Leningrad	Leningrad University	telepathy with twins, psychokinesis, telepathy and hypnosis
Moscow	Popov Society	telepathy, electromagnetic forces, hypnosis
Moscow	Department of Technical Parapsychology	underwater and long-distance telepathy, psychokinesis, precognition

CARL JUNG
BLENDING SCIENCE AND MYSTICISM

A PIONEER OF PSYCHIATRY PAVES THE WAY
FOR THE NEW AGE MOVEMENT.

Sigmund Freud (front row left) and Carl Jung (front row right) with other analysts at Clark University in 1909.

JUNG'S PREMONITIONS

Did one of the world's most amazing dream analysts have psychic dreams himself?

→ In 1913, Jung experienced a disturbing vision of a flood covering Europe, with floating debris and bodies. When World War I broke out the next year, Jung concluded his vision had been a premonition.

→ In 1944, Jung believed he had a near-death experience when he saw himself floating 1,000 miles above Earth. Jung's physician appeared in the vision as the Greek god of medicine and insisted that Jung return to Earth. A few days later, the doctor became ill and died. Jung's interpretation was that the doctor sacrificed his own life to save Jung's.

At the turn of the 20th century, psychology was in its infancy. One of its earliest practitioners was psychiatrist Carl Jung, a scientist who, like many of his Swiss peers, believed in a world beyond science. During his long career, Jung explored both the medical and spiritual aspects of mental illness as well as parapsychology or spiritualism, as the field was then known.

Two profound experiences Jung had as a student helped shape his thinking. One day while studying at his parent's house, Jung heard a loud bang that sounded like a gunshot. He ran to the dining room, where he found his mother. She told him that the sound had come from close by.

Looking around, the

Jung explored the medical and spiritual aspects of mental illness.

Jungs discovered that the solid oak dining room table had split wide open. Since the wood was aged, they concluded it was unlikely the top would have separated on its own. They ruled out weather as a catalyst since the temperature, air pressure, and humidity had been constant.

A week later, Jung came home to find his whole family upset. An hour earlier, they had heard another loud explosion in the dining room. This time, Jung found a basket that contained the shattered pieces of a heavy steel bread knife. According to the family, the knife had been used a short time before the incident.

Jung took the pieces to a knife maker, who could find no flaws in the metal. The forger told Jung that it would have taken tremendous force to break the knife into shards. Jung began

going to séances led by his 15-year-old cousin, who he believed might somehow be connected to the incidents.

Yet even as his interest in the séances waned, Jung became increasingly fascinated by the paranormal. He began to research Eastern and Western philosophy, religion, and psychic phenomena. He studied astrology and the I Ching, a Chinese oracle dating back thousands of years. Eventually, Jung developed what he described as a

Carl Jung, shown here in 1960, was renowned for his analysis of dreams.

"philosophical, spiritual, and mystical" treatment for patients that was meant to match up an individual's conscious mind—or ego—with his unconscious and to instill in patients a sense of fulfillment and harmony.

Jung's work significantly influenced the 20th century's New Age movement, which blended Eastern and Western spiritual and metaphysical traditions with psychology, self-help, holistic health, and the paranormal.

THE RULE OF THREE

The relationship between the two founders of psychiatry deteriorated when they began to disagree on principles.

Psychiatry's founding father, Sigmund Freud, and his protégé and collaborator Carl Jung agreed that the psyche was made up of three distinct parts. But the two men disagreed on what those divisions were and eventually had an acrimonious falling-out.

Freud:

Id: Basic human instinct, present from birth.

Superego: Internalized, learned cultural norms and behavior.

Ego: Mediates between the desires of the id and the brakes supplied by the ego.

Jung:

Ego: Conscious mind of an individual.

Personal unconscious: Forgotten or suppressed memories of an individual's past.

Collective unconscious: Innate memories and experiences shared by all people.

PSYCHIC SURGERY

SHADY PRACTITIONERS CLAIM TO OPERATE WITHOUT LEAVING INTERNAL OR EXTERNAL WOUNDS.

It's like a scene out of a science-fiction novel: A man in a white coat stands beside a young woman lying on a table with her shirt unbuttoned. Prodding her belly with his bare hands, the man seems to locate what he's looking for and pushes his fingers into the woman's body. Blood pools around his fingers, and after a moment he pulls back his hand, holding a small bloody mass. He tosses it into the trash and wipes the blood away; the patient sits up in a daze and looks down at her belly. There's no incision and no scar. Could such an operation have taken place?

Practitioners of psychic surgery claim they can, and do, thanks to their abilities to channel the spirits of deceased doctors or other healers. Operating without anesthetics and often without instruments, these paranormal physicians say they remove tumors, organs, and foreign matter with no discernible aftereffect.

The centers of psychic surgery are Brazil and the Philippines—many tourist hotels employ house "surgeons" in those countries—but the practice can be found around the world, including in the United States. In the Philippines, practitioners generally use their bare hands to work on patients, while in Brazil they favor instruments such as scissors, kitchen knives, and forceps. The specialists perform in improvised clinics, hotel rooms, and homes, sometimes before an audience, finishing their procedures in just a few minutes. Hundreds of patients may pass under their hands in a single day.

Reputable scientists maintain that psychic surgery is a hoax, and a dangerous one at that. In 1976, a review of the research by the Federal Trade Commission concluded that it is "pure fakery. The body is not opened, no 'surgery' is performed with the bare hands or with anything else, and nothing is removed from the body."

Medical doctors and public-health officials warn that psychic surgery can be fatal for seriously ill patients who reject or delay conventional medical care. In the 1970s, the Canadian Embassy in Manila issued death certificates for three people who died while on "miracle tours" there. Canadian authorities have also convicted numerous psychic surgeons and tour operators of fraud or illegal medical activity, as have the governments of the United States, Australia, the Philippines, and Brazil. Bottom line: As appealing as the prospect of quick, non-invasive psychic surgery may sound, it should not be considered an alternative to more conventional treatments.

A Reiki master giving energy for a body healing in southern India.

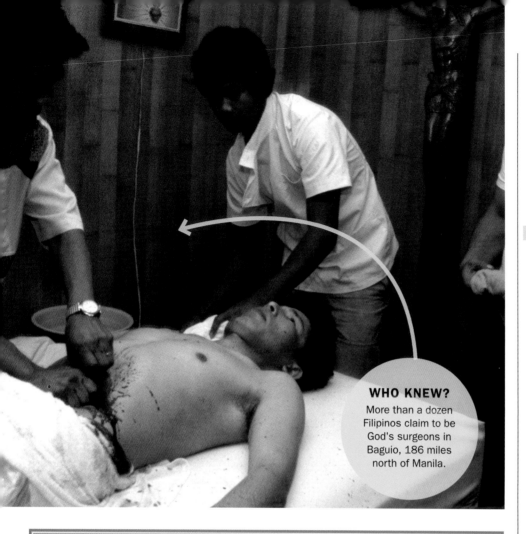

Faith healers in Manila.

WHO KNEW?

More than a dozen Filipinos claim to be God's surgeons in Baguio, 186 miles north of Manila.

ANY WAY YOU SLICE IT

Skeptics and believers alike have come up with explanations of psychic surgery.

It's the power of suggestion.
→ Some clinicians who see an improvement in a patient's condition after psychic surgery ascribe it to the placebo effect.

It's the power of faith.
→ Some compare psychic surgery to the laying on of hands often practiced by faith healers.

It's the power of the body.
→ Many alternative healing practices embrace the notion that illness arises from an imbalance in the body's energy field. In this view, healing—by ancient techniques such as acupuncture or New Age ones such as Reiki—is achieved by rebalancing energy.

It's the power of illusion.
→ James Randi, an ex-illusionist who now works to debunk paranormal claims, says psychic surgery relies on standard magician's tricks. Some former psychic surgeons admit to using sleight-of-hand to deceive patients and spectators.

TRICKS OF THE TRADE

Want to know how the debunkers say that psychic surgeons make it look so real? Read on.

THE INCISION: To create the illusion that he is inserting a hand into the patient's body, the surgeon first presses his fingertips into the skin to create a hollow. His hand partially camouflaged, he slowly flexes his fingers back toward the palm of the hand so it looks as if they're sliding into the flesh. Once he's formed a fist, it looks like his fingers are knuckle-deep in the patient's body.

THE BLOOD: Further camouflage for the hand's activity is provided by "blood" that appears to be oozing from the incision. The surgeon might be wearing a false thumb—stock equipment for a magician—filled with animal blood or another red liquid that can be released when he chooses. Alternatively, his assistant might conceal tiny balloons or sponges filled with red liquid that she hands to him during the procedure.

THE GUTS: Animal entrails generally stand in for the tumors and other diseased tissue supposedly removed from the patient. The assistant might surreptitiously pass them to the surgeon or he might simply palm the material or take it from nearby hiding places. Once the material has been "removed" from the patient, the surgeon quickly discards it so the patient and audience can't see exactly what it is.

MIND OVER METAL

PSYCHOKINESIS HAS LONG FASCINATED HUMANITY. IS IT REALLY POSSIBLE TO THINK A FORK OUT OF SHAPE?

Uri Geller bends a spoon.

SPOON-BENDING PARTIES

The public's fascination with psychokinesis transformed the phenomenon into a party game.

Much of spoon-bending's continuing appeal can be attributed to Jack Houck, a California aerospace engineer who in the 1980s began hosting "PK parties," at which guests could test their PK, or psychokinetic, abilities. Participants each chose a spoon and rubbed the top of the handle between forefinger and thumb while chanting, "Bend, bend, bend." The warmed handles became pliable, convincing partygoers that their mental energy had transformed physical matter.

WHO KNEW?

Spoonbending was featured in the blockbuster movie *The Matrix* (1999).

In the 1970s, all things paranormal went mainstream. Many people were proud to be into astrology, eager to talk to spirits during séances, and convinced that they possessed psychic powers.

The climate was perfect for Uri Geller. An ex-soldier in the Israeli army, Geller was handsome and charismatic, sporting a fashionable bush of black hair, patterned polyester suits, and enough of an accent to seem just a little exotic. Boasting about his extraordinary telepathic abilities, he became an international star, appearing on magazine covers and television shows around the world. Geller professed to be able to read minds and identify hidden objects—but

Johnny Carson as Carnac the Magnificent, a spoof of the kind of psychics he often invited to his couch.

what most excited his fans was his ability to bend metal with intense concentration. Before astonished audiences, he appeared to use psychokinetic powers to twist house keys, mangle the tines of forks, and, most famously, bend silver spoons in half.

Psychic or Fraud?

In 1973, Geller appeared on *The Tonight Show* starring Johnny Carson, who had begun his show-business career as a magician. Not wholly convinced of Geller's psychic talents, Carson beforehand consulted with James "The Amazing" Randi, a onetime magician turned debunker. Following Randi's advice, Carson presented Geller with spoons and other objects rather than allowing him to use his own props. The audience watched anxiously as Geller's customary confidence melted away. He stammered and hesitated, fell silent for long stretches, and seemed to stall for time. Finally, he explained that he did not "feel strong" that evening, implying that Carson's skepticism rendered him momentarily powerless.

In spite of this failure, Geller has remained popular as a performer and author and appeared on television in the United Kingdom on *Noel's House Party*, in the United States on *The View*, and in Israel on *The Successor*, throughout the 1990s and 2000s.

Geller holds two spoons at a March 27, 1973, demonstration. One spoon is already slightly bent.

HOW TO BEND A SPOON WITHOUT USING YOUR MIND

The jury is out on whether spoon bending by psychokinesis is truly possible, but every magician knows how to pull off the illusion.

→ Prepare the spoon by bending it back and forth at the point where the handle meets the bowl. Be careful to weaken but not break it.

→ Straighten the spoon handle so it appears normal.

→ Before your audience, rub the spoon between your forefinger and thumb where you have previously bent it. Pretend you are concentrating hard as your fingers heat the handle.

→ When the handle is warm, use the fingers of your other hand to push down lightly on the bowl of the spoon, which will begin to droop—creating the illusion of psychic spoon bending.

PARANORMAL MILITARY INTELLIGENCE

The U.S. military establishment doesn't seem like a natural home for New Age ideas, but it, too, was caught up in the spoon-bending craze.

In the early 1980s, the United States Army Intelligence and Security Command (INSCOM), then headed by General Albert Stubblebine, also started investigating psychokinesis. Colonel John Alexander, one of INSCOM's highest-ranking officers, began holding spoon-bending parties in his Virginia apartment for staff and invited psychics. Alexander was skeptical until he watched one guest's spoon, held upright at the base with two fingertips, bend to a 90-degree angle. "At that instant," he later wrote, "General Stubblebine and I knew for sure that the stories and results we had heard about the potential application of psychokinesis were, in fact, true." While spoon-bending parties remained popular with INSCOM personnel, the U.S. Army never found a practical use for its psychokinesis research.

UNLOCKING THE MYSTERY OF QIGONG

THIS ANCIENT CHINESE PRACTICE COMBINES MEDICINE, PHILOSOPHY, AND MARTIAL ARTS.

LUMOKINESIS: THE BENDING OF LIGHT

Some qigong practitioners claim they can use their thoughts to manipulate light, heat, or fire, abilities known as lumokinesis and pyrokinesis. Believers in lumokinesis insist that the mind can bend and scatter photons, the tiny packets of electromagnetic radiation visible to the eye. Despite a number of homemade videos purporting to show people making flames and lightbulbs flicker with their mind, lumokinesis has a long way to go before physicists consider it anything except the stuff of science fiction.

Qigong is an ancient physical and philosophical practice that combines elements of martial arts with Chinese medicine. The term comes from the Chinese words *gong*, meaning "skill," and *qi*, meaning "life force." Studied throughout China for centuries, qigong is gaining new fans today as the mysterious powers of its masters are discussed on the internet and in social media.

Harmony of Opposites

Practitioners of qigong adhere to the Chinese philosophy of Tao (*the way*), the belief that harmony between opposites—yin and yang—is the energetic essence of the seen and unseen world. The physical practice requires intense concentration and focused breathing as the body progresses through a series of graceful, fluid motions to summon the yin-yang energy.

Qigong masters try to manipulate the yin-yang energies of others to treat a range of illnesses and conditions, from heart problems, cancer, and diabetes to migraines and insomnia. Many masters also administer acupuncture, the ancient Chinese practice of penetrating the skin with needles, to open up clogged energy channels and allow the qi to flow freely.

The practice of qigong is believed to promote good health and generate vitality, but many use it simply as a form of meditation and exercise. Others use it to produce sometimes astonishing feats of strength.

Qigong masters claim such strength is not merely muscular but comes from manipulating the qi—the body's powerful subtle energy.

Master Zhou

The qigong star best known to Americans is Master Zhou Ting-Jue, who has appeared on *Ripley's Believe It or Not* and *That's Incredible!* and been featured on *Stan Lee's Superhumans* on the History Channel. Zhou is said to be able to generate 202 degrees Fahrenheit from the palms of his hands and has appeared to slice through a brick with a sheet of paper in front of a live television audience. In recent years, Zhou has taught qigong in China and Tibet, where he has attracted crowds of more than 4,000, and treated the Dalai Lama. He is also in demand in the West and has treated members of the Los Angeles Lakers basketball team.

Hongyi Qiu

In China, one of the more controversial qigong masters is Hongyi Qiu, an 84-year-old from Wuhan, China, who has been accused of fakery and illu-

A qigong practitioner uses a single movement of his palm to break a jar filled with ice.

sion for his televised antics. In one video, Qiu stands several feet from the end of a long table, his right arm outstretched, palm facing forward. He rocks back and forth, then lets out a guttural yell and thrusts his open palm out hard. As if on cue, a bowl filled with water slides down the length of the table. It appears Qiu has pushed it from several feet away without touching it.

In another video, Qiu wraps a glass in red cloth and places it on the table. He makes similar motions and lets out a yell. The glass shatters. In another performance, he runs a sharp cleaver across his bare stomach without leaving a mark. He claims to be manipulating the energy of qi to accomplish these feats.

Some insist that Qiu's skills are well within the parameters of a qigong master's power. Others say he is using fakery and illusion and that his yelling is evidence that he doesn't understand the quiet, subtle practice of qigong.

Images of Qiu in action went viral globally, with more than 300,000 views, after a clip from Chinese TV was posted to YouTube in 2010. Numerous versions of the clip and others like it have generated millions of views.

Shaolin monk Shi Niliang meditates while hanging by the neck for nearly a minute.

SUPER
HUMAN

HOW DO YOU DEVELOP EXTRAORDINARY POWERS?
PRACTICE, PRACTICE, PRACTICE.

Purushkara Yantra, a Jain cosmic figure, circa 1780.

WHO KNEW?

In the United States, modern Jains are expanding the tradition's practice of nonviolence to include environmentalism, animal-rights activism, and corporate business ethics.

In 1936, an Indian yogi named Subbayah Pullavar levitated off the ground in front of 150 witnesses. For a full four minutes, he hovered horizontally, only very lightly resting his hand on a stick. A photographer took shots of the yogi from numerous angles, and witnesses inspected him for signs that he was being supported by props or cables but could find nothing. A report of the event appeared later in a London newspaper.

Can a person become so literally enlightened that he or she can float in the air? Modern science says no, but ancient Eastern traditions insist otherwise. In Buddhism, one can obtain extraordinary power and understanding through meditation and other spiritual practices. Buddhist *abhijnas*, or supernatural abilities, include metamorphosing into any shape or form, hearing all sounds and understanding all languages, reading thoughts, and remembering one's past lives. Another group of supposedly achievable powers includes the ability to pass through solid objects, walk on water, appear in various places at the same time, and fly through the air.

But these skills don't come overnight. Achieving them takes years of practice, and one must be at an advanced stage of spiritual progress.

In the most miraculous stage, called an *abhijna*, the devotee experiences freedom and liberation through the renunciation of worldly passions, the understanding of the true nature of reality, and the certainty that one has attained awakening. This, the ultimate goal of the Buddhist practitioner, is achieved only by Buddhas, or Enlightened Ones, and saints.

Hindu Superpowers

Some of the Buddhist *abhijnas* are related to the Hindu *siddhis* ("miraculous powers" in Sanskrit). According to this tradition, *siddhis* are magical virtues that one can acquire through the disciplined practice of meditation and yoga. They include the ability to make yourself bigger or smaller, lighter or heavier; the ability to travel anywhere; and power over the physical world. But in both Hinduism and Buddhism, striving for the attainment of these powers can tempt one to be proud and egotistical. They should never be seen as an end in themselves, but as steps— or even just by-products—of a journey toward enlightenment.

In a third ancient religious tradition, Jainism, the most enlightened practitioners allegedly achieve superhuman talents including invisibility, mind reading, faith healing, and shape-shifting. According to Jainism, these extraordinary abilities can be attained through spells and the chanting of mantras, but also through austerity, nonviolence, and strict self-discipline.

Biblical Levitation

It isn't just Eastern philosophy. Christianity, too, is full of gravity-defying miracles. Here are four of them:

Statuary outside a Hindu temple depicts the Hindu sage Patanjali, who wrote the *Yoga Sutras*, the foundational text of Ashtanga yoga.

JESUS: In the book of Matthew, Jesus walks on water to meet his disciples, who are in a boat on a lake. Peter gets out of the boat and walks on water to meet him, but he begins to sink. When he cries out in fear, Jesus reaches for him and catches him.

TERESA OF AVILA: The 16th-century Spanish saint would supposedly become airborne during times of intense prayer, but viewed the experience as a reprimand from God.

SAINT JOSEPH OF CUPERTINO: This 17th-century Franciscan friar reportedly levitated or flew on 70 different occasions, staying aloft for as long as six or seven hours at a stretch.

SAINT ALPHONSO LIGUORI: This 18th-century Italian Catholic bishop was allegedly lifted several feet in the air in front of an entire congregation as he delivered a sermon.

HARD ON THE KNEES, GOOD FOR THE SOUL

Siddhasana, or "perfect pose," is said to bring practitioners one step closer to enlightenment.

Sit down on the floor. Keep your spine straight and bring your legs out in front of you. Now bend your left knee and place your heel under your groin. Bend your right knee, and put your right foot on top of your left. Finally, place your hands, palms down, on your thighs. You are now in a pose considered by some yogis to be conducive to summoning your *Kundalini Shakti*, or divine spiritual power, at the base of the spine. Yogis also use this pose to meditate and to practice breathing exercises. A word of caution: Siddhasana is not for beginners. It is anything but comfortable for most people's knees and hips. But who said enlightenment was easy?

FIRESTARTERS
AND MATCHLESS
MAYHEM

HUMAN TISSUE THAT HEATS ON ITS OWN? PEOPLE WHO CAN USE THEIR BRAIN WAVES TO IGNITE MATTER?

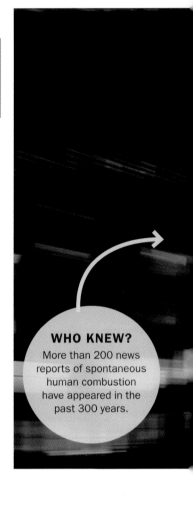

WHO KNEW?
More than 200 news reports of spontaneous human combustion have appeared in the past 300 years.

THE WICK EFFECT

A gory scientific theory proposes that spontaneous human combustion turns people into human candles.

A possible explanation for spontaneous human combustion is called the wick effect. According to this theory, the body is accidentally ignited by a cigarette, smoldering ember, or other heat source. The victim's hair and clothing catch fire and burn like a wick, while fatty acids act like candle wax, enabling the body to burn slowly without destroying surroundings.

THREE-MONTH-OLD BABY BURSTS INTO FLAMES WHENEVER HE SWEATS! FIRST IRISH CASE OF DEATH BY SPONTANEOUS COMBUSTION! Modern tabloids love stories of people who are allegedly able to ignite objects with the power of their minds or combust spontaneously.

But tales of such phenomena date to the 1400s, when Polonus Vorstius, an Italian knight, was described as drinking very strong wine, vomiting fire, and setting himself ablaze. Centuries later, when critics accused Charles Dickens of killing off an alcoholic landlord via spontaneous human combustion (SHC) in his novel *Bleak House,* Dickens pointed to research showing 30 historical cases.

So is there anything to pyrokinesis, the ability to ignite objects with thought, or SHC? Believers claim that pyrokinetic practitioners are made, not born, developing their skill by channeling intense emotions such as anger and fear. When a pyrokinetic focuses these feelings on an individual object, they reportedly produce flames.

If pyrokinesis exists, it means that individuals can use their brain waves to increase the thermal energy within the atoms of an object to the point of ignition. Scientists dis-

miss such theories, since brain waves generate very little energy—not even enough to light a lightbulb. For wood to ignite, it needs to reach a temperature of about 660 degrees Fahrenheit; for a human body to burn to ashes, it would have to reach a temperature of roughly 3,000 degrees.

People who swear that SHC is real refer to a mysterious condition under which human tissue supposedly heats on its own to the point of combustion, consuming the victim in fire while leaving the surrounding area virtually untouched. Believers theorize that the reaction is caused by an extremely small but high-powered subatomic particle they've dubbed the pyroton. Under the right conditions, pyrotons supposedly undergo nuclear fusion and release enough energy to ignite a human. To date, modern physics has been unable to locate these particles.

The character the Human Torch from the *Fantastic Four*.

In 1966, the remains of a Pennsylvania man were said to display signs of SHC.

HOT OFF THE PRESSES

Spontaneous human combustion has been featured everywhere from the cartoon *Calvin and Hobbes* to the TV program *ER*. But the news media have also carried reports of purported real-life examples.

→ In **September 2011** in Ireland, a man's burned body was found near his apartment furnace. According to the coroner, the furnace did not cause the blaze, nor was there any sign of foul play. The only burn marks were on the floor directly below the body and the ceiling directly above it—a common hallmark of spontaneous combustion.

→ In **1967**, a British woman on a bus noticed blue flames in an apartment building window. Fearing a gas fire, she got off the bus and called the fire department. When the firemen arrived at the scene, they found the body of a homeless man. One firefighter reported seeing blue flames coming from a slit in the man's stomach.

→ In **1974**, in Savannah, Georgia, Jack Angel claimed to have awoken from four days of sleep with strange burn marks on his body. His right hand, he said, appeared to be burned from wrist to fingertips, and he had "this big explosion in my chest. It left a hell of a hole. I was burned…on my ankle, and up and down my back, in spots."

HEATED DEBATE

Meet two real-life pyrokinetics, or "firestarters," said to have used their mental powers to create flames.

Hanky Panky
In 1882, L.C. Woodman of Paw Paw, Michigan, claimed to have discovered a man with pyrokinetic abilities. In a brief article in the *Michigan Medical News,* he described the case of William Underwood (born c. 1855), who could take a handkerchief, rub it vigorously with his hands while breathing on it, and cause it to burn until consumed. "It is certainly no humbug, but what is it?" Woodman wrote, sparking a round of debate in some medical and scientific journals of the day.

Hot Toddler
In March 2011, the *Philippine Daily Inquirer* reported that hundreds of people were flocking to a small city in Antique Province to see a three-year-old girl who had the power to predict or create fires. The mayor of the town stated that he'd witnessed a pillow ignite after a command from the toddler. "I can't explain it," he said. "I don't easily believe in this kind of thing, but I saw it."

The planets and other celestial bodies are thought by some to hold clues to life on earth.

CHAPTER 3

FUTURE FORETOLD

THE GUIDANCE OFFERED BY PALMISTRY, ICHING, FENG SHUI, TAROT, AND OTHER DIVINATION ARTS CAN AWAKEN THE IMAGINATION, SPARK HOPE—OR INSTILL FEAR.

SEEING
SIGNS
EVERYWHERE

ANCIENT ROMAN PRIESTS USED ANIMAL INNARDS, EGGS, FLYING BIRDS, AND DICE TO DIVINE THE WILL OF THE GODS.

Roman die, c. 1st–3rd century AD.

DICEY PREDICTIONS

The modern idea of rolling dice to determine the future may have begun with an ancient practice called *sortilege*, from the Latin words for *sort* and *choose*. Sortilege was a form of casting lots, where stones or pebbles were tossed to provide answers or guidance. In Rome, wood tablets were inscribed with names, phrases, or verses, and thrown into an urn of water. One would be extracted at random; the inscription on the retrieved tablet was believed to provide the answer to the question posed.

You have an important decision to make, such as where to found the capital of your empire, or whether to start a war. But you're not sure if the gods will bless your endeavor. What to do? If you lived thousands of years ago, you'd look for a sign from above using augury, a practice that involved observing the natural environment and interpreting it for clues to the future.

Some of the oldest forms of augury took guts, literally. The Etruscans, who flourished in the Tuscan region of Italy from the 8th to the 5th century BC, favored the examination of animal entrails. Known as haruspicy, this form of divination, or way of foreseeing the future, began with the ritual public slaying of a sacrificial animal. The seer would then inspect the butchered creature's organs, most often the liver and gall bladder. The color, size, shape, and markings on the organs would spell out the will of the gods.

The Answer Is in the Egg

If there were no entrails handy, there was always ooscopy, divination using egg innards. Under this practice, the various parts of the egg were examined for meaning. For example, blood in the yolk was an omen something bad would follow. Learning *ooscopy* was a lifelong undertaking, and ancient haruspices tended to avoid it because the practice failed to provide the requisite spectacle that accompanied sacrifice and dissection.

In ancient Athens and Rome, augury was performed by a priest who interpreted the will of the gods, mainly by studying the behavior of birds in flight. Were they flying in flocks or singly? What noises were they making? In which direction were they traveling? The study of these factors was known as "taking the auspices" and was considered essential in making decisions about personal matters such as marriage, or affairs of state or commerce.

Consulting the Gods

According to Roman myth, twin brothers Romulus and Remus used augury to determine whether to place Rome on the hill Romulus wanted or on the one Remus preferred. Romulus won. Centuries later, the Roman historian Livy stressed the importance of augury when he wrote, "Who does not know that this city was founded only after taking the auspices, that everything in war and in peace, at home and abroad, was done only after taking the auspices?"

It was not the role of the augur to determine what course of action should be taken. Instead, his job was to figure out what predetermined course had already met with the approval of the gods and should, therefore, proceed without the interference of man.

Pompeii wall painting, featuring a plate of eggs, from the 1st century AD.

THE FUTURE IN AN EGGSHELL

Ritual ooscopy is not as easy as it's cracked up to be.

→ **According to the ancients, before performing an egg reading, a priest had to...**

Be sober
Fast for 12 hours
Bathe
Put on clean, festive clothes

→ **To perform the ceremony, a priest needed...**

A pure, white, clean, unblemished egg
A vessel of water
A candle
Music, ideally that of the flute

→ **He then proceeded to...**

Carry the egg and water in a circle around an altar
Pour some of the water into his hands
Face south and extend his arms
Loudly invoke the gods, asking for an omen
Break the egg into the bowl of water

→ **Finally, he would inspect the egg for the answers he sought.**

WHO KNEW?
The terms *auspicious* and *inauspicious* are related to the concept of taking the auspices.

A Roman ceremony foretelling the future in the entrails of a sacrificial animal.

MAN OR MYTH

WAS THERE A REAL KING ARTHUR? FANS HAVEN'T STOPPED
SPECULATING FOR ALMOST 1,500 YEARS.

In Arthurian legend, Merlin was the great court magician and often by the king's side.

Repeat a story often enough, eventually people take it for fact. That adage certainly applies to the medieval legend of King Arthur, the heroic ruler of Camelot who is said to have triumphed over marauding Germanic invaders, established the Knights of the Round Table, and to have been tragically betrayed by his consort, Queen Guinevere. In the one of the most repeated Arthurian tales, the king was aided by a powerful wizard, Merlin, and wielded an enchanted sword that he pulled from a stone in order to prove himself the true ruler. When Arthur was gravely wounded during battle, he was taken by boat to the island of Avalon, where he vanished in the mists of time.

Did It All Really Happen?

As with much folklore, Arthur's tale is fantastical, full of magic, and larger than life. It is also a story that has recurred throughout literature. There are references to Arthur in 9th- and 10th-century texts. He plays a pivotal role in Geoffrey of Monmouth's *Historia Regum Britanniae* (The History of the Kings of Britain), a 12th-century work that today is considered more fiction than fact. Still, no definitive proof of the existence of this romantic king has ever been discovered.

Grains of Truth

Still, it has never been proven that he didn't exist, either. As with much of mythology, Arthurian legend probably contains at least some grains of truth. Historians have ar-

gued that Arthur is based on a 5th-century Romano-British king named Riothamus, a 6th-century Scottish king named Artur, and many other real-life figures. Some characters in the tale seem to have been borrowed from other lore: Merlin seems to spring from the Welsh legend of Myrddin, a lunatic and prophet. The sorceress Morgan leFay, one of Arthur's antagonists, is said by some scholars to be based on Modron, a Welsh earth goddess.

Timely Discovery

The exact whereabouts of Arthur's resting place is up for grabs. About 800 years ago, locals in what is now Glastonbury, England, began to claim that their landlocked town originally had been the Isle of Avalon. Their evidence: A high hill in Glastonbury at some point in time had been surrounded by swampland, proving that the hamlet was once an island. Further bolstering the story, in the 1190s monks at Glastonbury Abbey claimed they had unearthed a coffin containing the remains of Arthur and his queen, Guinevere, along with a cross identifying them. The convenient timing of the discovery—which just happened to occur when the monks were in financial difficulty following a devastating fire at the abbey, and needed to raise funds to rebuild it—has led scholars to conclude that the Tomb of Arthur is a medieval fake, perpetrated to attract tourists and their money. Today, the mystery could be solved by analyzing the bones and the cross, but those have since vanished.

The Lady of the Lake Telleth Arthur of the Sword Excalibur, illustration by Aubrey Beardsley for J.M. Dent's book *Le Morte d'Arthur* (c. 1894).

WHO KNEW?
According to *Historia Regum Britanniae*, the rocks of Stonehenge were magically transported from Ireland to England by Merlin.

HAPPILY EVER AFTER IN CAMELOT

Somebody important once lived at Cadbury Castle. Just who that somebody was is an ongoing mystery.

It doesn't look like much now, but a rectangular hill in Somerset, England, was once the site of an ancient fort called Cadbury Castle—perhaps King Arthur's legendary Camelot. The 16th-century English historian John Leland proposed the idea, and it has stuck ever since. Archeologists have uncovered proof that the fort, built around 400 BC, underwent a grand renovation around the 6th century and probably served as a king's palace. From a military perspective, it would make sense to locate a castle on a hill to offer protection from attackers in the lowlands. Whether the king who lived there was Arthur is debatable.

PRETENDERS TO THE CUP

Historians have dismissed claims made by many who said they possessed the Holy Grail.

According to the legend of King Arthur, the Holy Grail was the cup that Christ drank from at the Last Supper. Arthur's knights searched endlessly for the Grail, but never found it. Over time, many have said they possessed the Grail, but their claims have been discounted.

→ The Biblical Explanation

Claim: Joseph of Arimathea, who in the Bible donated his tomb for Jesus's burial, took possession of the Grail. He traveled to Britain, settled in what is now Glastonbury, and secured the Grail in a well at the foot of the town's sacred hill. The well water is warm and runs red because it contains drops of Christ's blood.

Counter-explanation: Ancient historical texts do not mention Joseph going to Britain. Iron in the water accounts for its red color.

→ Just a Really Old Cup

Claim: In the 16th century, the Grail was transported from Glastonbury to Herefordshire and stashed at a mansion called Nanteos House. The house has changed hands over the centuries, and the current owner keeps the Grail off-site.

Counter-explanation: There really is a Nanteos Cup associated with Nanteos House. It's a fragment of a wooden vessel, and naysayers insist it isn't the Grail, just a really old cup.

→ Hidden in Spain

Claim: The Grail found its way to Spain via a Spanish soldier. In the 15th century, the brown agate cup was given to the cathedral in Valencia, where it remains today.

Counter-explanation: The Valencia cup does date back to the 1st century BC, but a Vatican historian says it's too fancy to have been used at the Last Supper.

THINGS CHANGE

CONSULTING THE CHINESE TEXT KNOWN AS THE I CHING BEGINS WITH A TOSS OF THE COINS.

Confucius consults the I Ching.

OPPOSITIONAL FORCES

Yin and yang are constantly in flux and present in everything in the universe.

In the I Ching, the interlocking shapes of the yin and yang represent life in harmonious balance. Everything that exists is made up of these two energies. Yin, represented by the black swirl, is feminine: gentle, slow, relaxed. Yang, represented by the white swirl, is masculine: focused, strong, and fiery. The two opposite forces are dependent on each other and are constantly in flux.

The I Ching, the Chinese system of divination, is based on an anonymous text that translates as *Book of Changes*. But the system itself has remained the same for over 3,000 years. The complex calculations, which are based on a set of special diagrams and accompanying text, are used as a tool in solving personal and professional problems and attaining answers to philosophical questions. Interpreting the I Ching is an art in itself: The text is laden with arcane symbolism and opaque language, both in the original and in the many dozen translations that have followed.

The Future Is Uncertain

According to Chinese philosophy, the balance of the universe is ever-shifting between chaos and order. Since the two states coexist, change in nature, society, and human life is inevitable. This fundamental truth "should not constitute occasions for sadness but…for awareness, so that one may be happy in the interim," according to the I Ching. In other words: Things change, and that is the way of the world.

In the I Ching, there is no absolute, preordained destiny. People have the ability to alter the future, at least to some extent.

The purpose of the text, therefore, is to help humans consider and make sense of all the uncertainty, and reach thoughtful decisions about what is to come.

It does this first by identifying eight primary natural forces: Earth, Heaven, Water, Mountain, Thunder, Fire, Lake, and Wind.

The text then combines these forces in pairs to make 64 possible combinations: Earth with Thunder, Water with Mountain, and so on. Finally, it provides descriptions of what each combination means.

To discover the combinations that will offer the relevant guidance, seekers cast a series of lots. The I Ching offers instructions on how to do this and how to record the various pairings. Those seeking advice then consult the interpretation associated with their particular combinations.

Tossing Your Lots

The process of casting lots was once done in a complicated and time-consuming ritual involving counting piles of sticks, but the modern and simpler way is to use three coins, tossed six times. The configurations in which they land—the combination of heads and tails—correspond to specific pairs of I Ching symbols.

In modern times, the I Ching is often consulted by tossing three coins six times. Its text describes an ever-changing balance between opposing forces, yin and yang.

The answers within the I Ching text are typically complex, dense, and opaque. Nowhere does the I Ching say, "Yes, ask her to marry you." Rather, a reader might find a phrase like, "The time for action has come." Does that mean, "Yes, pop the question" or "Run away"? Interpreting the advice forces readers on a journey of self-discovery and discourages compulsion, or asking the same question repeatedly in order to get a better answer.

If the poetic text of the I Ching in the original seems daunting, there are simplified versions of the book available. Nowadays, there are even websites where those seeking answers can cast their coins virtually and be presented with "instant" interpretations—though that seems antithetical to the process, which is meant to be not only a tool for divination but also a form of meditation.

WHAT THE SYMBOLS MEAN

At its most fundamental, the I Ching can be broken down into eight elements. Each one is represented by a symbol made up of a combination of three lines called a trigram, each either solid or with a gap in the middle—a little like an ancient Morse code. No two symbols are alike. The eight elements represent qualities of nature and of personality.

Element	Symbol	Attribute
Earth		Receptivity
Mountain		Stillness
Water		Danger
Wind		Gentleness, flexibility
Thunder		Initiative, excitement
Fire		Radiance, motion
Lake		Pleasure
Heaven		Creativity, expansion

WHAT'S IN THE CARDS

WHICH INTRIGUING IMAGE WILL PROVIDE SPIRITUAL GUIDANCE FOR YOUR LIFE'S JOURNEY?

You've asked the tarot reader about your love life. She asks you to shuffle. Then she begins to place cards on the table in a cross-shaped pattern. The first card reflects your present. The second, your immediate challenge. The third is your distant past. She continues displaying cards. At first they seem auspicious: There's a star, a priestess, the moon. Then she lays down the tenth and last card: Death.

But all is not lost. This imagery could be more philosophical than physical and might suggest the closing of a phase in your life. In tarot readings, a divination technique with roots as a game, the answers are all about nuance and interpretation.

Tarot is derived from ordinary playing cards, which are thought to have originated in China and made their way to Europe in the late 1300s. The actual tarot deck was developed in the 1400s in northern Italy, when 22 symbolic characters and situations, such as the Emperor, the Pope, Love, the Wheel of Fortune, and Death were added to the existing pack.

Starting in the 18th century, fortune-tellers began using tarot cards in their practices, and by the 1780s French writers had published books describing occult uses of the tarot deck. During the occult revivals of the Victorian era and the early 20th century, tarot surged in popularity, metamorphosing into a practice close to the version used today.

Symbols into Meaning

The most common tarot deck has 78 cards, made up of four suits—usually wands, swords, cups, and pentacles (a five-pointed star inside a circle). Each suit ranges from aces to kings as in a standard deck of cards, but with one extra court card. These are referred to as the Minor Arcana. There are also 22 symbolic archetype cards referred to as the Major Arcana. Interpreting the cards is a complex process: During a reading, the cards can be organized, read, and understood in countless ways.

It isn't impossible to learn the tarot, and you need not be psychic, but mastering its many subtleties can take years of study. There is neither a standardized tarot style nor a universal deck. The suits can differ depending on the deck, and there aren't even always 78 cards. Even after a lot of practice, a certain amount of subjectivity enters into the process. Two readers might emerge with different interpretations of the same spreads.

The most recognizable deck today is probably the one created by Arthur Edward Waite, a British poet and mystic, and Pamela Colman Smith, a British artist, and first published by the Rider Company in 1910. But dozens of decks and styles exist, including versions with Shakespearean, fairy tale, Native American, mythological, and myriad other themes. Collectors of the cards view them as an art form as much as a divination tool.

A card from the Visconti tarot deck.

An assortment of tarot cards from the popular Rider-Waite tarot deck.

WHO KNEW?

There's a superstition that says it is bad luck to buy a tarot deck for yourself, but many professional readers dismiss this notion.

NO SHUFFLING ALLOWED

This famous tarot deck is accented in real silver and gold.

One of the oldest surviving tarot decks is also a beautiful work of Renaissance art. It has 67 extravagantly hand-painted cards, each featuring a miniature portrait accented in real silver and gold. The Visconti tarot deck, named after the wealthy Italian family for whom it was made, is more than 500 years old and is one of the earliest packs in existence. The deck is thought to have been created by Renaissance artist Bonifacio Bembo for the Viscontis, who apparently were avid tarot card users. The family had at least 15 decks, parts of which are now kept in various libraries, museums, and personal collections around the world.

ABOUT THAT DEATH CARD . . .

These trump cards are some of Tarot's most recognizable images. But what do they really signify?

The Magician	**Wheel of Fortune**	**The Lovers**	**The Fool**	**Death**
The second of the Major Arcana cards, the Magician is a hero, embodying will, creativity, and new adventures.	You may be taking an unpredictable ride on an emotional rollercoaster or embarking on an exciting life change.	Love and romance, of course, but it can also symbolize a significant either/or decision for which you require guidance.	The first Major Arcana card, the Fool isn't necessarily foolish, just inexperienced; it can signify a new beginning in your life.	The 13th Major Arcana card can be frightening, but its appearance usually means transformation, endings, or rebirth, not physical death.

LIFE LESSONS

Different schools of palmistry apply different significance to the various creases of the hand, but there is a consensus on these three:

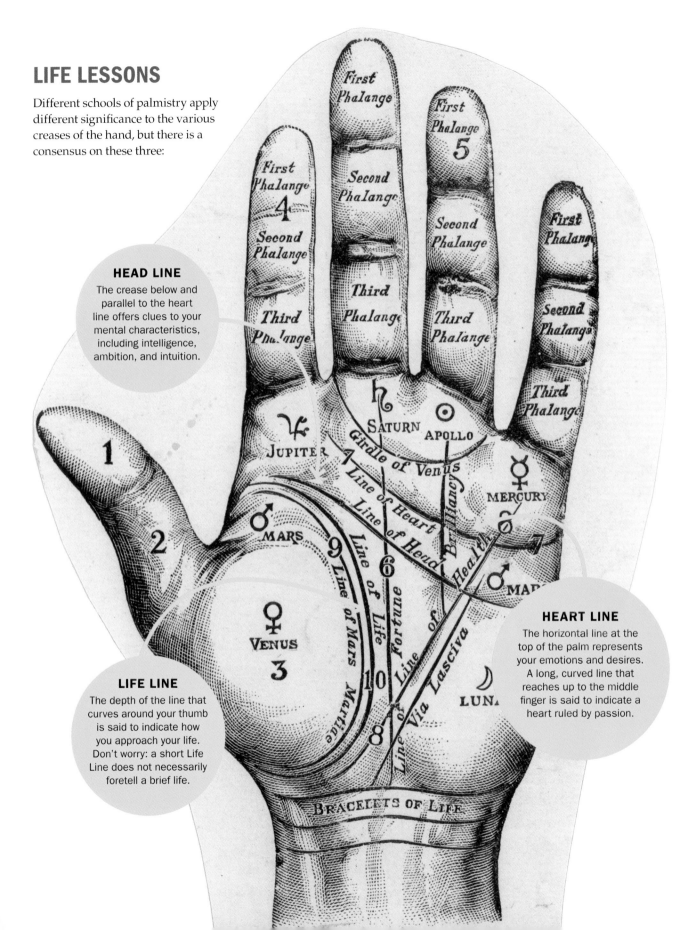

HEAD LINE
The crease below and parallel to the heart line offers clues to your mental characteristics, including intelligence, ambition, and intuition.

LIFE LINE
The depth of the line that curves around your thumb is said to indicate how you approach your life. Don't worry: a short Life Line does not necessarily foretell a brief life.

HEART LINE
The horizontal line at the top of the palm represents your emotions and desires. A long, curved line that reaches up to the middle finger is said to indicate a heart ruled by passion.

First Phalange 4
Second Phalange
Third Phalange

First Phalange
Second Phalange
Third Phalange

First Phalange 5
Second Phalange
Third Phalange

First Phalange
Second Phalange
Third Phalange

SATURN
APOLLO
JUPITER
Girdle of Venus
Line of Heart
Line of Head
Brilliancy
MERCURY
MARS
Line of Head
Line of Health
MARS
VENUS 3
Line of Life
Line of Mars Martia
Line of Fortune
Line of Via Lasciva
LUNA
1
2
9
6
10
8
7
BRACELETS OF LIFE

YOUR FATE IS IN YOUR HANDS

ACCORDING TO THE ANCIENT ART OF CHIROMANCY, YOUR CHARACTER AND FUTURE ARE ETCHED ON YOUR PALM.

Every crease and wrinkle of the hand can be interpreted.

Your long, flat Head Line shows that you're prone to overthinking decisions. Your short, curved Heart Line says you're an introvert who prefers one-on-one conversations. And your shallow Life Line means that you need to slow down and take time every day to relax. If you've ever had your palm read, you've probably heard such statements. If you believe the claims truly reflect your innermost self, you are in good and plentiful company.

Palmistry, also known as chiromancy, has been around for thousands of years, beginning with the ancient cultures of China, India, and the Middle East. The term itself comes from the Greek words for "hand" and "divination," and some practitioners claim that even the ancient Greek philosopher Aristotle was a fan: According to legend, he found a treatise on the subject in a temple altar and presented it to Alexander the Great.

Interest in palmistry waned after classical times and practically disappeared until the 19th century, when Cheiro, an Irish palm reader, gained fame divining information from the hands of clients including Mark Twain and Thomas Edison. The practice soon became so popular in Europe that it attracted charlatans. Established palmists then tried to legitimize the field by founding palmistry societies and issuing standardized guidelines.

The Palmist's Art

During a chiromancy session, the reader examines a number of physical characteristics. The shape of the hand and the relative size of the palm to the fingers are considered the most important predictors of personality. For example, a long palm and fingers might indicate sensitivity and emotional turbulence; a broad, square palm similar in length to the fingers might imply patience and reliability.

The lines on the palm and fingers are said to provide clues to one's innermost soul. In addition to scrutinizing the four most prominent creases—the Heart, Head, Life, and Fate lines—palmists look at a variety of smaller ones. The number of horizontal creases at the bottom outer edge of the palm is supposed to indicate the number of important trips a person has or will take during his or her lifetime, while the number of short horizontal creases at the outer edge of the palm above the heart line supposedly indicates the number of children a person will have. Chiromancers also sometimes analyze the size and characteristics of the bumps or *mounts* on the surface of the palm.

As for which hand to read, that is up to the reader. Some prefer to read their subject's dominant hand. Others view the left hand as showing the potential a person was born with and the right as what he or she has done with that potential.

BALANCING ACT

ACCORDING TO FENG SHUI, A CLUTTERED SPACE CAN'T ATTRACT OR KEEP THE ENERGY OF WEALTH.

GEE, NICE CHI!

Tap into the power of feng shui with these decorating tips.

→ Paint the front door the optimal color based on the direction it faces: red for south; blue for north; green or brown for east; white or gray for west.

→ No large furniture should face the front door; back and front doors should not align—chi will flow in and out again.

→ Keep the home tidy! Clutter confounds the flow of chi and causes stagnation.

→ Mirrors at the end of a hallway keep chi circulating, but if placed facing the front or back doors will ping-pong the chi in and out.

→ A sink opposite the stove in the kitchen can lead to disharmony in relationships.

→ Always close the toilet lid or risk having your money "flushed away."

→ No electronics or exercise equipment in the bedroom. They create negative chi and interfere with restful sleep.

For more than 5,000 years, the Chinese have been relying on feng shui (pronounced *fung shway*) to balance energy so that the *chi, o*r life force, flows properly in a given space. Need good luck, good health, or good fortune? Buying an aquarium, hanging a painting of a waterfall, or just moving a mirror might help. These days, the practice is popular in the West as well, and some interior decorators even specialize in offering commercial and residential clients feng shui services.

Directing the Flow

According to the ancient Chinese, all places exuded a particular chi. Long before the magnetic compass was invented, early mystics looked to the heavens to orient themselves in their environment. They believed that the flow of positive and negative chi could be harnessed by particular shapes and colors and by certain arrangements of natural elements and man-made objects.

The earliest feng shui practitioners started by choosing an auspicious piece of land. It was considered important to find a "dragon's energy" by examining mountains, hills, valleys, and water formations characterized by animal shapes, according to the first-century feng shui master Yang

Yun Sang. In Yang's view, a well-positioned house would optimize energy flow and be harmonious with the universe. A century later, feng shui master Wang Chih built on Yang's work by introducing the *bagua*, an octagonal, directional energy map that could be combined with the floor plan of a specific space to coordinate the elements, colors, and shapes that might best serve its residents.

Western practitioners of feng shui have adopted a simpler approach. Instead of emphasizing the land formations and astral cycles that were so important to the ancients, Westerners rely on a set of so-called aspirations. These are positions that correlate to specific aspects of life, such as north for career and south for health and wealth.

By placing the bagua over the floor plan of a house, the owner can see if the rooms align with the appropriate areas of aspiration. If a bathroom or laundry room falls within the wealth grid of the bagua, this is considered negative chi because any money coming into the home will tend to "go down the drain."

Once the floor plan is made harmonious, extend a home's feng shui with the right furnishings and decorative objects. Bringing in the elements with things like fountains and candles can boost a room's positive chi.

Use a *luopan*, a Chinese compass, to determine the proper direction for a piece of furniture or architectural feature.

A feng shui compass and crystal on a house plan.

IT'S ELEMENTAL

The first step in basic feng shui is harnessing the power of wood, fire, earth, metal, and water.

All five elements should be used in a home, each in its most auspicious area. Begin by lining up the bagua so that the front door is north, then map out where each element belongs. Employ the material, color, and shape appropriate for each room.

→ Lessen the power of an ill-placed water element by placing a plant (earth) in the room.

→ Introduce a fire element by using reds and vivid yellows or by adding triangle-shaped candles.

→ If there is a fireplace in a wood area, which may cause burnout and stress within the family, install a small fountain.

→ If the wood element is missing, add wooden window boxes and green or brown paint.

A DREAM COME TRUE

A VISION COMES TO YOU IN YOUR SLEEP. THEN YOU LIVE IT. HAVE YOU SEEN THE FUTURE?

A portrait of Aristotle, who wrote that dreams foretelling the future were mere coincidence.

You are in the middle of an experience that you recall precisely from a recent or recurring dream. What's going on? Did you subconsciously predict the future? Did you alter your behavior to fit your dream without realizing it? Did you even have the dream at all?

The precognitive dream, related to the been-there-done-that feeling known as *déjà vu* (see page 68), is called *déjà rêve* (French for "already dreamed"). It's very common, but the experience is sometimes given religious underpinnings. The first known mention of precognitive dreaming can be found in *Gilgamesh*, a 4,000-year-old epic poem that mixes myth and historic events. In it, the warrior-king Gilgamesh has multiple prophetic dreams in which he communicates with the gods. In the Bible, God speaks to many prophets through dreams. And the 5th-century Christian theologian Saint Augustine considered such dreams definitive proof of life after death.

Advanced Communication

Jumping ahead through the centuries, when the ship *Titanic* sank in 1912, hundreds came forward to report that they'd had dreams predicting the disaster. Ordinary people have also claimed to have had *déjà rêve* about the September 11, 2001, terrorist attacks; about Hurricane Sandy in 2012; and about the disappearance of Air Malaysia Flight 370 in 2014.

Dream Teams

Déjà rêve has been the subject of a variety of scientific and psychological studies. In a study published in 2010, researchers in Germany surveyed hundreds of university students. More than 95 percent of respondents reported having had at least one dream that came true. Most respondents said this happened between two and four times a year, but 7 percent said that they had precognitive dreams at least once a week.

Some theorists turn to physics to explain the phenomenon. In physics, time is not a linear progression of past, present, and future, the way we perceive it. Rather, all of time can be said to exist simultaneously and can therefore be experienced out of order. Dream theorists who view the human brain as essentially an information-

A woman in a multiple exposure of several positions during sleep.

WHO KNEW?
People who frequently remember their dreams tend to be those who wake up often during the night.

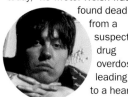
processing system posit that our subconscious can navigate time in nonlinear ways. In a nutshell, we can time-travel as we sleep and get glimpses of the future. This, not surprisingly, is a controversial theory in need of much more study.

As far back as 350 BC, the Greek philosopher Aristotle wrote that precognitive dreams were simply happenstance. Modern skeptics echo that notion and say these dreams are examples of confirmation bias, in which we forget the thousands of times our dreams didn't come true but remember the very few that coincidentally did.

Detail from *The Last Judgment* (15th century), Novara Cathedral, Piedmont, Italy.

END TIMES

NOTHING LASTS FOREVER—BUT SO FAR, PREDICTIONS OF THE WORLD'S DEMISE HAVE BEEN GREATLY EXAGGERATED.

The New Testament famously predicts that Jesus Christ will return to establish a messianic kingdom and reign over it for 1,000 years before the Last Judgment. But Christianity isn't the only religion to foresee apocalypse after the appearance of a redeemer, and through the ages many have auditioned for this role.

One of the first false Messiahs was the Jewish leader Bar Kokhba, who led a revolt against Rome in 132 AD. Hailed as the savior by Akiva, the greatest rabbi of the time, Bar Kokhba was killed by the Romans and his revolt violently suppressed. Centuries later, Sephardic rabbi Sabbatai Zevi was believed by many Jews to be the Messiah until the Ottoman sultan forced his conversion to Islam in 1666.

For Muslims, the Day of Judgment will be preceded by the arrival of the Mahdi—prophesied redeemer—riding a white horse. Perhaps the most famous claimant to the title was Muhammad Ahmad (1844–1885), a Sudanese Sufi sheikh who, in 1881, declared himself the Mahdi. From 1883 to 1885, Ahmad won a series of military battles against Anglo-Egyptian forces, culminating in victory over the British at Khartoum. Six months later, Ahmad died of typhus.

Over time, claims of being the savior seem to have given way to doomsday prophecies. On October 22, 1844, thousands of Americans gathered in meeting places across the country to await the end of the world and the glorious return of Jesus Christ. Many of these "Millerites," followers of William Miller, a New York farmer and Baptist lay preacher, had abandoned their possessions and said good-bye to loved ones. When October 22 passed without incident—an episode known as the Great Disappointment—some Millerites regrouped and started the Seventh-Day Adventists.

Harold Camping, a U.S. Christian radio personality, issued many erroneous dates for the world's end before his own demise in 2013. Camping's most famous prediction was that Christ would return on May 21, 2011, when the saved would be taken to heaven in the "rapture."

Celebrations for the end of the Mayan cycle known as Bak'tun 13 and the start of the Maya new age, at Chichen Itza, Mexico.

AGE OF ANXIETY

In 2012, the world was on edge when a reading of the Mayan Long Count calendar—used by ancient Mayans to track long periods of time—led millions to fear the planet's destruction on December 21. Even as astronomers, historians, and archaeologists discounted the scenarios of impending apocalypse, television programs, books, and the Internet helped spread hysteria.

CRYSTAL CLEAR

WANT TO SEE THE FUTURE? START WITH A SMALL QUARTZ GLOBE AND AN OPEN MIND.

Portrait of Nostradamus, by Cesar de Nostredame.

FUTURE SHOCK

A famous French occultist is thought to have used mirrors and water in his forecasts.

Nostradamus is the 16th-century French seer famous for "predicting" events such as the French Revolution, the Great Fire of London, and Hitler's reign of terror, among others. He reportedly used a black mirror and reflective bowls of water in his work,which he expressed in poems. Today, many of Nostradamus' prophesies seem strangely accurate—in hindsight anyway.

When a fortune-teller looks into a crystal ball, it is called scrying—that is, gazing intently into a reflective surface to achieve insight. The act is less mystical than it might appear.

Books and movies often portray mediums looking into a ball and seeing pictures inside. But a crystal ball is not a magic television set. It's simply a tool for sending the user into a deep, meditative trance. The seer may then have visions inspired by natural flaws in the crystal, or by reflective flickers of light on the surface. These visions can awaken the imagination and help subconscious answers form to address the question or problem at hand.

I Scry with My Little Eye

If you want to try scrying yourself, you'll of course need a crystal ball. They are surprisingly available, if not necessarily cheap. You might pay $800 or more for a 5-inch solid quartz sphere, or $200 to $500 for an 8-inch globe made of quartz. The shape and material are important: Crystals are said to have a special energy that connects them to the spiritual realm, and if it is formed into a ball, the energy can radiate out from all directions. Finally, the price also may depend on the ball's history and magical aura.

There are also smaller, very inexpensive crystal balls available, but those in the know warn against trying to scry on a globe less than 3 inches in diameter; it's not easy to focus on a small surface. If you simply can't afford the real deal, you can always try using a glass ball instead.

Having a Ball

Once you've acquired your crystal ball, you should clean it using warm water and a soft cloth to purify its energies. You might also wave some burning sage around it in another energy-cleansing ritual, known as smudging. Charge your ball monthly by placing it in the light of the full moon, and make sure no one but you touches it, so as not to contaminate its aura. When you're not using the crystal ball, store it away from all light.

When you're ready for a gazing session, prepare a quiet, candlelit space, relax, and hold the ball in both hands. Ask it, either aloud or silently, the question to which you are seeking answers. Then place the ball on a dark surface, such as a piece of black velvet, open your mind, and stare into it. The goal is to achieve a trancelike state in which thoughts or images come to you. If that doesn't happen, keep trying.

Artist John William Waterhouse depicts a woman gazing into a crystal ball (*The Crystal Ball*, 1902).

CRYSTAL METHOD

Crystals of all sorts have long been said to be associated with special powers. Here are a few:

→ **Amethyst:** magic, mysticism, past lives

→ **Apache tears:** transformation, release of negative energy

→ **Blue lace agate:** patience, understanding

→ **Carnelian:** personal power, growth

→ **Citrine:** travel, communication

→ **Garnet:** passion, sexual energy

→ **Green aventurine:** prosperity

→ **Hematite:** wisdom

→ **Moonstone:** clear thinking

→ **Rose quartz:** love, friendship

→ **Sodalite:** protection, sleep, healing

→ **Smoky quartz:** stability

INVESTING BY THE STARS

SOME PSYCHICS AND ASTROLOGERS CLAIM TO HAVE OTHERWORLDLY INSIGHT INTO BUSINESS AND FINANCE.

Does Venus rule the worlds of fashion and luxury goods?

SPHERES OF INFLUENCE

Some believe that each celestial body in the solar system rules particular aspects of the economy.

In financial astrology, the solar system is responsible for the various commercial sectors and for leadership qualities, investment opportunities, and luck.

→ **The Sun:** confidence, leadership

→ **Mercury:** transportation, communications, technology

→ **Venus:** cash, currency, fashion, luxury goods

→ **The Moon:** investor and consumer confidence

→ **Mars:** ambition, competition, physical labor, the military, weapons

→ **Jupiter:** banking, investing, law, prosperity

→ **Saturn:** steel, the financial status quo, misfortune

→ **Uranus:** inventions, new technology, mass media

→ **Neptune:** long-term assets, real estate, natural resources, water, shipping, health care

→ **Pluto:** investment banking, venture capital

It's a list that reads like an honor roll of business titans: Wall Street financier J.P. Morgan, steel tycoon Andrew Carnegie, entertainment giant Walt Disney, oil baron H.L. Hunt Jr., media mogul Oprah Winfrey, and software magnate Bill Gates. But the members of this exclusive club reportedly have more in common than just successful investment portfolios. These Americans, like many wealthy individuals since ancient times, are said to have consulted clairvoyants and astrologers about money matters. In an appropriate metaphor, many are referred to as "wizards" for their prescient business insights.

What role do specialized financial psychics and astrologers have in guiding the economy and those who benefit from it?

Corporate Crystal Ball

Commercial seers, many of whom prefer to be called "intuitives," focus on reading the business vibrations and energies swirling around their clients. They base their readings on hunches and general business acumen, rather than on any specific knowledge of their clients' operations. Their clients—who might be private individuals, fund managers, or CEOs—tend to recognize that spreadsheets and algorithms provide all the answers, and that they're most successful when they add instinct into the equation.

Companies of every size and type, from manufacturing to health care, are known to rely on intuitives for advice on strategic planning, human resources, and other issues. Investment bankers are thought to have been especially receptive to working with diviners who claim they can predict market fluctuations and economic trends.

Profit in Loss

Business for corporate psychics is particularly brisk during economic downturns. In these times, old forecasting models stop working and established rules fly out the window. So, the thinking goes, why not try some more radical methods of interpreting the markets?

The recent recession helped spur the expansion of the psychic service industry, which grew at an annual rate of 2 percent between 2007 and 2012, according to industry research firm IBISWorld. Today, with the economic recovery still spotty, some psychics are touting their forecasts to boost business further. Fiscal psychic Mary T. Browne has said she predicted the collapse of the U.S. housing market three years ahead of time and advised her clients to get out of real estate and invest in gold. She also says she cautioned job-seeking clients not to join Lehman Brothers or Bear Stearns, both of which subsequently collapsed.

Wall Street titans seeking a bull market are known to consult astrologers in their insatiable pursuit of wealth.

In India, the astrological signs are used to maximize profitability.

CELESTIAL GUIDANCE

Indians have a long tradition of relying on the stars to guide their business decisions.

Astrology has pervaded every aspect of Indian life, including business, for thousands of years. Believers follow a special system, called Hindu or Vedic astrology, which employs the same 12 zodiac signs as the Western version but interprets them in uniquely Indian ways.

It's common for Indian entrepreneurs to ask astrologers to bless their new ventures. Businesses seek astrological advice on launching new products, including what to name them and when to release them. Financial astrologers offer predictions on the performance of specific investments and the fluctuating value of the rupee. Claiming success rates of 80 percent or more, consultants often blame any errors on faulty information supplied by their clients.

Not everyone buys into Vedic predictions, of course, and the government agency that regulates the stock market warns investors not to make decisions based on astrology.

Corporate intuitive Laura Day, a best-selling author and television personality, says she maintains five corporate clients at any given time, charging each of them $10,000 a month. Day claims to have counseled her clients to pull out of the stock market a year ahead of the 2008 nosedive.

All That Glitters

Financial astrologers or "astrological economists" use the cosmos to analyze markets and companies. Working from significant dates such as when a company was founded, they construct astrological charts just as a conventional astrologer might do for an individual. According to this system, planetary cycles and the movement of the stars provide clues to future market developments and a client's optimal business and investment strategies.

One of today's most influential financial astrologers is Raymond Merriman, who estimates that more than 7,000 subscribers read his monthly forecasts. Another well-known Wall Street astrologer, Arch Crawford, studied sunspot activity, scrutinized star charts, and crunched numbers, and said he successfully predicted the stock market crash of 1987. Grace Morris claims to have been accurate as well: At the beginning of 2009 she declared that the S&P 500 stock index would plunge on or around March 9, and it did so on March 6. Similarly, she predicted that the U.S. stock market would reach a low on or around July 13, 2010, and begin rising that November—which also turned out to be right. Was it skill, chance, or the stars?

BEEN THERE, DONE THAT

MOST OF US HAVE EXPERIENCED DÉJÀ VU, THE SENSE THAT WHAT IS HAPPENING IN THE MOMENT HAS HAPPENED BEFORE.

WHO KNEW?
St. Augustine, the 4th-century AD Christian theologian and philosopher, wrote of malignant and deceitful spirits sowing "falsae memoriae" (false memory).

Déjà vu (French for "already seen") is that eerie sensation of having already lived through a particular experience. We suddenly feel a perplexing sense of familiarity. Every detail seems duplicated. We're that we have visited a place, met a person, or seen, heard, or smelled this thing before.

According to numerous surveys, most people have experienced déjà vu. It's especially prevalent between ages 15 and 25. Fatigue and stress, conditions that compromise short- and long-term memory, typically increase the likelihood of its occurrence. The uncanny sensation tends to last a few seconds or minutes at most, although a feeling of disorientation can linger. An episode of déjà vu is often accompanied by a sense of premonition.

Déjà Vu Under the Microscope

Prominent psychologists first attempted to distinguish and codify various "paramnesias," or errors of memory, in the 1890s in France. Today, many psychologists believe déjà vu is psychogenic, originating in fantasy, memory, or dreams. By its very nature, déjà vu is extremely difficult to document and analyze in a laboratory setting because it comes on without warning or cause, lasts only briefly, and involves no physical manifestations. Research data has been mainly anecdotal, limited to personal descriptions and recollections.

Recently, however, researchers have found ways to induce an approximate illusion of déjà vu in study participants through hypnosis and tightly controlled, conducive environments. They have experimented

WHEN THE BRAIN MISFIRES
Why is déjà vu common in epileptics?

Research has shown a higher incident of déjà vu in people with epilepsy than in the general population. The sensation can occur during seizure activity or between convulsions and can continue for hours or days. It is possible that déjà vu is linked to seizure activity in the medial temporal lobe, the area of the brain associated with sensory perception, speech, and memory. When neurons misfire in that lobe, scrambled information is transmitted to various body parts, creating seizures and possibly scrambled sense information as well. Some epileptics who have undergone brain surgery to prevent seizures no longer experience déjà vu.

Déjà vu can make people feel as if they are experiencing a double take.

with the use of photographs, memorization, and brain scans to hone their findings and conduct large-scale anecdotal surveys.

Out of these efforts have come several theories. One of them, the "dual processing" theory, suggests that déjà vu is the result of mental processes being out of sync for just a moment. This is possible because the human brain transmits visual data that arrive via the retina through at least two circuits. Due to a timing lapse in this process, thoughts may be experienced twice, resulting in an inexplicable sensation of repetition.

Another theory holds that déjà vu occurs when a forgotten memory (whether from real life, a dream, or something one has read or viewed) is subconsciously evoked in our present experience. For example, when visiting the Louvre Museum in Paris for the first time, you have a sudden, unsettling sense that you have been there before. But you've forgotten that you recently watched *The Da Vinci Code*, a film with vivid scenes set there.

Some researchers explain déjà vu as simply the result of a momentary attention lapse. Our brain rapidly registers a subconscious impression. When we become conscious of it, it feels oddly familiar because we've already processed it on a deeper cognitive level.

Paranormal Theories

The ancient Greek philosophers Aristotle, Plato, and Pythagoras contemplated the mysteries of déjà vu. Today, paranormal researchers cite it as evidence of reincarnation. They theorize that déjà vu occurs when fragments of past-life memories, stored deep in the unconscious, are suddenly thrust to the mind's surface by unfamiliar surroundings or experiences. Others point to clairvoyance, out-of-body experiences, or even alien abduction as possible causes of that "been there, done that" feeling.

Belief in the curse of the evil eye dates to ancient times.

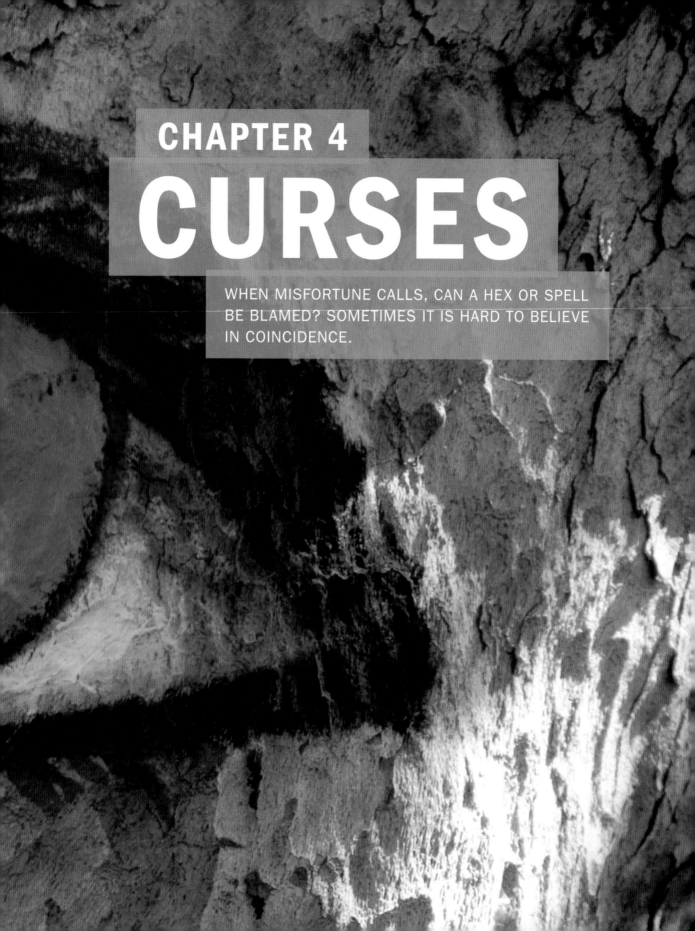

CHAPTER 4
CURSES

WHEN MISFORTUNE CALLS, CAN A HEX OR SPELL BE BLAMED? SOMETIMES IT IS HARD TO BELIEVE IN COINCIDENCE.

I PUT A SPELL ON YOU

WHEN TOMBS OF ANCIENTS ARE DISTURBED,
THE DEAD MIGHT STRIKE BACK WITH A CURSE.

WHO KNEW?
Belief in the curse of the evil eye dates to ancient times. With a single stare, a spiteful person could afflict anyone with bad luck or physical harm.

Human history from biblical times has been filled with stories of curses and spells. The Old Testament has Adam, Eve, and the serpent. In ancient Hawaiian tradition, those who take rocks from volcanic sites risk the wrath of the goddess Pele. In Iron-Age Assyria, "book curses" were invoked to protect written documents, threatening potential thieves with the wrath of God. Horror writer Steven King is famous for the creative hexes in his books. In the 1996 film *Thinner,* based on a King novel, a fat man accidentally kills a gypsy and is cursed with rapid weight loss by the woman's father.

In everyday life, people who believe in voodoo and witchcraft still seek to use ancient incantations to bring harm to those they hate or fear. Sometimes, hexes from the distant past seem to reach into the present day.

King Tut's Curse

In the 1920s, British archaeologist Howard Carter had been combing the Egyptian Valley of the Kings for years without results, and had fallen into disfavor with his benefactor. His luck seemed to improve

Lord Carnarvon, the patron of the Howard Carter expedition to the Tutankhamen Tomb.

in 1922, when he finally uncovered and opened the tomb of ancient Egypt's King Tutankhamen, a marvel of gold and ebony treasures. But was it really a fortunate find? Some believe Carter's discovery unleashed a curse of unimaginable proportions.

The gossip started soon after Carter opened Tut's tomb, when a cobra—symbol of the Egyptian monarchy—almost killed Carter's pet canary. A few weeks later, George Herbert, 5th Earl of Carnarvon, who had financed the Tut project, died of blood poisoning after he nicked himself while shaving. Believers claimed the cut was in the same place as a mark on Tut's cheek, but Herbert was buried before it could be confirmed.

Soon, Carter presented his dear friend Sir Bruce Ingham with a symbolic gift, a paperweight made of a mummified hand wearing a scarab bracelet with the inscrip-

Born circa 1341 BC, King Tut reigned only eight or nine years and died at the age of 18.

Israeli extremists pronounce a death curse on Prime Minister Ariel Sharon.

THE PULSA DENURA

Although Jewish law forbids praying for another's death, some believe in the tradition of the *pulsa denura* (Aramaic for "lashes of fire"), a curse against those who break God's commandments.

→ Two Israeli prime ministers have died after supposedly becoming the target of the pulsa denura. The right-wing Israeli group Gush Emunim believed that Prime Minister Yitzhak Rabin dishonored God by recognizing Palestinians and by agreeing to a partial Israeli withdrawal from the West Bank. On October 6, 1995, Gush Emunim claimed to have invoked the pulsa denura against Rabin. A month later, the prime minister was assassinated.

→ On July 26, 2005, a group of Israeli radicals gathered in a cemetery to bring the pulsa denura down upon Prime Minister Ariel Sharon for promoting the establishment of a Palestinian territory on the West Bank. A few days before the 2006 election, Sharon suffered a stroke and went into a coma. He never regained consciousness and died eight years later.

tion, "Cursed be he who moves my body. To him shall come fire, water and pestilence." Carter's house burned down, then was flooded after he rebuilt it.

Other supposed victims of King Tut's curse were murdered or assassinated, committed suicide, or died of unidentified illnesses. Within 12 years of discovering the tomb, 8 of the 58 who had been there for the opening were dead. Carter himself, who never believed in the curse, passed away at age 64 in 1939, of lymphoma.

Curse of the Iceman

In 1991, two hikers in the Ötztal Alps stumbled upon the frozen body of a prehistoric man dressed in animal furs and surrounded by various tools and weapons. When scientists investigated the exceptionally well-preserved mummy, they found it was about 5,300 years old; they named him Ötzi: the Iceman. Today he's on display in a custom freezer-casket in Bolzano, Italy.

Researchers working with the Iceman soon started dying, and a rumor spread that Ötzi may have been angry at having his 53-century rest interrupted and cursed all those who had interfered with him. Believers think that seven people so far have died as a result of the curse.

The first to go was forensic pathologist Rainer Henn, who perished in a car crash while driving to an Ötzi conference. Helmut Simon, one of the hikers who had found the body, died in a 300-foot fall in the Alps and was found frozen in snow and ice. One of those who discovered Simon succumbed to a heart attack after the hiker's funeral. Various accidents and diseases felled the other supposed victims of Ötzi—though scores of researchers investigating the case are still alive.

THE DIAMOND OF DEATH

THE MOST FAMOUS DIAMOND IN THE WORLD BROUGHT TROUBLE UPON MANY WHO CAME IN CONTACT WITH IT.

When French princess Marie Thérèse de Lamballe refused to denounce King Louis XVI in 1792, she was dragged from court and thrown to a violent mob. The crowd stripped, tortured, and decapitated the princess, placing her head on a pike. They then paraded their prize in front of the Louvre, where the former queen of France Marie Antoinette was under house arrest.

Both women once wore the Hope Diamond, reputed to have been cursed in 1642, when it was acquired—or stolen—in India by Jean Tavernier. The Frenchman is said to have brought the large, rough-cut blue stone to Paris and to have sold it to King Louis XIV in exchange for a noble title and gold. The king ordered the diamond cut into a 69-carat gem known as the French Blue, and it entered the royal collection.

THE HOPE CURSE

A chronicle of 400 years of woe.

1642

French jeweler Jean Tavernier acquires a 115-carat rough blue diamond in India. Legend has it that Tavernier gained the stone by deception and perhaps even murder, only to be torn apart by a pack of wild dogs on a later journey. In fact, he died of natural causes at age 84.

1668

Tavernier sells the stone to King Louis XIV.

1791

The crown jewels are stolen during the French Revolution; their owners, King Louis XVI and Marie Antoinette, are beheaded the following year. The diamond disappears.

1812

London jeweler Daniel Eliason receives a message telling him to go to an impoverished section of Soho, where he finds a destitute and dying Francis Beaulieu with a large blue diamond in his hand. Eliason offers far less than the stone is worth, but Beaulieu dies before payment is made. Eliason later allegedly kills himself, but not before disposing of the diamond.

1839

The stone appears in a catalog of the collections of British banker Henry Philip Hope, who dies that same year. The gem becomes known as the Hope Diamond.

1901

After gambling away his multi-million-dollar fortune, losing his foot in a hunting accident, and being left by his wife, actress May Yohé, Lord Francis Hope sells the diamond.

1902

The diamond is bought by Ivan Kanitowsky, a Russian prince, who loans it to his lover, Folies-Bergère actress Lorens Ladue. He allegedly shoots her to death while she wears it on stage. Kanitowsky is murdered soon after by Russian revolutionaries.

1908

The Hope Diamond passes to New York diamond dealer Simon Frankel, who resells it to the Turkish sultan of the Ottoman Empire for $400,000. The sultan is deposed shortly after, and the diamond is sold at auction to settle his debts.

Hope Diamond pendant

The Black Orlov/Eye of Brahma.

For the next century and a half, misfortune would befall many owners of the French Blue, from amputations to death by starvation to suicides. The origin of the stone's curse is unknown and its travels uncertain, but the gem is widely described as the most famous diamond in the world.

Eventually it would be purchased by jeweler Harry Winston, who in turn gave what today is called the Hope Diamond to the Smithsonian Institution in Washington, D.C., where it is on display. If there is a curse, it seems to be dormant—at least for now.

BEWARE THE EYE OF BRAHMA

Karmic retribution? Stones that begin in theft seem to cause death.

While the Hope Diamond reigns supreme on the gemstone curse list, the Black Orlov, aka "The Eye of Brahma Diamond," ranks a close second. The stone allegedly became cursed when it was plucked from the eye of a statue of the Hindu god Brahma. Three of its owners are said to have leapt to their deaths.

The diamond was then cut into three pieces in hopes of breaking the curse. Did that do the trick? Actress Felicity Huffman decided not to take any chances. When offered the opportunity to wear jewelry made from the diamond to the 2006 Academy Awards, Huffman declined.

1921

May Yohé writes and produces a film called the *The Hope Diamond Mystery*, blaming her troubles on the curse and calling the diamond "the most sinister jewel in history."

1911

Washington Post heiress Evalyn Walsh McLean purchases the diamond from Pierre Cartier, setting off a string of family tragedies.

1958

After purchasing the Hope Diamond from the McLean estate, jeweler Harry Winston sends the gem through the U.S. mail from New York to the Smithsonian Institution, to help establish a national jewel collection. Postman James Todd, who delivered the package, later is injured in two car accidents and loses his wife and dog to untimely deaths. Subsequently, part of his house burns down.

DID AN HEIRESS PAY THE PRICE FOR ACQUIRING THE HOPE DIAMOND?

Evalyn Walsh McLean had the gem blessed by a priest, but her life would soon unravel in tragedy.

The decades after heiress Evalyn Walsh McLean acquired the Hope Diamond brought her much sorrow. Not long after the purchase, McLean's son was hit by a car and killed. In 1931, McLean filed for divorce from her husband, Ned, on the grounds of his infidelity. The next year, the family newspaper, *The Washington Post*, went bankrupt and was sold at auction. Even as her fortune dwindled, McLean paid a conman a $100,000 ransom for the kidnapped Lindbergh baby. Soon after, Ned was committed to a sanitarium, where he later died. In 1946, McLean's 25-year-old daughter killed herself with an overdose of sleeping pills. Nevertheless, McLean never believed in the curse. "What tragedies have befallen me might have occurred had I never seen or touched the Hope Diamond," she said.

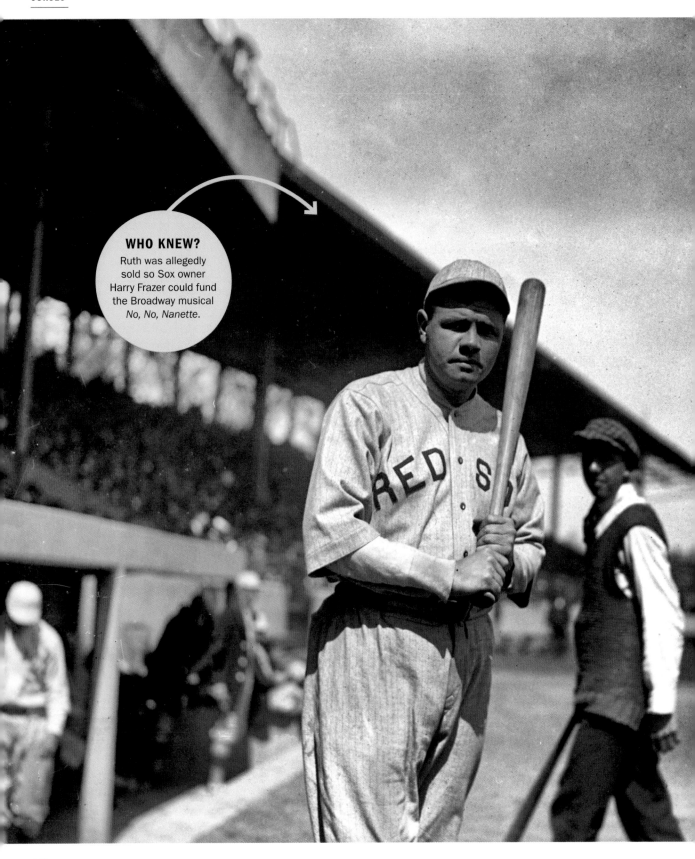

WHO KNEW?
Ruth was allegedly sold so Sox owner Harry Frazer could fund the Broadway musical *No, No, Nanette*.

THE CURSE OF THE
BAMBINO

IT MAY SEEM EASY TO BLAME A CURSE ON THE TRADE OF ONE PLAYER—BUT 86 YEARS OF LOSSES ARE HARD TO CHALK UP TO COINCIDENCE.

In 1918, the Boston Red Sox won their fifth World Series title, a victory attributed to Babe Ruth, the legendary player known to fans as the Great Bambino. During that series, Ruth, a pitcher and outfielder for the Sox, threw an impressive 17 scoreless innings. Yet two years later, Boston would sell Ruth to the Yankees in the off-season for $100,000 in cash and a $300,000 loan, thus setting in motion the most notorious sports curse of all time.

Ruth would go on to become one of the most prolific sluggers in baseball, knocking out 714 career home runs and earning the moniker "The Sultan of Swat." He would draw legions of fans to Yankee Stadium and turn the team, which had until then never won a Series, into an American League leader. With Ruth's help, the Yankees would snag seven American League pennants and take home four World Championships. The Ruth effect would endure even after the slugger left the team: In the following decades, the Yankees would go on to win 23 World Series. The once mighty Red Sox, in comparison, would be defanged, suffering a string of definitive losses and humiliating misses. The Curse of the Bambino would become a central theme in the Yankees–Red Sox

Babe Ruth in his Boston Red Sox uniform, 1919.

Fenway Park's left field scoreboard wall is nicknamed the Green Monster.

A POX ON THE SOX

The team suffered a long series of mishaps and near-misses.

→ **1949** Boston needed to win one of two final games against the Yankees for the American League pennant—but lost each by a single run.

→ **1978** In July, the Red Sox led the Yankees by 14 games. A summer slump led to a tie-breaker game against New York in September, which they lost by a single run, ending their season.

→ **1986** One win away from the Series title, a slow grounder rolled through Red Sox first baseman Bill Buckner's legs, allowing the winning run and forcing Game 7, which Boston lost.

→ **2003** With Boston up 5–2 late in Game 7 of the American League Championship Series, the Yankees tied it up, then hit a homer for the win.

John Madden

THE MADDEN COVER JINX

Injury often seems to befall athletes soon after they are featured on the cover of a video game named after John Madden, former NFL player, coach, and commentator. Here are just a few examples:

→ **1999:** San Francisco 49ers running back Garrison Heart appeared on the cover. He badly broke his ankle in a playoff game.

→ **2002:** A potential MVP, Viking's quarterback Daunte Culpepper, appeared. He later had a season-ending injury and Minnesota had a losing season.

→ **2004:** Atlanta Falcons quarterback Michael Vick appeared. He broke his leg in the preseason.

→ **2008:** Seattle Seahawk running back Shaun Alexander appeared, then broke his foot in the third week of the season.

→ **2009:** Retired quarterback Brett Favre appeared, then came out of retirement—only to suffer a torn bicep.

rivalry over the decades, and the subject would be explored in multiple books and videos.

People tried to break the curse. A Red Sox cap was left atop Mount Everest while a Yankees hat was burned at base camp. Catholic priests were brought in to exorcise Fenway Park. Former Red Sox pitcher Bill Lee had the idea "to dig Babe up, bring him back to Boston, and apologize to him."

In the end, they didn't have to. In 2004, the Red Sox broke the curse, finally winning the World Series again—in the 100th Series matchup, against the St. Louis Cardinals.

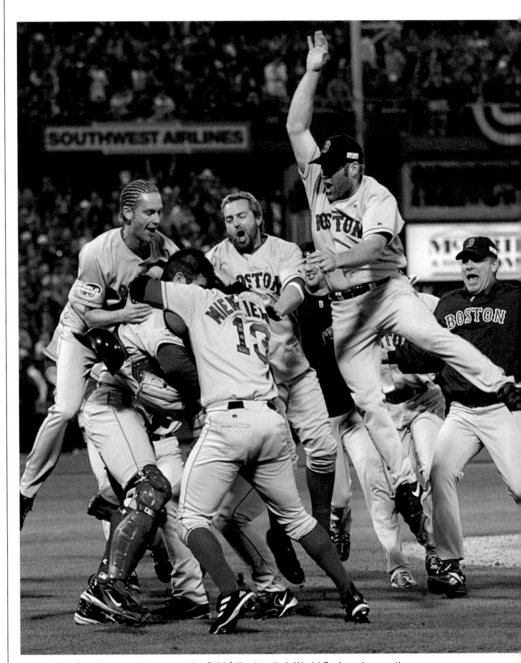

Boston Red Sox players celebrate on the field following their World Series win over the St. Louis Cardinals in St. Louis on October 27, 2004.

TRIPLE PLAY

More great baseball curses.

Chicago Cubs

The Chicago Cubs, considered the most cursed franchise in baseball, supposedly got that way because of a smelly goat. When William Sianis, owner of the Billy Goat Tavern, showed up for Game Four of the 1945 World Series with his pet goat in tow, team owner Phillip K. Wrigley told him he was welcome but his four-legged companion was not.

"Why not the goat?" Sianis asked.

"Because the goat stinks."

An enraged Sianis left, uttering the following infamous words: "The Cubs ain't gonna win no more. The Cubs will never win a World Series so long as the goat is not allowed in Wrigley Field."

At the time, the Cubs were leading Detroit 2 to 1. They promptly lost game four, and the Lions swept the series. Sianis sent Wrigley a telegram: "Who stinks now?"

Several attempts have been made to break the curse by bringing a goat into the stadium, to no avail. The Cubs fell into a slump from which they apparently cannot recover: Since 1945, the team has never made it to another World Series.

Philadelphia Phillies

In Philadelphia, a long-standing gentlemen's agreement prevented developers from erecting any structure taller than City Hall, a building topped by a statue of city founder William Penn. The agreement was broken in 1987 with the opening of 945-foot-tall One Liberty Place. For more than two decades, Philadelphia's professional sports teams failed to win any championships until communications giant Comcast placed a small figure of William Penn atop its 975-foot-tall skyscraper, opened in 2007. The following year, the Philadelphia Phillies won the World Series.

New York Giants

New York Giants outfielder "Captain Eddie" Grant was the first Major League Baseball player to die in World War I. The team honored him with a plaque at Polo Stadium, and the Giants went on to win the World Series four times. When the team relocated to San Francisco in 1957, the plaque was lost in the move and the Giants didn't win again for decades. To remove the curse of Captain Eddie, the team owner ordered a replacement plaque installed in AT&T Stadium in 2006. The Giants finally won the World Series again in 2010.

Chicago Cubs fans stand outside Wrigley Field after being denied entry for bringing a one-year-old goat to opening day, April 13, 2009.

DEAD PRESIDENT

AS TRAGEDY PILED ON TRAGEDY FOR THE KENNEDYS, SOME WONDERED IF THE FAMILY WAS CURSED.

BAD LUCK OR BAD JUDGMENT?

The family's apparent curse was inseparable from its undeniable aura of privilege.

On July 18, 1969, U.S. Sen. Ted Kennedy drove his car off a bridge on Chappaquiddick Island, Martha's Vineyard. The accident fatally trapped Kennedy's passenger, Mary Jo Kopechne, underwater and would haunt Kennedy for the rest of his political career. He was criticized for exhibiting bad judgment in the days following the crash, and the Kennedy family was accused of a cover-up. The incident destroyed his presidential aspirations, though he would serve as a senator from Massachusetts for 47 years. A week after the "Chappaquiddick incident," Kennedy described his experience in a televised statement: "All kinds of scrambled thoughts...went through my mind...including...whether some awful curse did actually hang over all the Kennedys."

Joseph P. and Rose Kennedy on the beach at Hyannis Port, Massachusetts, with their eight children.

As the iconic American political family of the 20th century, the Kennedys have been referred to as "America's Royal Family"—but fame, wealth, and political power have their dark side. The Kennedys have endured more than any one family's share of tragedy, with not only multiple assassinations, but plane crashes, car accidents, and fatal diseases. Some believe they are cursed.

In 1960, John Fitzgerald Kennedy Jr., known as JFK, was 43, and the youngest U.S. president ever elected. His energy and good looks, his glamorous wife, Jacqueline, and their two young children, John and Caroline, enthralled the nation and ushered in an era of youthful idealism. As part of the larger Kennedy clan—a wealthy and powerful Irish-American dynasty from Boston—the First Family seemed almost too perfect to be real. They leveraged their image brilliantly, offering the press unprecedented access to their private as well as public moments, endearing the fractious family to the world.

Behind the scenes, the Kennedy curse had already been set in motion. In 1941, Rosemary Kennedy, JFK's first sister, was debilitated for life by a botched lobotomy. JFK's brother, Joseph P. Kennedy Jr., a naval aviator, was killed during World War II. Another sister, Kathleen, died in a plane crash in 1948. But it was President Kennedy's November 22, 1963, assassination in Dallas, Texas, that would break the world's heart and forever undo the aura of Kennedy invincibility. The event shocked the American public and the world, and many people today can still recall where and when they heard the news. Five years later, tragedy would strike again when JFK's brother Robert F. Kennedy was shot and killed in Los Angeles while campaigning for president.

A Dedication to Public Service

The Kennedy catastrophes, however, didn't dampen the family's dedication to public service, a tradition started by patriarch Joseph P. Kennedy Sr. and his wife, Rose Fitzgerald Kennedy. Rose's father, John Fitzgerald, was mayor of Boston and served in the U.S. House of Representatives. Kennedy Sr., a businessman, was also Franklin D. Roosevelt's ambassador to Great Britain and the first chairman of the Securities

UNHAPPY HISTORY

Rose Elizabeth Kennedy and Joseph Patrick Kennedy Sr. married in 1914 after a seven-year courtship. Joe Sr. would live until 1969, and Rose until 1995, but many of their children and grandchildren would die tragically before their time.

JOSEPH PATRICK KENNEDY SR.   M.   **ROSE ELIZABETH FITZGERALD**

JOSEPH P. KENNEDY JR.

1915–1944. Eldest son and naval aviator. Killed in action during World War II at age 29.

JOHN F. KENNEDY (JFK)

1917–1963. Assassinated at age 46 in Dealey Plaza, Dallas, Texas, while riding in a motorcade with his wife, Jacqueline, and Texas governor John Connally.

ARABELLA KENNEDY

1956. JFK's wife, Jacquelyn "Jackie" Bouvier Kennedy, gave birth to a stillborn daughter.

PATRICK BOUVIER KENNEDY

1963. JFK and Jackie's son, born while Kennedy was president, died at just 3 days old.

ROSEMARY KENNEDY

1918–2005. The third child of Joe Sr. and Rose was considered unstable by her family. At 23, she was given a lobotomy. The procedure was botched, rendering Rosemary nonfunctional. She spent the rest of her life in an institution.

JOHN F. KENNEDY JR.

1960–1999. JFK and Jackie's son died along with his wife, Carolyn, and her sister when the plane he was piloting crashed into the Atlantic Ocean. He was 38 years old.

ROBERT F. KENNEDY JR. (RFK)

1925–1968. Assassinated at age 42 by Sirhan Sirhan on the night he won the California Democratic presidential primary.

DAVID KENNEDY

1955–1984. At 28, the fourth of RFK's 11 children died of a drug overdose.

KATHLEEN KENNEDY

1928–1948. The second daughter and fourth child of Joe Sr. and Rose, Kathleen was killed in a plane crash in France at age 28.

MICHAEL KENNEDY

1958–1997. At 39, the sixth of RFK's 11 children died in a skiing accident.

and Exchange Commission. Of Joseph and Rose's nine children, five would either hold public office or play an active role in politics. Edward M. "Ted" Kennedy, the youngest son, served in the U.S. Senate for 47 years. Ted's son, Patrick, was elected to the U.S. House of Representatives in 1995; Robert's son Joe was elected to the House in 2012. Robert's daughter Kathleen Kennedy Townsend served as lieutenant governor of Maryland. Robert F. Kennedy Jr. is a high-profile environmental activist. The late John F. Kennedy Jr. was the publisher of the political magazine *George*, and Caroline Bouvier Kennedy, his sister, became the U.S. ambassador to Japan in 2013. Their cousin Maria Shriver—daughter of Eunice, one of JFK and RFK's sisters—is the former first lady of California and an award-winning television journalist and producer.

Robert Kennedy, Jacqueline Kennedy, and Edward Kennedy during the funeral of President John F. Kennedy on November 25, 1963, in Washington, D.C.

THE DAY THE MUSIC DIED

LOOKED AT THIS WAY, SINGING THE BLUES TAKES ON A WHOLE DIFFERENT MEANING.

The wreckage of a twin-engine Convair 240 with 26 people on board, including three members of Lynyrd Skynyrd.

Frank Sinatra

A PARANORMAL "MY WAY"

In the Philippines, karaoke fans fear the famous song is cursed.

"My Way," the classic Frank Sinatra anthem about approaching death, is popular in karaoke bars in the Philippines, but singing it can be fatal, according to *The New York Times.*

Over the years, six people have been reported killed over their karaoke versions of "My Way," according to *The Times.* In San Mateo, a security guard shot a man who refused to stop singing the song off-key. In Manila, an off-duty cop pulled a gun when another table laughed at his rendition.

Some locals believe "My Way" is cursed, and the opening lyrics are rather ominous: "And now, the end is here." The song is banned in many Filipino karaoke bars.

As a little kid growing up in Robinsonville, Mississippi, in the 1930s, legendary blues singer Robert Johnson couldn't play the guitar to save his life. But after leaving the town for a period, he returned with an almost miraculous talent—or so said the locals who knew Johnson. Rumors began to circulate that the young man's newfound skills were the result of a Faustian pact: that he had sold his soul to the devil at a crossroads in exchange for musical success. Some said that Johnson made a deal with Papa Legba, a Haitian trickster.

Johnson's ballad "Crossroad Blues," released in 1937, supposedly revealed the place where the guitarist made his deal with the devil. In certain circles, it is thought that anyone who covers "Crossroad" and includes it on an album will be cursed—and believers point to some famous victims.

During the period 1965–1967 when the Allman Brothers were going by the name the Allman Joys, the band recorded a version of "Crossroad Blues." Then, in 1971, band leader and guitarist Duane Allman was killed in a motorcycle accident. The following year, band bassist Berry Oakley also died in a motorcycle crash, just three blocks away from Allman's accident. In 1976,

Southern rockers Lynyrd Skynyrd covered "Crossroad Blues" on their album *One More From the Road.* En route from Greenville, South Carolina, to Baton Rouge, Louisiana, a plane carrying the band's lead singer, guitarist, and others ran out of gas and crashed in October 1977. Six aboard died.

The most famous "Crossroad" cover was recorded by a young Eric Clapton and

Robert Johnson with blues musician Johnny Shines, circa 1935.

Duane Allman playing guitar.

Cream in 1968. Tragedy later befell Clapton in 1991 when his four-year-old son fell from a window in a New York City high-rise.

As for Johnson himself, he died the year after he wrote the fateful song. The prevailing story is that he was poisoned by the jealous husband of a lover. He was only 27, and barely known outside the Mississippi Delta. But Johnson would be discovered decades later and become one of the most influential American musicians, with fans including Bob Dylan, Eric Clapton, and the Rolling Stones' Keith Richards.

THE 27 CLUB

A startling number of rock musicians have died at the same age. Is there a connection?

"Live fast, die young, leave a good-looking corpse." Sadly, this brash rock-star dictum has proved all too prophetic, with an unusually high number of famous rockers perishing at the same young age. The phenomenon has given rise to rumors of a curse—and the moniker The 27 Club. Various theories about the significance of the club have been floated, with fingers pointing to numerology, astrology, and pacts with Satan. Some grim conspiracy theorists even believe that Nirvana's Kurt Cobain deliberately timed his suicide to join the group.

Here are some of the most famous members of The 27 Club, whose number has now surpassed 30.

BRIAN JONES
Guitarist for the
Rolling Stones;
drowning, 1969

JIMI HENDRIX
Guitarist and singer;
asphyxiation, 1970

JANIS JOPLIN
Singer/songwriter;
drug overdose, 1970

JIM MORRISON
Lead singer of
The Doors;
drug overdose, 1971

KURT COBAIN
Lead singer of
Nirvana;
suicide, 1994

AMY WINEHOUSE
Singer/songwriter;
alcohol poisoning, 2011

83

The northern lights (aurora borealis) reflected in a river in Iceland.

CHAPTER 5
MYSTIC
GEOGRAPHY

WE HAVE UNLOCKED HUMAN DNA AND SENT THE HUBBLE TELESCOPE INTO SPACE. BUT WE STILL DON'T KNOW HOW THE PYRAMIDS WERE BUILT OR WHO MOVED THE EASTER ISLAND MOAI.

The pyramids at Giza in the Giza Necropolis, near the city of Thebes.

PYRAMID SCHEME

MUMMIES, MARVELOUS TOMBS, AND THE GREAT SPHINX.
HOW DID THE ANCIENT EGYPTIANS DO IT?

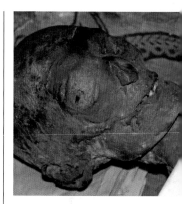

Mummy of Asru, a temple chantress from Thebes.

Standing 455 feet tall, with a base of 592,000 square feet, the Great Pyramid of Giza in Egypt is one of the Seven Wonders of the Ancient World and the only one of the structures to remain intact. That this imposing edifice has survived more than 7,000 years is indeed a marvel.

Building Blocks

Giza dates to around 2550 BC, when the Egyptian king Khufu ordered construction to begin on a tomb for his family, which would become the largest pyramid in the land. It was to be the centerpiece of a group of smaller pyramids and buildings in the town, about ten miles north of what is now modern-day Cairo. Built over roughly 20 years, the pyramid was made from some 2.3 million stone blocks, ranging in weight from 2 to 50 tons each. To this day, no one is quite sure precisely how the Egyptians pulled it off. But historians believe that it took thousands of workers—rather than slaves, as biblical stories suggest—placing the blocks at the rate of one every two-and-a-half minutes to complete the task.

Alternate Theories

Although the ancient Egyptians were excellent record-keepers, no documentation exists showing how the pyramids were built. Most Egyptologists believe the stones were pulled with ropes over gradually sloping ramps. Others think levers were used. How the blocks were transported from the quarry is an even bigger mystery. Some historians think the stones were moved via wooden sledges, or carts without wheels, over wooden tracks—but this is difficult to believe, because there is very little wood in Egypt.

Recently, evidence has emerged supporting a theory that the Giza pyramid was constructed from the inside out, using a spiraling tunnel. Images from a 1986 survey indicate a spiraling feature within the outer walls, but the evidence is not conclusive.

To date, no theories have been proven.

Detail of the Great Pyramid blocks.

MUMMIES UNWRAPPED

After burying their dead in the Sahara for years, the ancient Egyptians discovered that the dry desert conditions were halting the bodies' decay. Before long, priests developed a preservation process, and the Egyptian mummy was born.

Early Egyptians believed that post-mortem preservation provided a good start in the afterlife, so a well-performed mummification was of the utmost importance:

→ All interior organs were removed from the deceased, except for the heart, the supposed organ of intellect.

→ The corpse was rinsed out with wine and spices.

→ The body was covered with a salt-like substance called natron.

→ The corpse dried out for 70 days, or a shorter time for those who paid less.

→ The departed was wrapped in linen and placed in a sarcophagus.

The Great Sphinx and the Pyramid of Khafre on the Giza Plateau, on the west bank of the Nile River in Egypt.

What Lies Beneath

In October 1995, the Egyptian Antiquities Organization was refurbishing the parking lot east of the Sphinx when workers made a startling find: a series of underground chambers and passageways, one of which led deep underneath the Sphinx. The secret corridor, estimated to be ten feet wide and 200 feet long from north to south, dipped mysteriously at the eastern end before vanishing into the ground.

Since restoring the Sphinx was considered more important than other work, the passageways were blocked with stones to prevent treasure hunters from stealing artifacts. Giza antiquities chief Zahi Hawass has stated that he doesn't believe there is anything in the tunnel but rocks, but the mystery of the chambers remains alluring to all.

One person who has managed to explore the tunnels is Egyptologist Robert Bauval, the author of two controversial books about the Sphinx, who claims the massive structure was actually built more than 10,000 years ago. In 1995, before the

The Missing Nose

Upon viewing the Sphinx in profile, you can't help but notice its missing facial feature. Researchers have yet to "sniff out" when or how the Great Sphinx lost its nose. They do know that it originally was painted red and that it had been reported missing as early as the 15th century. Researchers have also discovered rod or chisel marks in the meter-wide area where the nose was, indicating that it was hammered off.

The most popular theory has Napoleon blasting the nose off with a cannonball while using the Sphinx for target practice during the French campaign in Egypt. This makes for an interesting story but has no factual basis. The French campaign took place from 1798 to 1801, a few hundred years after the nose was documented as missing.

The account accepted by most scholars comes from the Arab historian al-Maqrizi, who wrote in the 15th century that the nose was chiseled off by Muhammed Sa'im al-Dahr, a fanatical Sufi Muslim, in 1378 AD. Apparently, al-Dahr became enraged at local peasants' worship of the Sphinx. The peasants hung al-Dahr for vandalism before burying him near the Sphinx.

The Grand Gallery inside the Great Pyramid of Khufu, Giza.

area was closed off, Bauval spent time inside where he said he found a "very curious manhole in the main artery." Made of limestone, the manhole was cracked in the corner and Bauval said he could see running water flowing toward the Sphinx and the Valley Temple.

Bauval connects the tunnels with an ancient Egyptian myth that describes two sphinxes guarding the gates to the afterlife, with an underground stream beneath them.

Greek winged goddess.

RIDDLES OF THE SPHINX

The world's largest monolith may just be the most mysterious, too.

Drawings with clues to the age and purpose of other ancient tombs have been discovered in Giza, but to date, no such images of the Great Sphinx have been unearthed. No Old Kingdom inscriptions refer to it, and there is no clue to how its contemporaries referred to it. By the time a New Kingdom pharaoh named Thutmose IV excavated the front paws in 1400 BC, the body had already been covered in sand for centuries.

What is known is that the Sphinx takes her name from a fearsome creature in Greek mythology, a winged lion with a woman's face who strangled all who could not answer her riddles. The Sphinx in Egypt has become a riddle herself, puzzling the ancients as well as present-day archeologists.

SACRED SUNCATCHER

ONCE A YEAR, AN ANCIENT TOMB SEES THE LIGHT OF DAY.

A detail of stone carvings at the temple of Newgrange.

ETCHED IN STONE

Many of the kerbstones surrounding Newgrange, as well as the entrance and the walls within, are decorated with various spirals, circles, and diamond shapes. They may have symbolized phases of the moon and sun, or the changing seasons. The most well-known is the *triskele*, the triple spiral. One is carved on the entrance stone, perhaps as a sign that inside is another, sacred world.

In 1699, Charles Campbell, a landowner in County Meath in eastern Ireland, stumbled upon an entrance in a massive stone mound, as he and a group of workers cleared the land for a road. Campbell and his crew had uncovered a 200,000-ton structure dating from 3200 BC: the ancient sacred temple of Newgrange.

The mound and its history were shrouded in mystery. Was it a supernatural site? The abode of ancient Irish gods? In spite of intermittent interest, it wasn't until the 1960s that an exhaustive excavation of the acre-wide site began. Eventually archeologists identified a so-called passage tomb, a structure 36 feet high and 300 feet in diameter, containing a long narrow passage, a chamber in the shape of a cross, and huge stones with multiple burial chambers within.

The researchers discovered the mysterious tomb had fallen into disuse for centuries after it was constructed. Romans coins were discovered within, possibly left by invaders as a sign of respect. When the Danes invaded Ireland in the 9th century, they apparently left the structure alone. By the time Cistercian monks acquired the land around the passage tomb in 1142, its secret was already hidden. The monks named the area Newgrange, which meant "new farm."

From Darkness, Light

Like Stonehenge in England, Newgrange is oriented to the celestial calendar. On the winter solstice, through an opening carved above the entrance, the sun completely illuminates both the passage and the chamber. The process begins on December 19, when a narrow shaft of light appears. It gradually widens until, for 17 extraordinary minutes on December 21, the longest day of the year, the sun fills the entire chamber. How did the ancient builders develop such precise astronomical knowledge and architectural expertise? The answer is unknown, though professor Michael J. O'Kelly, who led the excavation of the site in the 1960s, estimated that it would have taken 400 people about 16 years to construct it.

Newgrange, now part of a UNESCO World Heritage Site, continues to be of immense interest. Archaeologists have proposed many ideas about the passage tomb, but many questions remain about its original purpose and use.

Newgrange is at least 500 years older than the Great Pyramid of Giza and 1,000 years older than Stonehenge.

Inside a burial chamber at Knowth, the passage tomb complex.

A RIVER RUNS BY THEM

Brú na Bóinne is an ancient Gaelic name that means "Palace of the Boyne." Along a stretch of the River Boyne, about 36 miles north of Dublin, are the three ancient stone passage tombs that make up this "palace," a UNESCO World Heritage Site.

Newgrange
The most thoroughly excavated and restored, with a remarkable show of sunlight on the winter solstice.

Knowth
The most artful, with more than 200 decorated stones. Some carvings inside have been identified as moon maps.

Dowth
Between November and February, the rays of the sunset reach into the passage.

WHO KNEW?

Visitors can enter a lottery to see the shaft of sunlight that penetrates Newgrange's interior at the winter solstice. Each year, 35,000 people vie for just over 100 spots.

Candles illuminate a passage in the Newgrange tomb.

THE LOST CONTINENT

TALES OF ATLANTIS HAVE ENDURED FOR MORE THAN 2,000 YEARS. WHERE IS IT?

One psychic's visions of Atlantis spurred modern interest in the legend.

AMERICANS = ATLANTEANS?

Tales of reincarnation and technology thrilled Cayce's listeners.

The famous 20th-century American psychic Edgar Cayce often spoke of Atlantis, claiming that many Americans were reincarnated Atlanteans. He believed that the historical records of the lost continent were hidden beneath the Egyptian sphinx, and that the ultimate destruction of Atlantis was caused by giant laser-like crystals that had been employed by its people as power sources.

"Timaeus" and "Critias," two famous dialogues by the Greek philosopher Plato, provided readers with a detailed description of the long-lost island of Atlantis and the advanced culture that flourished there. Plato wrote of the isle's lush and fertile farmland, abundant mineral resources, plentiful fruits and vegetables, and exotic animals. He described the beautiful capital city, also known as Atlantis, as being ringed with canals that separated wide bands of land filled with racetracks, gymnasiums, warehouses, and harbors.

Some subsequent scholars believed Plato's account of Atlantis was fiction, while others were certain it was real. Most modern academics believe that the philosopher's story was meant as a myth or allegory to educate readers about ideal societies—one of his favorite themes. Either way,

Plato's story of Atlantis has proved remarkably durable over the centuries. Many have attempted to provide details that Plato left ambiguous, including the date of the island's destruction (estimated to have been more than 9,000 years before his time), as well as its location (somewhere "beyond the Pillars of Hercules"). In the popular imagination, Atlantis is no longer a Platonic creation but instead is thought of as the quintessential example of an advanced, yet tragically lost ancient civilization. The idea continues to fire imaginations, and the fanciful island is often depicted in books, movies, television shows, and other works.

A New Atlantis

The interest in Atlantis today can be traced to the 1882 publication of *Atlantis, the Antediluvian World,* by Ignatius Donnelly. A U.S. congressman and amateur scientist, Donnelly wrote about an Atlantis that was more technologically sophisticated and culturally superior to Plato's, and that was the mother of all known ancient civilizations, including the Egyptians, Mayans, Mexicans, Irish, and the Chinese. According to Donnelly, whose book became a best seller, Atlantis sank into the middle of the Atlantic Ocean during

"There occurred violent earthquakes and floods, and in a single day and night of misfortune all your warlike men in a body sank into the earth, and the island of Atlantis in like manner disappeared into the depths of the sea." —Plato

The legend of Atlantis has inspired immensely creative visions. Here, an illustrator imagines dinosaurs feeding around the famous city, which is about to sink beneath the waves.

the great flood of the Old Testament.

As the geological theories of plate tectonics and continental drift gained acceptance during the 1960s, most "lost continent" theories were discarded, but the search for Atlantis didn't end. Over the years, there have been dozens of locations proposed for Atlantis, including the environs of Cuba, the Andes, Spain, Turkey, the Arctic, the Antarctic, the Mediterranean, Central America, central Africa, and central Asia. Reputable organizations, most notably the National Geographic Society, are still involved in searching for Atlantis, and ongoing theories regarding its existence and collapse thrive to this day.

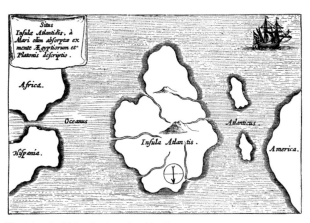

The island of Atlantis described by Plato.

MIRACLE WORKER

THE WATER AT A FRENCH SHRINE TO THE VIRGIN MARY IS SAID TO HEAL THE SICK.

A pilgrim fills bottles at taps carrying water from the Grotto of Massabielle at Lourdes.

People come from all over the world to drink it, bathe in it, or just be near it. In thousands of cases, the healing water of Lourdes is said to have cured everything from broken bones to blindness, multiple sclerosis, and cancer. Thorough analysis of the water that emanates from the spring shows that it's nothing more than ordinary H_2O. But the faithful are certain that the liquid in the shrine to Our Lady of Lourdes is something special, and even the Catholic Church has verified that it has given rise to more than 60 miracles.

The shrine is located in a cave in the Pyrenees mountain town of Lourdes, France, near the border of Spain. One of the world's most popular pilgrimage sites, Lourdes has had about 200 million visitors since the shrine was established in 1860. Of those, about 7,000 claim to have been cured of illness.

The watery miracle was first discovered by a local teenager named Bernadette Soubirous. On February 11, 1858, Bernadette was searching for firewood near a cave called the Grotto of Massabielle. Preparing to cross a stream, the 14-year-old stopped in the grotto to remove her shoes and socks. There, she later said, she heard "a noise like a gust of wind" and suddenly saw "a small young lady" smiling at her, wearing a white dress and veil, a blue belt, and "a yellow rose on each foot." After reciting the rosary with Bernadette, the apparition vanished.

Bernadette visited the grotto many more times over the next several months. On each visit she saw the lady in white, who ultimately revealed herself to be the Virgin Mary. The now-famous spring appeared on Bernadette's ninth outing, when the apparition told her to dig at the ground and drink the water that welled up.

Gaining a Following

As word spread of Bernadette's visions, crowds began to follow her on her visits to the grotto. The first healing attributed to Lourdes water occurred when a woman with a dislocated arm dipped it into the spring; afterward, she could move it again. As thousands of people began following Bernadette, the police threatened to arrest her, believing she was a fraud. The mayor of the town barricaded the grotto, but a few months later it was reopened by order of Emperor Louis Napoleon III. Pilgrims flooded into Lourdes and began to describe miraculous healings.

After 18 visits, Bernadette's visions ceased, and she stopped going to the grotto. She maintained that the water had no special powers, and that faith and prayer were healing the visitors. Bernadette soon joined the nearby Convent of St. Gildard of Nevers, where she died in 1879. But her story wasn't over.

Considering her for beatification, the Catholic Church opened Bernadette's

Millions of pilgrims have visited the Grotto of Massabielle at Lourdes.

Saint Bernadette at age 15.

grave in 1909. Thirty years after her death, her body was inexplicably intact. It was exhumed again in 1919 and 1925 and remained pristine—a testament, perhaps, to the water. Bernadette was made a saint in 1933. Her body, encased in a glass casket, is on display at her former convent.

Hope Springs Eternal

Today, approximately five million people come to the Sanctuary of Our Lady of Lourdes every year. Surrounding the grotto are chapels, churches, and facilities for the sick. A system of *piscines* (baths) and taps dispenses the Lourdes water. As it has since 1905, the church-run Lourdes Medical Bureau examines claims of cures for authenticity, accepting as miracles only those with no other physical or psychological explanation.

HARD TO SWALLOW

Water covers most of the Earth's surface and makes up much of our bodies.
We can't live more than a few days without it. No wonder so many cultures
believe it has healing powers. But does it? Not in these three cases.

H_2O	The Story	The Truth
Mystery Tree Water	"Holy" water began to gush from the trunk of a San Antonio, Texas, woman's backyard oak in 2006.	The tree had grown down into a water pipe in the yard.
Miracle Spring Water	TV evangelist Peter Popoff claims his water can bring prosperity and healing.	Requestors get a sample of the "free" water, followed by multiple appeals for financial donations.
Zam Zam Water	In 2007, bottles of water supposedly from a sacred well in Mecca popped up in the United Kingdom.	Tests on the bottled water showed it was contaminated with arsenic. The authentic water, from the real Well of Zamzam, is not.

MATH MARVELS

THE MAYANS BUILT PYRAMIDS TO CAST SHADOWS
SHAPED LIKE ANIMALS. THEIR SECRET?

Not far from the contemporary sun worshippers in the resort of Cancun, Mexico, a very different kind of adoration occurred, millennia ago. The place was Chichen Itza, an ancient Mayan city considered to be one of the seven wonders of the world. What the cathedrals were to Europe, the temple pyramids were to the Maya.

The Mayan culture thrived in parts of Meso-america from about 1500 BC to 1697 AD; remnants of their architecture can be found in such places as Tikal, Copán, Palenque, Caracol, and Uxmal. The sacred Temple of Kukulkan that dominates the site of Chichen Itza is the clear-est example of the Maya's genius for mathematics and astronomy.

Equinox Magic

Both the design and the orientation of the pyramids were determined by the Ma-yas' knowledge of the path of the sun. Twice a year, on the days of the spring and autumn equinoxes, a long shadow cast by the sun takes the shape of a snake winding across the pyramid at Chichen Itza. The viper curls its way down the pyramid to the base, where the stone head of a serpent has been carved.

The serpent shadow may represent the supreme Ma-

THE FEATHERED SERPENT

The Mayan's flying serpent deity may have been inspired by a local bird.

A sculpture of a human atop a winged serpent at Temple of the Warriors, Chichen Itza.

The Mayas' supreme god, Kukulkan, was identified with the image of a feathered snake and was known as Quetzalcoatl in the ancient Mesoamerican Nahuatl language. Quetzalcoatl was also associ-ated with the brilliantly colored quetzal, a native bird known for its spectacular plumage. At Chichen Itza, visitors can stand at the base of the pyramid, clap their hands, and hear an echo caused by the alignment of the steps. The sound resembles the call of the quetzal!

The Temple of Kukulkan pyramid at Chichen Itza, in the Yucatán, Mexico (circa 9th–12th centuries AD).

The Mayan calendar.

"DAYS WITHOUT NAMES"

The Mayan solar calendar, presented in the round, perceives time as cyclical rather than linear.

Like our Gregorian calendar, the Mayan solar calendar, the Haab', had 365 days. The Maya divided their year into 18 months of 20 days each, plus 1 month of five days. The first month of the year, Pop, began on the winter solstice.

The five unfortunate days in the 19th month were called Wayeb, "days without names," and were thought to be an unlucky time during which evil spirits from the Underworld might cause disaster. To avert calamity, the Maya avoided leaving their houses on these days.

yan god Kukulkan, which was typically depicted as a flying snake whose tail moved the winds, and symbolized the divinity of the state. The darkened form was clearly intentional and the result of careful calculation by the ancients.

Do the Math

To unlock more secrets of this sacred pyramid, one must understand the calendar used by the Mayans and other pre-Columbian Mesoamerican societies. The calendar was a sophisticated set of three interlocking measures that were pegged to the movements of the sun. The Long Count calendar calculated so-called universal cycles of time, each of which was about 7,885 solar years. The ancient Maya believed that the universe was destroyed and recreated at the end of each universal cycle. The 260-day sacred calendar, or *Tzolk'in*, was used for timing ceremonial events, while a 365-day solar calendar, or *Haab'*, divided years into months and days in much the same way that our Gregorian solar calendar does.

The temple pyramid at Chichen Itza was built to sync with the solar calendar. It has four outside stairways, each with 91 steps. Combine those with the single step at the entrance, and the total is the number of days in the solar year: 365.

OFF WITH THEIR HEADS

ARE PRESERVED SKULLS AT NAZCA BURIAL SITES THOSE OF REVERED ANCESTORS, OR REVILED FOES?

This female mummy may have been a Nazca elite.

WAR TROPHIES OR HUMAN SACRIFICES?

The Nazca heads were once thought to be trophies gathered from particularly unlucky losers in wars with the Nazca. But today some archaeologists believe the decapitation victims were Nazca who were sacrificed for the good of their people, powerful offerings to spirit beings for an abundant harvest. According to this theory, the Nazca spilled blood to ensure their own fertility and that of their land.

The lowland region along the coast of southern Peru is among the driest places on earth. This forbidding environment was the home of the Nazca civilization from about 1 to 750 AD. With little water or arable land, merely surviving was a continual struggle.

The extreme aridity of the Nazca's lands, however, has helped to protect the artifacts for which these ancient people are best known—the Nazca heads. About 150 human heads have been found at Nazca burial sites, some so well preserved that their skin and even their hair remains intact.

Each head was prepared in the same way. After decapitation, the Nazca clubbed away the back of the skull and removed the tongue and throat. They then reached into the opening to pull out the brain and eyes. To retain the shape of the face, they filled the empty skull with cotton. Finally, they pinned the lips shut with spines from a huarango tree—possibly to prevent the escape of a powerful spirit they believed to be inside.

What Was Their Purpose?

All Nazca heads have a small hole in the center of the forehead through which the Nazca threaded a rope that they secured with a knot or wooden toggle. The rope provided an early clue to scholars as to why the Nazca made and collected these heads. Many Nazca pots are painted with mystical figures holding a club in one hand and a head suspended from a rope in the other. Archaeologists concluded that the heads came from people the Nazca had conquered, and that carrying them around was a way to celebrate their victories over their enemies.

Recent discoveries, however, suggest that the victims were not foreigners. In 2009, archaeologists compared the tooth enamel of Nazca heads in the collection of Chicago's Field Museum to mummified bodies at Nazca sites. The chemicals found

WHO KNEW?

The tombs of the Chauchilla Cemetery contain many mummified Nazca corpses, all similarly dressed and posed in a seated upright position.

The Nazca remains were wrapped in embroidered cotton and then painted with a plant resin. The resin is thought to have repelled insects and slowed bacterial decomposition.

WEIRD PERU

In Peru, a number of strange discoveries and phenomena have inspired even stranger theories.

→ Several elongated skulls with huge eye cavities have been unearthed in the city of Andahuaylillas. Some speculate they are the remains of ancient aliens.

→ The Nazca Lines are enormous drawings etched into the desert floor. Because the images can only be seen from the air, one theory is that extraterrestrials created the designs.

→ Workers at a temple of the ancient Chavin culture have reported sighting ghostly figures. Many locals thought the figures were the spirits of human sacrifices who had been killed inside the building.

A BLOODY CRAFT

The Nazca memorialized their gory practice in their art.

A woven rug shows Nazca holding heads after decapitation.

A few rare pottery paintings and other artifacts suggest how the Nazca decapitated their victims. The most vivid shows the killer holding a dead man's hair after slicing through the back of his neck with a long blade made of obsidian, a black volcanic rock. Specks of red paint splattered over the pot suggest the bloody gore of a decapitation with such a primitive tool. After discovering and examining a corpse at a Nazca burial site in 2004, archaeologist Christina A. Conlee explained, "Someone spent quite a bit of effort cutting off the head."

in the teeth were nearly identical, indicating that both the mummies and the beheaded victims had eaten the same diet. The scientists concluded that the heads came not from foreign enemies but from the Nazca themselves. If they were war trophies, they were the victims of civil wars among small Nazca chiefdoms vying for scarce farmland and water.

Other, less bloodthirsty theories exist. Perhaps the heads were a means of preserving and honoring revered ancestors, or were used in religious rituals. We may never know for sure.

THE EASTER ISLAND MOAI

THE GIANT LONG-FACED HEADS OF EASTER ISLAND HAVE STUMPED RESEARCHERS FOR CENTURIES.

On Easter Sunday in 1722, the Dutch explorer Jacob Roggeveen came upon a tiny 63-square-mile island more than 2,000 miles off the coast of South America, in one of the most isolated spots in the world. Roggeveen and his crew were the first outsiders to visit the island in at least 500 years.

In his ship's log, Roggeveen wrote approvingly of the islanders he encountered, noting that they were "big in stature" and had "well proportioned limbs, with large and strong muscles." But he was even more impressed by what he saw ringing the island's jagged coast: hundreds of enormous stone figures, some "a good thirty feet in height and broad in proportion."

"[T]hese stone figures," Roggeveen wrote, "caused us to be filled with wonder, for we could not understand how it was possible that [these] people…had been able to erect them." Roggeveen may have been

The moai monoliths were positioned to gaze across the islanders' clan lands.

Signs of erosion are visible on some of the moai.

NO BOTOX, BUT GETTING SOME WORK DONE

Some moai may be getting a facial.

Made of porous volcanic rock, many moai are crumbling from exposure to winds, rain, and sun. Researchers are experimenting with water repellents and other chemical coatings to keep the moai's faces from being worn away completely by the elements.

101

the first foreigner to marvel at the massive statues, but he was far from the last.

Modern archaeologists have concluded that the figures' creators were the descendants of a few dozen Polynesians who had navigated some 1,000 miles of ocean to arrive on the island sometime between 800 and 1200 AD. The best theory about their significance to date is that the figures, or *moai*, represent the carvers' deified ancestors. Their creators placed most of the moai in sacred places along the island's coast.

But Roggeveen's question remains unanswered: How did a people possessing only Stone Age technology erect the massive monuments? Archeologists now know that most of them were carved from the sloping bedrock of a single quarry some 11 rocky miles from where they sit. How did these early people push, pull, or drag them to the stone platforms, or *ahu*, on which many of them still stand?

One theory was posed by moai expert Jo Anne Van Tilburg in 1998. She believed the Rapa Nui, the island's native people, adapted the technology they used to transport large canoes to the beach to move the moai. Tilburg and her team of volunteers created a 10-ton replica of a moai and laid it face up on a triangular wooden sled. They discovered that by pulling ropes tied to the sled, just forty people could easily move it down a track made of felled palm tree trunks.

More recently, archaeologists Terry Hunt and Carl Lipo came up with another idea, inspired by a legend of the Rapa Nui. The Rapa Nui believe that the sculptures were brought to life through *mana*, a powerful spiritual force, and walked to their final destinations. In 2012, Hunt and Lipo tied three ropes around the head of a five-ton moai replica that was standing upright. A team of 18 volunteers pulled the ropes to rock the monument from left to right, causing it to slowly "walk" forward—just as the Rapa Nui said the great moai did long ago.

MORE THAN HEADS

Archaeologist Jo Anne Van Tilburg has spent more than 30 years trying to solve the mysteries of the Easter Island sculptures.

People the world over have seen photographs of the colossal Easter Island "heads" without realizing that they have bodies as well. Erosion over the centuries buried the moai so that only their heads are now visible. Archaeologist Jo Anne Van Tilburg has led the excavation of two of these monuments, revealing that they indeed have arms and torsos. The excavated statues are etched with petroglyphs, which might provide new clues about their sculptors. The archeological team also found red pigment in the ground, suggesting that long ago the moai were painted in much the same way their creators painted their own bodies for ceremonies.

This moai stands facing inland at the Ahu Akapu site on Rapa Nui.

DISAPPEARING ACT

By the end of the 19th century, the Rapa Nui population had plummeted to just over 100 people. What happened to the famed sculptors of Easter Island?

→ Eco Disaster

According to some, the Rapa Nui needed logs to move the moai, so they cut down the dense forests of palm trees that once covered the island. In doing so, they unwittingly created ecological and social disaster. Without a source of wood, they could no longer build canoes and fish in the ocean, and the erosion caused by deforestation made it nearly impossible to grow enough food.

→ It Was the Rats

Others blame the disappearance of the forests on Polynesian vermin. If even a few rats had stowed away on the boats that brought the first people to the island, the rat population could have quickly spiraled into the millions. A bestial feeding frenzy on the tree roots and seeds might have destroyed the forests in little time.

→ Going Viral

A third camp defends the rats, arguing that even if they did destroy the forests, they also provided a new source of protein. What's deadlier than rats? Foreigners. Under this theory, the Rapa Nui almost died out because of diseases brought to the island by non-natives, much as Native Americans were almost wiped out by European smallpox and other illnesses.

WHO KNEW?
Believers say there are numerous energy vortices in and around Sedona, including Bell Rock, the Sedona Airport, Boynton Canyon, and Cathedral Rock.

Bell Rock, considered a vortex by New Age metaphysicists, in Sedona, Arizona.

LIVING ON
THE GRID

ARE THE WORLD'S SACRED SITES AND MONUMENTS ALL CONNECTED BY A VAST, INVISIBLE ENERGY MATRIX?

The Great Pyramid. Stonehenge. Uluru, the massive sandstone formation in Australia. Sedona, Arizona. Glastonbury, England. What do these natural and man-made landmarks have in common? Exceptional spiritual power, according to New Age theory. And despite being scattered all over the globe, believers say, these sites and other spiritually important places are all part of a massive psychic energy grid.

Geometric Patterns

The idea that spiritual places are somehow related was first proposed by an English antiquarian named Albert Watkins. Standing on a hill, he noticed that ancient monuments in the landscape could be con-nected by straight lines that he called ley lines—though Watkins believed them to be simply ancient roads or pathways. In the 1970s, a trio of Russian theorists took the concept further by marking Earth's oldest sacred sites on a map, connecting the points, and noting that a surprisingly large number of them fit into a geometric pattern, creating a 20-sided structure called an icosahedron. The team suggested that Earth was once an energy-charged, crystal-shaped heavenly body, the edges of which had supposedly worn down into a sphere over time. Ancient holy locations, the theorists said, were positioned at points where the flow of this energy was, and still is, strongest.

SACRED SEDONA

One of Earth's most intense energy spots is located right here in the U.S.A.

Sedona is located amid the dramatic buttes, spires, and red sandstone mesas of the northern Arizona desert. From pre-Columbian times, the Native American Yavapai and Apache peoples living there have considered Sedona sacred ground. Indian tradition also holds that the area is an interdimensional portal. People from around the world have reported seeing UFOs in the area, in the form of strange lights, sounds, and shapes.

Since the 1950s, the town has been a center of alternative spiritual activity. During an August 1987 event called the Harmonic Convergence, which coincided with an exceptional alignment of the planets, thousands of seekers gathered at a butte called Bell Rock to await the predicted arrival of a spaceship. It did not show up, but most in the unfazed crowd considered the event a success.

VIKINGS AND ALIENS

Do monuments in Scandinavia actually map out flight paths for ancient spaceships?

Norse mythology tells of gods and goddesses who criss-crossed the heavens in chariots and ruled over thunder and lightning. UFO enthusiasts speculate that these mythical gods were actually extraterrestrials. As proof, they point to a geometric pattern of ancient forts and megaliths in the area. What accounts for these landmarks, which crossed terrain too rough for roads and lay too far inland to be of use to the seafaring Vikings, unless they served to guide spacecraft?

The region seems to have been a hotspot for UFO sightings for thousands of years. The aliens that supposedly visited the Vikings are said to have traveled to distant sacred places as well, guided by a ley line that connects four of Denmark's 10th-century Viking ring castles.

The perfectly straight line, spanning about 140 miles in Denmark, continues south across the Alps to the site of Apollo's temple in Delphi, Greece, which ancient Greeks believed to be at the center of the world. The ley line then continues to Egypt's Pyramids of Giza. Maybe it's just a coincidence.

Glastonbury Tor, Somerset, United Kingdom

Into the Vortex

According to this theory, when many lines come together, they create a vortex—a point of intense positive or negative force that can invite paranormal events and attract extraterrestrials. Around a negative vortex, such as the Bermuda Triangle, bad things tend to happen. A positive vortex, such as Machu Picchu, is conducive to spiritual enlightenment or contact with the world beyond. Visitors to such places are said to receive visions or physical healing and to experience intense emotion, heightened awareness, or simple contentment. Might nonbelievers sense anything out of the ordinary? Some reportedly do. At the very least, they can enjoy a spectacular view.

Spiritual Glastonbury

Even sites that aren't directly on a vortex can reputedly have great power. One such location is a small town in southern England. It lies along one of Watkins's ley lines, on the ridge of the Malvern Hills. The line passes by Glastonbury Tor, a distinctive cone-shaped hill.

In Celtic mythology, the Tor was the home of the Lord of the Underworld and

THE VILE VORTICES

In 1972, a paranormal enthusiast and writer named Ivan Sanderson plotted the locations of numerous disappearances of ships, planes, and civilizations and noted 12 "Vile Vortices." These spots, Sanderson said, had the most intense negative energy on Earth. The map identifies a few, in case you want to stay away.

Devil's Triangle
The Japanese government has this designated as an area of great hazard.

Bermuda Triangle
Ships and aircraft have disappeared here, some say mysteriously, for hundreds of years.

Great enclosure courtyard, Zimbabwe
Millennia-old, huge monoliths are all that remain of this little-known African civilization.

Loyalty Islands, New Caledonia
Strange currents and ocean vortices of water have been observed here.

The South Atlantic Ocean
This part of the Atlantic is an area of great danger to ships and planes alike.

Easter Island, Chile
The civilization of Easter Island that built the giant moai disappeared without a trace.

a gateway to Avalon, land of the fairy folk. The area has also been linked by some to the legend of King Arthur. Encircling the hill are terraces possibly built by Neolithic inhabitants for defensive, agricultural, or religious purposes. The hill is topped by a stone tower, a remnant of a 13th-century church. The Tor is also believed by some to represent the sign of Aquarius in the Glastonbury Zodiac, an enormous astrological diagram supposedly carved into the landscape by Sumerians in 2700 BC.

Today, the purported Earth energy of Glastonbury Tor attracts neo-pagans, neo-druids, New Agers, and possibly UFOs. Visitors and locals have noted strange colored lights spiraling and hovering around the Tor. And in 1981, several people said they saw an undulating light arcing from the top of the stone tower.

WHO KNEW?
Some ley lines correspond to tectonic fault lines, cracks in Earth's surface that supposedly release magnetic energy.

WHO KNEW?
Sailing stones can leave tracks 600 feet long, but no one has ever seen them move.

THE SAILING STONES
OF DEATH VALLEY

IN THE HOTTEST PLACE IN NORTH AMERICA, HUGE ROCKS TRAVEL ACROSS THE DESERT OF THEIR OWN ACCORD.

Death Valley is famed for its severe climate, where daytime temperatures can reach a scorching 190 degrees and swing to below-freezing conditions at night. Yet deep within the national park, an even more remarkable geological phenomenon has quietly stumped scientists for over 100 years.

In the extremely flat, remote area of Death Valley National Park known as Racetrack Playa, rocks of all sizes have been documented creeping across the floor of a dry lakebed. Some are small stones the size of golf balls; others are boulders that weigh up to several hundred pounds. They have left tracks that are straight, others that zigzag and change direction, and still others that curve and wind back on themselves. Some stones have moved only a few inches, while others have traveled thousands of feet.

What causes these odd and wildly varying tracks? And why haven't scientists been able to observe the stones moving, even though some have dedicated their careers to studying the phenomenon?

In the century since the mysterious movements were first documented, a variety of explanations have been offered, ranging from the effects of strong winds and mysterious energy fields to the earth's magnetism or alien intervention. An experiment in 1948 involved flooding part of the playa using an airplane propeller to create strong winds to see if air currents could be responsible—but they weren't. Another scientist visited Racetrack Playa annually from 1987 to 1994 and eventually proposed that giant sheets of ice moved the rocks. A third experiment used GPS to track the stones' courses. None of the investigations have yielded a convincing answer.

One plausible theory is linked to the climate conditions unique to Racetrack Playa. Scientists posit that when temperatures drop precipitously after a rainfall in this area, ice forms around a rock, changing its buoyancy and permitting it to float on the surface of the mud. As the air temperature increases, the ice melts around its outer edges, and the combination of a lighter stone and watery ice makes the rock vulnerable to strong winds that can push it smoothly over the mud, leaving tracks behind it. As the wind changes direction, so do the rocks, which could explain the variation in trails. If this theory is true, it might be more accurate to describe the "sailing" rocks as ice rafts.

According to close observers, the stones move only every two to three years, probably for only about ten seconds at a time, which might account for the lack of eyewitnesses. Contemporary photo technology may finally allow scientists to record the movement of the sailing stones one day, and perhaps the mystery will be settled once and for all.

Tracks of sailing stones, Racetrack Playa, Death Valley, California.

KITCHEN TABLE PLAYA

In 2006, Ralph Lorenz, a scientist at Johns Hopkins University, was working on a NASA project, testing weather stations in Death Valley. He became intrigued by the sailing stones at Racetrack Playa and wondered if he could re-create the effect in his own kitchen.

Lorenz put a small rock in a piece of Tupperware and filled it with water, leaving a bit of the rock sticking out. He froze the container, then popped out the contents, a slab of ice with the rock embedded in it. Placing the icy rock in a tray of water with a sand-covered bottom, he found he could blow on the rock and cause it to slide over the sand—creating conditions similar to those at Racetrack Playa.

Some crop circles in Wiltshire, England, appear to be based on fractal geometry.

AROUND
AND AROUND

MORE THAN 700 CIRCLES OF FLATTENED CROPS APPEARED IN ENGLAND IN THE LATE 1900S. WHERE DID THEY COME FROM?

In the 1970s, farmers across southern England began awakening to find large areas of their grain fields flattened into series of perfect spheres and other geometrical forms. Among the wheat, barley, corn, and rye, lyrical patterns of smashed stalks mysteriously took shape.

Overnight, the crisp, sharp designs seemed to spread from farm to farm. The shapes ranged in width from just ten feet to hundreds of feet. Some patterns included dozens of orbs in a spiral. Other formations had right-angled corners and lines or even images of sea life. Soon, crop circles appeared around the globe, in Japan, the United States, Canada, and countries of the former U.S.S.R. The more complex and beautiful geometrically patterned ones attracted huge crowds of curious viewers.

But where did they come from? Initially, speculation ran wild. Some believed they were caused by UFOs and related to so-called saucer nests, areas of flattened reeds observed in Australian marshes in the 1960s. The nests were linked to alleged UFO sightings, and it was said that the round depressions were caused by rays or exhaust from circular UFOs. Others thought that governments might be experimenting with precisely targeted microwaves that caused the plants to collapse.

Crop circle appearances were not entirely new. In 1678, in Hertfordshire, England, a printed pamphlet told of a farmer who made a deal with the devil, who then mowed the farmer's field in circles. Another report in a 1880 *Nature* magazine attributed round circles of flat crops to cyclonic winds.

In recent years, however, farmers and others whose land has been marked with the fanciful patterns have agreed that the crop circles are the handiwork of human pranksters. In 1991, Dave Chorley and Doug Bower, two residents of southern England, claimed that they alone had made all the circles in England until 1987. Once the two men demonstrated how they had made the patterns, copycats took over and the number of crop circles around the world shot up. By the 1990s and 2000s, corporate-funded logos were appearing in crops, and artists began working in the medium.

Still, a small minority of crop circles seem to defy explanation, and a few scientists state they have observed irreversible changes in crops where circles have been found.

An aerial view of crop circles in Wiltshire, England.

Gaston Julia (right), a World War I veteran who lost his nose in battle, wore a leather strap around his face where his nose had been.

GASTON JULIA AND HIS SET

Fractal geometry, based on the work of Gaston Julia, informs some of the most beautiful crop circles.

In 1996, a formation of numerous circles known as the Julia Set appeared in a field in Wiltshire, England, across the road from the mystical ancient site of Stonehenge. The design appeared to be modeled after patterns created in fractal geometry, an area investigated by 20th-century French mathematician Gaston Julia. In fractal geometry, curves and other features recur, based on a mathematical function. A snowflake, with its geometric patterns, is a good example of a fractal.

Spiraling Mystery
Snowflakes materialize naturally, but how was the Julia Set in Wiltshire formed? The circles were discovered by a doctor who claimed that he had piloted a small plane over the area one afternoon and saw an undisturbed field of wheat. When he returned 45 minutes later, 149 separate circles were arrayed in a huge spiral measuring 500 feet wide and 915 feet in length along a curve.

Over the years, various circle artists have claimed responsibility for the Julia Set, but no conclusive evidence has been offered to support their claims.

NO PROTRACTOR REQUIRED

Making a crop circle is a low-tech affair. All you need is a plank, rope, wire, and baseball cap.

When Britons Dave Chorley and Doug Bower came forward in 1991 to claim responsibility for the earliest crop circles in England, they demonstrated their methods for the public. The equipment was fairly low-tech: a wooden plank with a loop of rope at each end and a wire attached to a baseball cap. One member of the team stood still, anchoring the wire, as the other walked around him in a circle, flattening the grass. Other imprints were made with the edge of the plank, with Chorley and Bower looping the rope over their shoulders and pressing down the plank with their foot to flatten the plants. Later, artists developed slightly more sophisticated methods, using surveyor's tape, pipe or broomsticks, and stepladders.

A group of amateur researchers examine crop circles in the Czech Republic.

Commercial, private, and military aircraft and ships have mysteriously
disappeared into the seven seas.

CHAPTER 6
MYSTERIOUS VANISHINGS

HOW DOES AN ENTIRE BATTALION OF SOLDIERS, AN AIRPLANE, OR EVEN A CARGO SHIP DISAPPEAR? SCIENCE DISMISSES THE PARANORMAL, BUT MANY SUCH EVENTS REMAIN UNEXPLAINED.

THE LOST COLONY

WHAT HAPPENED TO THE COLONISTS ON ROANOKE ISLAND 400 YEARS AGO? THE TRUTH IS BEGINNING TO EMERGE.

LIFE ON THE ISLAND

→ **1584** An English expedition finds and explores Roanoke Island.

→ **1585–1586** A party of Englishmen, including John White, attempt to build a settlement on Roanoke, but abandon the site when food becomes scarce.

→ **July 1587** John White leads a third expedition to Roanoke to establish a permanent colony there.

→ **August 1587** John White returns to England to obtain supplies for the struggling colony; his granddaughter Virginia becomes the first baby born to English parents in North America.

→ **August 1590** John White returns to Roanoke to find that the colony has vanished—but bad weather forces him to leave before he can search for the colonists.

→ **1602** England sends another expedition to Roanoke, but this final attempt to build a colony on the island quickly fails.

In the late 16th century, England was desperate to get a foothold in North America before Spain could gain control over more territory there. As part of this effort, artist and mapmaker John White was charged with founding the Roanoke Colony, a small settlement of some 100 men, women, and children. But even with strong support of Queen Elizabeth I, Roanoke struggled. The colonists had arrived in July, too late to plant crops. White was forced to sail back to England for supplies, leaving the settlers to fend for themselves until his return.

White expected to be away a few months, but soon after he reached England, a naval war broke out between England and Spain. When he returned three years later, in 1590, the colonists and all of their possessions had disappeared.

White discovered only two clues to what had happened: the letters CRO carved on a tree and the word CROATOAN cut into a wooden fence post. He concluded that the colonists had journeyed to the villages of the Croatan Indians on what is now Hatteras Island, about 50 miles south. Stormy weather made it impossible to reach the islands, so White returned to England and never again saw any of the Roanoke colonists, including his own daughter and granddaughter.

False Lead

In the late 1990s, one archaeological team believed they were finally close to solving the mystery of Roanoke. At a dig site on Hatteras Island, they found a variety of English coins, pipes, and, most tantalizingly, a gold ring embellished with an image of a lion. The design, which dated from the 16th century, suggested that it might have belonged to one of the lost colonists. More research revealed that the lion was the crest of the Kendall family—but there were no Kendalls among the lost Roanokeans. Researchers have identified two men named Kendall who might have owned the ring—a member of one of the first explorations of Roanoke Island, or a Jamestown colonist who was executed for treason in 1607.

Gold signet ring with an engraved prancing lion crest attributed to the Kendall family.

John White painted this watercolor of the orderly Indian village of Secotan during a 1585–1586 English expedition to what is now North Carolina.

Their rype corne

Their greene corne.

Corne newly sprong.

A man watches over a field of corn, pumpkins, and sunflowers, waiting to chase away any animals that might disturb the crops.

The Secotan villagers dance, sing, and play instruments during what is probably a harvest ritual.

Their sittinge at meate

prayer

The house wherin the Tombe of their Herounds standeth.

SECOTON.

John White's watercolor of the village of Secotan.

A Ceremony in their prayers w strange gestures and songes danssing abowt posts carued on the topps lyke mens faces.

For four centuries, there were few new clues about the Lost Colony of Roanoke, but that has not stopped the curious from developing their own theories. Here are the leading contenders.

→ They moved to Hatteras Island (or further inland) and were taken in by a friendly tribe.

→ They died from starvation or disease.

→ They were abducted and killed by hostile Indians.

→ Spaniards discovered the colonists and murdered them.

→ A hurricane swept over the island, destroying the settlement.

→ The colonists tried to sail home in their small boats and were lost at sea.

A New Clue

Archaeologists and historians are still searching for evidence of the Lost Colony. One of the most promising discoveries was found at the British Museum in 2012.

Brent Lane of the First Colony Foundation was examining *La Virginea Pars*, a map drawn by John White, when he noticed a large paper patch glued onto the map. Placing the document on a lightboard, Lane could see what was underneath—a red and blue diamond, a symbol the English once used to designate a fort, at the confluence to the Chowan and Roanoke rivers. Archaeologists are planning to dig at the site in search of evidence that at least some of the lost colonists survived and built a new fort and settlement there. In the meantime, researchers have a new puzzle to solve. Who papered over the fort on White's map, and what were they trying to hide?

In the Genes

In recent years, science has provided a new tool for the centuries-long search for the Roanoke colonists: genetic testing.

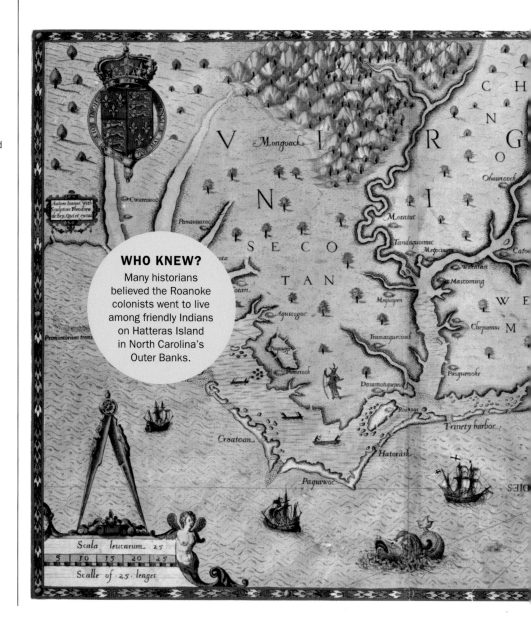

WHO KNEW?
Many historians believed the Roanoke colonists went to live among friendly Indians on Hatteras Island in North Carolina's Outer Banks.

Roberta Estes, the owner of a company that interprets genetic tests, began collecting DNA samples from volunteers in the area near Roanoke Island in 2007. Estes looks for subjects whose family history suggests that they had an ancestor who in the 16th century lived on Hatteras Island, where the lost colonists might have sought refuge. Estes hopes to discover Caucasian and Native American descendants with a common ancestor among the Roanoke colonists. If she is successful, she might finally be able to prove that they found a new home among the Indians on the island.

THE DARE STONES

In 1937, a man gathering hickory nuts along a North Carolina highway found a peculiar slab of stone. Carved into it was a desperate story of disease, murder, and misery, signed with the initials EWD.

Professor Haywood J. Pearce Jr. at Emory University identified EWD as Eleanor White Dare, daughter of John White, governor of Roanoke Colony. The carvings were a letter to her father, which explained that, after he retuned to England, all but seven of the colonists had died, mostly at the hands of hostile Indians. A local stonecutter named Bill Eberhardt then came forward with 42 similar carved stones that completed Eleanor's story. According to the stones, the Roanoke survivors wandered through South Carolina and Georgia. Eleanor eventually married an Indian chief before dying in 1599.

The discovery of the Dare Stones was celebrated as the key to unlocking the Roanoke mystery, until 1941, when the *Saturday Evening Post* published an investigative report revealing the stones were fakes. Pearce admitted he had been tricked by Eberhardt, and the Dare Stones went down as one of the greatest hoaxes in American history.

Some historians now believe that the first stone, the only one not "discovered" by Eberhardt, deserves another look. According to historian David La Vere, "Whoever [carved] it knew the history and knew Elizabethan English. If it's a forgery, it's a pretty good forgery."

"From hence we went thorow the woods...untill we came to the place where I left our Colony in the yeere [1587]....[W]e entred up the sandy banke upon a tree, in the very browe thereof were curiously carved these faire Romane letters C R O: which letters presently we knew to signifie the place, where I should find the planters seated...for at my comming away they were prepared to remove from Roanoak 50 miles into the maine."

—From John White's account of his return to Roanoke Island

NAVAL MANEUVERS

COULD ALEXANDER THE GREAT'S ARMADA HAVE TRAVELED HALFWAY AROUND THE WORLD? ITS FATE REMAINS UNKNOWN.

The Flotilla of Alexander the Great, from *Vie d'Alexandre le Grand* (c. 15th century).

Mosaic from Pompeii depicting Alexander the Great at the Battle of Issus.

Almost 2,500 years ago, Alexander III of Macedon, aka Alexander the Great, commanded an enormous war machine. Thanks to the might of his undefeated military, Alexander expanded his empire from Greece across three continents and two million square miles. He became king of Persia, Babylon, and Asia, and Pharaoh of Egypt. He was unstoppable.

In 326 BC, hoping to reach what he called the ends of the world, Alexander led his army from present-day Afghanistan into Pakistan and northwest India. He wanted to press on, but his troops, exhausted from ferocious battles, refused to go any farther. Alexander decided to turn back. He would lead some of his army home by land, and his admiral, Nearchus, would transport the others by sea.

Alexander's navy departed in November to travel down the Indus River to the Indian Ocean, westward into the Persian Gulf, and up the gulf to the Euphrates River. And here's where things get odd: Alexander died in Babylon (of either illness or poisoning) a year later, and though Nearchus apparently made it back to land, the fate of the navy is unclear. Modern historians tend to believe that most turned back to explore the coast of India and make more conquests. Still, some amateur theorists speculate that the ships made it all the way to Australia, 5,000 miles away, across whole a lot of open sea.

Gone Missing

Could a navy from thousands of years ago pull this off? Certainly, there might have been enough personnel. Though historians of the time gave widely varying assessments of the size of Alexander's navy, it included anywhere from 30 to 80 warships, plus dozens of supporting vessels. Some of the ships were huge, able to hold 600 or more crewmembers and passengers. The navy included experienced sailors from across Alexander's empire, including Greeks, Phoenicians, and Egyptians.

The veteran seafarers knew how to navigate by the heavens and how to harness seasonal currents and winds. They might

A trireme, from *Della militia maritima* (*On the Maritime Militia*), a treatise by Cristoforo Canal (1560).

THE HIGH-TECH TRIREME

Alexander's warships were state-of-the-art, but they weren't meant for ocean travel.

At the heart of the lost fleet of Alexander the Great was a deadly warship known as a trireme. Powered by three tiers of oarsmen—up to 200 at once—the 120-foot-long trireme was built for speed. It could travel 125 miles in a day and was extremely maneuverable. In the typical battles of antiquity, it was lethal. The bronze ram on its prow could hammer into opposing craft, making it possible for Alexander's armed soldiers to jump aboard and crush the enemy in hand-to-hand combat. These battles usually unfolded close to shore, though, and the lightweight vessel was not well-suited to open ocean waters. Storms, or even strong winds, claimed more triremes than fighting did.

have skirted India and continued along the northern shore of the Bay of Bengal, past present-day Bangladesh and Myanmar, then south past Thailand, Malaysia, and Indonesia. From there, it might have been possible for the fleet to reach New Guinea, Australia, and New Zealand. The wildest theories put the fleet as far afield as Polynesia, Hawaii, and even Easter Island.

The Evidence

If Alexander's men made all or part of this very long voyage, they would have had to trade with people they met along the way, and some sailors likely would have settled in various places they visited. Lost-fleet buffs say that's exactly what happened, and that there is evidence of an ancient Greek presence in Southeast Asia and Oceania.

European explorers centuries later who first encountered the people of the South Pacific reported that some of them had Mediterranean, Middle Eastern, or North African physical characteristics. According to Dutch explorer Jacob Roggeveen, who landed on Easter Island in 1722, the natives spoke of white ancestors arriving in ancient times.

Some lost-fleet theories point to numerous archaeological finds throughout the Pacific Islands. Pottery from Phoenicia, Babylonia, and ancient Egypt and Greece has been discovered in the region, as have coins, tools, and other artifacts.

Some discoveries, though, have turned out to be hoaxes, and there's a more logical explanation for the appearance of these objects so far away from their origins: trade. Perhaps these items and even genetic material spread across the world one person at a time, over many years, by a process of international "pass-it-on." Or maybe, just maybe, the lost fleet of Alexander really did find its way to faraway lands.

A CLOUD OF
SMOKE

IN 1915 AN ENGLISH REGIMENT WAS DISPATCHED TO BATTLE. THE MEN CLIMBED A HILL, THEN WERE GONE.

Sandringham.

CAPTAIN COURAGEOUS

The men from Sandringham were valiantly led by a 54-year-old land agent.

The Sandringham Company was formed in 1908 at the request of the British king, George V, with Sandringham's land agent, Frank Beck, serving as captain. The king quickly had second thoughts about sending the 54-year-old Beck to war and begged him to stay at home, but the new captain was steadfast. "I formed them," he said. "The lads will expect me to go with them; besides, I promised their wives and children I would look after them."

Like the rest of the Sandringhams, Beck perished on Gallipoli. While Beck's body was never found, years after the war his gold pocket watch was recovered by the army, which returned it to Beck's daughter on her wedding day in 1922.

On August 12, 1915, the men of the Sandringham Company were awaiting orders as they sweated in the harsh Turkish heat. Exhausted, thirsty, and terrified, the inexperienced British soldiers were far from home. Only months before, they had been butlers, gardeners, farmers, and servants at the Sandringham estate of King George V.

But with the outbreak of World War I, the men were sent halfway around the globe to the peninsula of Gallipoli, as part of the First Fifth Battalion of the Norfolk Regiment. The Sandringhams were preparing for a bloody battle against the Turks.

Lost in a Cloud

Late in the afternoon, the Sandringhams and other members of the First Fifth Battalion took the field and began advancing toward the Turkish army. Their orderly battle lines soon dissolved in chaos as the Turks turned their machine guns on the British troops and Turkish snipers picked off officers one by one. The surrounding brush was set ablaze and smoke filled the air. Other battalions fell back in the face of heavy enemy fire, but the Sandringhams and their comrades pressed on. As they headed toward a forest, the soldiers were engulfed in a yellowish cloud of smoke. When the smoke lifted, the men were gone. More than 250 soldiers—many of them from the Sandringham estate—were never heard from again.

Some believe that the men, faced with certain and painful death as they walked

into a wall of enemy fire, were spirited to heaven by a merciful God. Others think that the cloud was a type of UFO and aliens abducted the soldiers, saving their lives in the nick of time.

Casualties of War

Historians have far less dramatic theories about what happened to the missing soldiers. The bodies of about 100 men were later found near the battle site, believed by some scholars to be battalion members taken as prisoners of war by the Turks. The skull of each corpse bore a single

1915 map of Gallipoli Peninsula and the Dardanelles, Turkey, from *The War Illustrated Album deLuxe*, published in 1916.

"There happened a very mysterious thing....Nothing more was ever seen or heard of any of them. They charged into the forest and were lost to sight or sound."

—From an official dispatch, dated December 11, 1915, from Sir Ian Hamilton

King George V, whose Sandringham regiment disappeared at Gallipoli

DISAPPEARING ARMIES

History tells of other armies that disappeared mysteriously during the heat of battle.

→ According to the ancient Greek historian Herodotus, a 50,000-man Persian army vanished in the Egyptian desert in 525 BC. He wrote that a great wind blew up "vast columns of whirling sand, which entirely covered up the troops."

→ In the 2nd century AD, 5,000 soldiers of Rome's Ninth Legion set out for Britain to end a rebellion. Legend holds that they vanished into the mists of Scotland and were never seen again.

→ In December 1937, 3,000 Chinese troops were sent to the Yangtze River to stop a Japanese advance. The following day, a unit dispatched to find out what had happened found no trace of the men.

bullet hole, suggesting that they had been executed—though Turkish records make no mention of the executions.

Stoking the Myth

The myth of the "vanished battalion" took hold in April 1965, 50 years after the supposed disappearance.

At a commemoration for the soldiers lost at Gallipoli, a New Zealand veteran named Frederick Reichardt shared his recollections. Backed up by three other soldiers, he testified that "six or eight" seemingly solid clouds hovered over the battlefield. One cloud lowered to the ground, and the men walked into it. After about an hour, the cloud rose and hovered among the others before they all sailed into the sky. Reichardt was confused about many details, including the location and date of the battle and the name of the battalion involved.

Still, his account made its way into the magazine *Flying Saucers*. From this unlikely source, the tale transformed from a fringe theory into a widely accepted part of World War I lore.

Amelia Earhart in the cockpit of her autogiro after setting a new altitude record for women in planes of this type.

INTO THIN AIR

HOW DOES AN ENTIRE AIRPLANE TAKE OFF INTO THE WILD BLUE YONDER ... AND NEVER RETURN?

It was midnight, July 2, 1937, when Amelia Earhart, 39, and her co-pilot Fred Noonan, 44, took off from Lae, New Guinea, in their small Lockheed 10 Electra aircraft. The famous aviator was just two stops from achieving her goal of circum-navigating the globe and was heading for Howland Island, a uninhabited chunk of coral in the middle of the Pacific Ocean 2,556 miles away. From there, Earhart planned to continue home to Oakland, California. But that plan was not to be: No one would ever see Earhart alive again.

A month prior, Earhart and Noonan had taken off from Miami amid a hail of flash photography, on their second attempt to fly around the world. The run so far had been successful: The pair had covered 22,000 miles without a hitch and had only 7,000 to go.

Despite forecasts for good weather, the *Itasca*, a U.S. Coast Guard cutter stationed near Howland Island, detected trouble and began signaling Earhart. It seems likely the messages were never received, since Earhart, at 7:42 AM, radioed the *Itasca*, "We must be on you, but we cannot see you. Fuel is running low. Been unable to reach you by radio. We are flying at 1000 feet." In her final transmission, Earhart told the *Itasca*, "We are running north and south." It was 8:45 AM on July 2.

The U.S. government deployed three air-craft carriers and spent $4 million searching roughly 250,000 square miles of the Pacific for Earhart and Noonan. No trace was ever found, and on July 19 the search was called off. The fate of the world's greatest female pilot remains unknown to this day.

Pilot Amelia Earhart and navigator Fred Noonan.

What Happened to Amelia?

Like many famous unsolved mysteries, theories abound about the fate of the legendary pilot.

MOST LIKELY: She crashed and sank in the Pacific. Many aviation experts, aeronautical engineers, and U.S. Navy officials concur that the Electra went into the sea somewhere offshore of Howland Island. Perhaps Earhart's stepson, George Palmer Putnam Jr., said it best: "The plane just ran out of gas."

NOT SO LIKELY: She landed on Gardner Island. Some believe Earhart and Noonan arrived on this uninhabited island 350 miles south of Howland and eventually died. Bronze bearings, a zipper pull, and even a female skeleton have been found there, but whether any of them belonged to Earhart remains unproven.

LEAST LIKELY: She crashed on the island of Saipan and was executed by the occupying Japanese. Evidence, including photographs of a captured Earhart, has all been deemed fraudulent. A related theory, that Earhart wasn't executed and became a "Tokyo Rose," was also discounted—by Earhart's own husband,

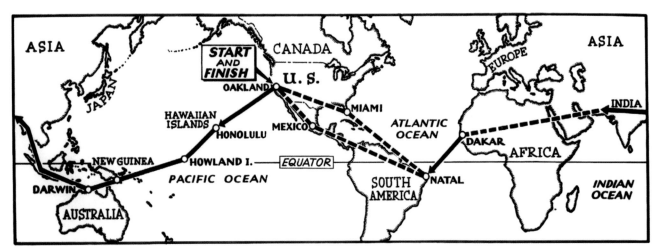

Earhart's proposed route in 1937.

NOW YOU SEE IT...

Amelia Earhart's may be the most famous flight disappearance, but it was by no means the only one. Some may have been the victims of foul play or terrorism; others, mechanical malfunction or pilot error. But many will never be explained.

AUGUST 2, 1947

While flying over the Andes, a British South American Airways Star Dust sent a message to a Santiago airport announcing its imminent arrival. The plane never landed, prompting theories of sabotage and UFO activity. More than 50 years later, remnants of the plane and its passengers were recovered by Argentinean soldiers, above. The plane had apparently been buried by an avalanche after crashing into a mountain.

JULY 21, 1951

A Canadian Pacific DC-4 on a United Nations flight from Vancouver, Canada, to Tokyo, Japan, reported to aircraft control in Anchorage, Alaska, 90 minutes before its scheduled stopover there. It never arrived in Anchorage. Despite wide-ranging searches by both the U.S. and Royal Canadian air forces, no trace of the plane or the 37 people on board has ever been discovered.

MARCH 16, 1962

Flying Tiger Line Flight 739, carrying troops from California to Saigon, disappeared over the western Pacific Ocean. A tanker near Guam reported a flash of light in the sky, followed by two red lights falling into the ocean, 90 minutes after the plane's last transmission. It is believed that the plane exploded in flight; the cause remains unknown.

who listened to hours of recorded broadcasts and never recognized the voice of his late wife.

LUDICROUS: She survived the flight, changed her name, and moved to New Jersey. This theory was proposed by Joe Klass in his book *Amelia Earhart Lives*, published in 1970, only to be debunked by researchers. The woman Klass claimed to be Earhart, Irene Bolam, sued him, and the book was removed from stores.

WHO KNEW?
American aviator Amelia Earhart (1898–1937) was the first woman to cross the Atlantic Ocean in an airplane.

Amelia Earhart atop her plane.

OCTOBER 21, 1978

Frederick Valentich was flying a Cessna 182L airplane en route to King Island, Australia, when he reported to Melbourne air traffic control. "There was a strange aircraft...on top of me again. It is hovering and it's not an aircraft," before he and his plane vanished without a trace. Theories range from a staged self-disappearance to alien abduction.

MAY 23, 2003

When a Boeing 727 took off from an airport in Angola, the only two people known to be on board were a Congolese mechanic and an American hired to repossess the plane. Neither had a commercial pilot's license. Witnesses reported "crazy ground maneuvers." The plane took flight over the Atlantic, never to be seen again. The pilot's family believes the aircraft crashed in Africa. Rumors that the plane is being held in Beirut for use in an attack on Israel remain unconfirmed.

JUNE 1, 2009

Air France Flight 447 crashed into Atlantic waters between South America and Africa due to an autopilot malfunction and pilot error. The plane descended in a terrifying three-and-a-half-minute free fall before impact. Seventy-four bodies remain missing.

MARCH 8, 2014

Malaysian Airlines Flight 370, scheduled to arrive in Beijing at 6:30 AM, disappeared over the Indian Ocean. There were 227 passengers, two of whom were using fake passports, and 12 crew on board. The plane's transponders were shut down shortly after 1:00 AM. Military radar registered dramatic altitude shifts from 45,000 to 23,000 feet.

THE ZONE OF NO RETURN

BEWARE THE BERMUDA TRIANGLE, WHERE SHIPS AND PLANES ARE SAID TO VANISH MYSTERIOUSLY.

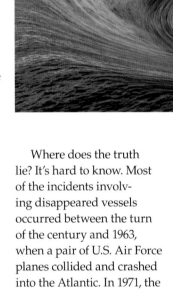

In February 1918, the World War I cargo ship U.S.S. *Cyclops* set sail from Rio de Janeiro, Brazil, to Baltimore, Maryland. After a brief stop in Barbados from March 3 to 4, the ship, along with its 306 passengers and crew members, disappeared without a trace.

Cyclops never sent an SOS distress call, and an extensive search failed to turn up any wreckage. "Only God and the sea know what happened to the great ship,"

President Woodrow Wilson later said of the incident, the single largest non-combat-related loss of life in U.S. naval history.

Strange Lights

Ever since Christopher Columbus reported seeing strange lights and erratic compass movements while sailing between Miami, Bermuda, and Puerto Rico, the Bermuda Triangle has been notorious for sailors and airmen alike. At least

four boats have vanished while passing through the 500,000-square-mile expanse of ocean, and many planes in the airspace above have met the same fate. During World War II, a squadron of U.S. Navy torpedo bombers and one of the naval planes dispatched to rescue them disappeared there. While some attribute the incidents to rough weather, human error, or piracy, others are convinced that supernatural forces are at work.

Where does the truth lie? It's hard to know. Most of the incidents involving disappeared vessels occurred between the turn of the century and 1963, when a pair of U.S. Air Force planes collided and crashed into the Atlantic. In 1971, the

The U.S. Navy cargo ship *Cyclops*.

The Lost Squadron and plane of Flight 19.

Rendering of the Bermuda Triangle in a thunderstorm.

Illustration of rogue waves as seen from an aerial viewpoint.

EARTHLY EXPLANATIONS

Skeptics chalk up Bermuda Triangle incidents to a variety of terrestrial factors.

→ **Human error:** One of the most frequently cited explanations is the simplest. Fatal mistakes were made by those in charge.

→ **Violent weather:** Tropical cyclones could have caused at least some of the disappearances, although several occurred when no storms were reported in the area.

→ **Methane hydrates:** Decreased water density due to fields of natural gas may have caused ships to sink, though no large releases are believed to have occurred in the area for 15,000 years.

→ **Rogue waves:** Waves up to 100 feet high can form spontaneously far out at sea. They could account for the loss of low-flying aircraft as well as seafaring vessels.

→ **Piracy:** Author Carl Hiaasen has suggested that more than a few disappearances may have been caused by modern-day pirates who commandeered the vessels.

Navy's U.S.S. *John F. Kennedy* was cruising in the waters when it encountered a UFO, according to Jim Kopf, a communications specialist aboard the ship. "We saw a large, glowing sphere," Kopf recalled. "It made no sound that I could hear. The light coming from it pulsated and was yellow to orange."

Kopf's account has helped fuel wild speculation that alien kidnappings, UFO attacks, or even devices developed by inhabitants of the lost continent of Atlantis have been responsible for Bermuda Triangle disappearances. The communications specialist said he was quickly ordered belowdecks by his captain, who later warned the crew that any incidents they had witnessed or heard about onboard were classified.

As fanciful as a paranormal explanation may be for these incidents, several of the bona fide disappearances continue to defy rational theories.

Case in point: the squadron of five Avenger planes that went missing toward the end of World War II. Referred to as U.S. Navy Flight 19, the group of bomber aircraft took off on a routine training mission from Fort Lauderdale, Florida, on December 5, 1945.

Four hours later, radio contact with the aircraft was lost, but not before an agitated flight leader transmitted an odd mes-

A map shows the area of the Bermuda Triangle.

sage: "Everything looks strange—even the ocean. We are entering white water. Nothing seems right." Upon hearing this, two naval air rescue planes took off for the area, but only one returned. No evidence of the five planes in Flight 19—or the missing rescue aircraft—has ever been found.

THE SURREAL SEAS

GHOST SHIPS CAN BE ACTUAL EMPTY CRAFTS OR PHANTOM VISIONS. EITHER WAY, THEY'RE SPOOKY.

In January 2014, an ominous ship appeared in the North Atlantic Ocean. The 300-foot cruise liner, called the *Lyubov Orlova*, had no life aboard except, reportedly, disease-infested rats. It seemed to be on a collision course with the coast of Ireland. Was the *Lyubov Orlova* a classic ghost ship, an unmanned vessel adrift on the high seas? As scary as the story sounded at first, it quickly turned banal. The *Lyubov Orlova*'s owners had fallen into debt and hadn't paid the crew, who had abandoned the ship in a Canadian harbor.

Paranormal Theories

History abounds with real ships whose crews have mysteriously vanished, seemingly without a struggle. When there's no obvious explanation for the missing people, the paranormal theories begin: sea monsters, the Bermuda Triangle, alien abductions. Some say ghost ships are supernatural apparitions—spectral visions of real ships that sank or were destroyed. If you see such a craft, beware: They are terrible omens that portend death and disaster. At least, that's what seafarers say. Skeptics dismiss such theories and say ghost ships can be explained with facts. In the case of real ships with vanished crews, they often point to mutiny or piracy.

The *Mary Celeste*

One famous example of a ghost ship is the *Mary Celeste*. In 1872, the charter vessel left New York City, bound for Italy. About a week later, it was found in the Atlantic Ocean. The sails were up, and the crew's belongings were still on board. So was the cargo, which included 1,700 barrels of liquor, most of them still full. Missing were the captain's logbook, the captain, and the nine other people who had been on board. Some speculated that the passengers and crew inadvertently ate poisonous food, became delusional, and jumped overboard. Others suggested that the crew was sucked out in a waterspout—a tornado-like storm

This artist's representation portrays a ship encountering the legendary *Flying Dutchman* at sea.

The *Joyita*, which was found adrift in the South Pacific.

that forms over water. But no definitive explanation for the abandoned *Mary Celeste* has ever been reached.

The *Flying Dutchman*

Perhaps the best known of all ghost ships is the *Flying Dutchman*, the nickname given to a vessel that set sail from Amsterdam in 1680. The ship's captain, Hendrick Vanderdeckenis, is said to have sailed arrogantly into a vicious storm near the Cape of Good Hope, destroying the ship and killing his crew. Lore has it that, as punishment, the *Flying Dutchman* is doomed to sail for all eternity, emanating a ghostly light. Many sailors claim to have seen it, including British royalty: As a teenager in 1880, King George V reported having spotted the *Flying Dutchman* on calm seas off the coast of Australia.

Science Steps In

There may be a simple explanation for ghost ships, say some scientists. They're a type of mirage, called a Fata Morgana, an Italian reference to the legendary sorceress Morgan leFay, who created mirages to lure sailors to their deaths. A Fata Morgana can occur during an unusual weather condition in which a layer of warm air rests on top of a layer of cool air. The strata act like a funhouse mirror, producing images for observers that may be flipped or distorted. Under these conditions, a real ship might appear ethereal and ghostly or seem to move in unnatural ways. In some cases, a nonexistent vessel might seem to appear and disappear.

As for the *Lyubov Orlova*, it has not been spotted since early 2014. It is believed to have sunk.

MARITIME MYSTERIES

What happened on board these abandoned crafts? Theories abound.

→ **THE SHIP:** *Kaz II,* 2007

THE CIRCUMSTANCES: The catamaran was found drifting off the coast of Australia. Its engine was running; a cup of coffee and a laptop were on a table. No bodies were recovered.
THE THEORIES: The three-man crew fell victim to pirates or drug smugglers, or faked their own disappearance.
THE CONCLUSION: The three accidentally fell overboard and drowned.

→ **THE SHIP:** *Bel Amica,* 2006

THE CIRCUMSTANCES: The $600,000 yacht was found adrift off the coast of Sardinia. On board was a half-eaten meal, clothing, maps, and a Luxembourg flag.
THE THEORIES: The ship was an antique haunted sailing vessel.
THE CONCLUSION: The owner, a Luxembourg man, ditched it to avoid paying taxes on it.

→ **THE SHIP:** *Joyita,* 1955

THE CIRCUMSTANCES: Five weeks after leaving Samoa for a two-day journey, this commercial ship was found adrift in the South Pacific. Its 25 passengers and crew members were gone.
THE THEORIES: The vessel was attacked by Japanese forces, or those aboard were kidnapped by Soviets.
THE CONCLUSION: When the *Joyita* took on water, everyone panicked and abandoned ship.

Some say that the seal of the United States, which appears on the back of the $1 bill, is the symbol of a clandestine alliance that controls America.

CHAPTER 7
SECRETIVE
SOCIETIES

AN AURA OF ILLICIT MYSTERY TRAILS GROUPS LIKE
OPUS DEI AND THE ORDO TEMPLI ORIENTIS. WHAT
IS IT THAT GOES ON BEHIND CLOSED DOORS?

INTERNATIONAL MEN OF MYSTERY

DARK KNIGHTS OR MORAL LEADERS? SEARCHING FOR THE TRUTH BEHIND THE WORLD'S MOST ENIGMATIC BROTHERHOODS.

In medieval times, powerful secret societies, with their roots in religion and connections to the dark arts, confounded the political establishment. The groups were often perceived as threats to the government and were persecuted and sabotaged. Some were accused of witchcraft, others of treason.

Today, an aura of illicit mystery continues to trail secret societies, though many now function as community-based charitable organizations. Where does the truth lie?

Heroes to Heretics

One of the most intriguing of the ancient societies was the Knights Templar, a group dating to the 12th century that inspired Arthurian tales of the Knights of the Round Table and films like *Indiana Jones and the Last Crusade*.

The Knights Templar was founded in France in 1118 to protect Christian pilgrims seeking to visit the Holy Land, at the time controlled by Muslim rulers. With the support of the Catholic Church, the Knights established their headquarters on Jerusalem's Temple Mount and eventually conquered the local Muslims and claimed the area for the Church.

In the wake of their triumph in Jerusalem, Knights became powerful bankers who financed the ventures of kings and popes. Their white tunics emblazoned with red crosses came to symbolize courage, honor, and chivalry, and they were admired and beloved throughout Europe.

But once the Holy Land returned to Muslim rule in 1244, the Catholic church's religious mili-

Procession of Crusaders around Jerusalem, 1099.

THE TREASURE OF THE COPPER SCROLL

An ancient document written on copper holds clues to the location of an immense, missing fortune.

Between the mid-1940s and 1950s, Bedouin herdsmen and archaeologists discovered more than 800 Hebrew documents in 11 caves near the Dead Sea in Israel. The manuscripts, dubbed the Dead Sea Scrolls, were written on parchment or papyrus and described ancient Jewish beliefs and practices. It is unknown for certain who wrote the texts, though some are thought to have belonged to Judaic sect called the Essenes. Among the manuscripts and fragments was a catalog, etched in copper, that described vast quantities of gold and silver stashed in 64 cryptic locations across the desert. Did the Essenes control this invaluable treasure?

Translations of the so-called Copper Scroll detail tons of precious metal that would be worth many millions in today's dollars. Some scholars speculate that the riches were from the Jewish temple in Jerusalem, hidden either from the Babylonians, who destroyed the structure in 586 BC, or from the Romans, who destroyed it in 70 AD. Skeptics dismiss the scroll as a forgery and the treasure as a hoax. Another theory is that the Knights Templar discovered the cache in the Middle Ages and took it back to their strongholds.

A fragment of the copper scroll.

tary campaigns trailed off and the Knights Templar foundered. Strange claims about them gained traction: It was said they had found the Holy Grail and the Ark of the Covenant. They were reputed to have hidden the Shroud of Turin and to own a piece of the True Cross. They were believed to be wealthy beyond imagining. Whether accurate or not, the rumors gained currency. King Philip IV of France, who was in debt to the Knights, set out to crush them, accusing them of idolatry, Satanism, sodomy, fraud, and other crimes. In 1307, he had hundreds of Knights arrested, tortured, and forced to confess. Some were burned at the stake. Finally, in 1312, Pope Clement V abolished the order.

A colored engraving of a Templar Knight on his horse, 1847.

WHO KNEW?
The headquarters of the Ancient Mystical Order Rosae Crucis are in San Jose, California. It operates a planetarium and a museum of ancient Egyptian artifacts.

GROUP THEORY

IS THERE AN ELITE, SECRET SOCIETY
THAT RUNS THE WORLD?

Through the ages, mystical groups such as the Rosicrucians and Opus Dei have claimed unique knowledge of secret truths. Since their ceremonies and initiation rites are known only to members, the general public has long wondered: What do the organizations do behind closed doors? Who are their leaders? What do they really do?

Rosicrucianism

The Brotherhood of Rosicrucianism, symbolized by the mysterious Rose Cross, claims to transmit exceptional knowledge to its members. This wisdom, they say, is unavailable to most people, explains the spiritual and physical worlds, and unravels great mysteries such as life after death. Rosicrucians find understanding through a combination of occult disciplines, including astrology, alchemy, magic, and spiritualism, as well as various Christian, Jewish, and pagan beliefs.

The society traces its origins to medieval Germany, when three anonymous manifestos about a fictional doctor and alchemist, Christian Rosenkreuz, began circulating. According to the documents, Rosenkreuz in the 15th century had founded a secret scientific and mystical order dedicated to the transformation of the arts, scholarship, religion, and politics. European intellectuals of the 17th century were fascinated by the legend, and a society of followers, dubbed the Rosicrucians, emerged.

The order flagged in the 18th century but reappeared during the spiritualist craze of the 19th century, with an emphasis on the mystical. As a new wave of Rosicrucians flourished, the groups competed with each other, fighting over which were the most authentic with actual ties to Rosenkreuz or his associates. Today, Rosicrucian brotherhoods such as The Ancient Mystical Order Rosae Crucis and the Rosicrucian Fellowship, both based in California, remain active. They initiate new members, promote them up the ladder of Rosicrucian knowledge, and are said to practice the same occult rituals as their earliest founders.

Pilgrims pray in front of the coffin of Josemariá Escrivá de Balaguer, the founder of Opus Dei, at the Roman Basilica of St. Eugene in Rome, Italy, 2002.

Ordo Templi Orientis

Thought to be one of Hollywood's favorite secret societies, the Ordo Templi Orientis splintered off of either the German or Austrian Freemasons around the turn of the 20th century. Early in its life, the order also adopted some Rosicrucian principles, but the emphasis changed once English occultist Aleister Crowley assumed control in the 1920s. Under Crowley's direction, Ordo Templi Orientis adopted a 16th-century philosophy known as *Thelema* (Greek for *will* or *intention*). Thelema's main tenet, "do what thou wilt shall be the whole of the law," directed adherents to find their real calling in life—their so-called True Will.

Members of Ordo Templi Orientis claimed to use science and symbols to pass secret knowledge onto members. As associates advanced in insight, they learned how to use the "supreme secret" to live successfully and to realize the divine in themselves. They found the truth through fellowship with other members, occult pursuits such as magic, and elaborate rituals. One of these was Liber XV,

a mass celebrated by the order's church, the Ecclesia Gnostica Catholica (Gnostic Catholic Church). Written by Crowley, the dramatic ceremony incorporated Egyptian gods, virgin priestesses, children, and the devil.

Though Crowley was dismissed by some of his contemporaries as a libertine,

Audrey Tautou and Tom Hanks in the film *The Da Vinci Code*.

ARE THEY, OR AREN'T THEY?

The secretive nature of the Rosicrucians, the Ordo Templis Orientis, and Opus Dei has long fueled speculation about membership. Who belongs—or might belong—to these groups?

ALLEGED MEMBERS

Rosicrucians

Dante Alighieri (1265–1321)
Italian author of *The Inferno*

George Washington (1732–1799)
American president

Walt Disney (1901–1966)
American animator and filmmaker

Édith Piaf (1915–1963)
French singer

Gene Roddenberry (1921–1991)
American creator of *Star Trek*

Ordo Templis Orientis

Wolfgang von Goethe (1749–1832)
German author of *Faust*

Richard Wagner (1813–1883)
German opera composer

Friedrich Nietzsche (1844–1900)
German philosopher

Jimmy Page (1944–)
English lead guitarist of Led Zeppelin

Jay-Z (1969–)
American rapper and entrepreneur

Peaches Geldof (1989–2014)
British model and TV personality

Opus Dei

Robert Hanssen (1944–)
American spy

Clarence Thomas (1948–)
American Supreme Court justice

Sam Brownback (1956–)
American politician

Rick Santorum (1958–)
American senator

Madonna (1958–)
American singer and entrepreneur

today's Ordo Templi Orientis lodges adhere to many of his philosophies and claim that they're his direct descendants. Often called a "sex cult," the order allegedly has replaced Scientology as the cult-du-jour of the entertainment industry.

Opus Dei

Does the Catholic Church include a cult? Critics of the order Opus Dei, Latin for "Work of God," think so. The order was founded in Spain in 1928 by Josemaría Escrivá, a Catholic priest whose philosophy was inspired by a vision. His teachings revolved around the belief that everyone was capable of holiness, and that anyone could become a saint. Godliness was attained through honest work, whether cleaning houses or running a company, as long as it was performed as a service to others and as an offering to God. To fulfill this ideal, the faithful were to live in the world, with ordinary jobs and traditional families. They were to follow a set of religious practices such as attending daily Mass, saying the rosary, reading religious texts, and prayer.

Despite its virtuous ideals, Opus Dei has been controversial both within and outside the Church. Detractors claim that it has many attributes of a cult and even a sinister hidden agenda. They describe it as extremely secretive, asserting that followers are forbidden to reveal their affiliation to outsiders without permission from higher-ups. Recruiting techniques are described as aggressive, designed to draw in the unhappy and vulnerable, and members are allegedly pressured to cut off contact with their nonbelieving friends and family.

A number of journalists who have reported on Opus Dei say that many of these allegations are unsubstantiated. But their voices have been largely drowned out by Dan Brown's extraordinarily successful novel *The Da Vinci Code*. Published in 2003 and released as a movie in 2006, it portrays Opus Dei as an immeasurably rich and powerful secret society that's part of an evil international conspiracy.

The Jewel of the Rose Croix, by J. Augustus Knapp.

137

Imaginary zombies haunt our movies and TV shows: have real ones walked in Haiti?

CHAPTER 8

VAMPIRES

AND

ZOMBIES

EERIE TALES OF THE UNDEAD AND HALF-HUMAN MIGHT
SEEM LIKE HARMLESS ENTERTAINMENT. BUT SOME OF
THOSE STORIES ARE BASED ON REAL-LIFE OCCURRENCES.

Portrait of Vlad III the Impaler, or Dracula.

VAMPIRES: THEY LIVED!

WHEN IT COMES TO THE UNDEAD, DRACULA WAS JUST THE BEGINNING.

WHO KNEW?
The father of Vlad the Impaler, or Dracula, was Dracul. *Dracula* means son of Dracul, or little devil.

Tales of blood-drinking demons have been with us for millennia, stretching from stories told by the Mesopotamians and ancient Greeks to current books, films, and television series. Despite the long passage of time, the stories are remarkably similar. Vampires are typically portrayed as surviving forever and subsisting on the blood of living creatures, preferably humans. With a single bite, they are able to transform their victims into new vampires. They are also virtually indestructible.

But each generation has also reimagined the bloodsucker in its own way. Vampires of the modern imagination tend to be pale, tortured, and dangerously sexy like Edward Cullen and Bella Swan of the *Twilight* series. Or, like Lestat de Lioncourt, the antihero of Anne Rice's *Vampire Chronicles* series, they are fallen aristocrats who live in feudal castles. They sport fangs and swirly capes.

In contrast, the bloodsuckers of Eastern European folklore of the 1700s were of peasant stock and resided, at least during the day, in the graveyard where they were buried, according to Paul Barber, author of *Vampires, Burial and Death: Folklore and Reality*. The undead in these tales were often laid to rest improperly and would return to stalk the living and

The notion of vampires has been around for millennia.

MEET THE REAL VAMPIRES: BATS

Vampire bats seek out prey with biological sonar called echolocation.

In 1565, early Spanish explorer M. Benzoni told of waking up in what is now Costa Rica to find a small, hairy creature sucking the blood from his toes. This chilling account was one of the first on record concerning the vampire bat. Today, much more is known about this creature.

→ It is roughly the size of a teacup.

→ It is able to drink blood from an animal for more than 30 minutes without waking it.

→ Every night, it must drink about half its body weight in blood or it will die.

→ It emerges at night to feed, mostly on livestock.

Today, there is a surprising subculture of people who believe themselves to be vampires.

in turn cause their death, writes Barber. The way to avoid unsettled souls returning and causing havoc was to lay a corpse to rest properly.

If a vampire materializes, the best way to get rid of it is staking—but only with the correct implement. In some traditions, the weapon must be made of a particular kind of wood, such as ash. In others, it must be steel or iron. As for the best body part in which to stick the stake, some cultures specify the stomach, others the mouth, and still others say the chest is best.

Today, there is a surprising subculture of people who believe they are vampires—or at the very least pretend to be. Some reportedly drink blood. Others call themselves "psychic vampires" and claim to feed off others' life energy through force of mind. "Lifestylers" might transform their appearance with makeup, contact lenses, and even artificial fangs. Are they truly vampires? Only time will tell, so check back in a few hundred years.

REAL-LIFE VAMPIRES IN HISTORY

For centuries, European folklore has included stories of bloodsucking monsters who are more than human.

1459
Vlad III, better known as Dracula, ordered his forces to impale 30,000 aristocrats as traitors. As his victims writhed in agony, Vlad allegedly dined on bread dipped in their blood.

1614
Elizabeth Bathory, a Hungarian aristocrat, was locked away in her castle for the torture and killing of at least 80 girls from nearby villages. She is believed to be the world's first and most prolific female serial killer.

1672
For 16 years after Jure Grando died, villagers claimed he rose from his grave every night, crept around town, knocked on a door, and someone in that household would die soon after. Official records from the period refer to him as a *strigon*, the regional term for vampire.

1725
Within eight days of Petar Plogojowitz's passing away in Serbia, nine other villagers died. Shortly before they expired, each of them reported being attacked and drained of blood by Plogojowitz.

1872
Italian serial killer Vincenzo Verzeni murdered two women and assaulted six others. According to testimony, Verzeni enjoyed strangling and sucking blood from his victims. Bite marks on the bodies were found to be from Verzeni's teeth.

Engraving of Florence during a 14th-century plague.

1890

While working on a novel about a vampire count, Bram Stoker discovered a book: *An Account of the Principalities of Wallachia and Moldavia*. A footnote inspired the name of his fictional character Dracula.

1892

A mass hysteria now known as the Great New England Vampire Panic was caused by a misunderstanding of tuberculosis. When Mercy Brown died of the disease, neighbors wondered why the rest of her family was dying off as well. Authorities dug up Mercy's grave and had her heart removed and burned. She was the last "vampire" officially investigated in North America.

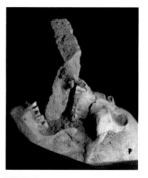

2006

The skull of an elderly woman dubbed the "Vampire of Venice" was found in Italy in a mass grave of plague victims. The mouth of the skull was stuffed with a brick, an exorcism technique used in the 16th century. Widows of the era, considered to be weak and susceptible to the devil, were often suspected of being witches in life and vampires in death.

2012

Remains of bodies pierced with iron stakes, dating from the 1200s and all belonging to male aristocrats or clerics, were found during the archaeological excavation of a monastery in Bulgaria.

2013

Four skeletons of suspected vampires from about the 16th century were discovered in Poland. The bodies had been decapitated and buried with their heads between their legs to prevent a return from the grave.

THE RABIES-VAMPIRE CONNECTION?

Did the vampire legend start with rabies?

In the late 1970s, Spanish neurologist Juan Gomez-Alonso was watching *Dracula* when he made a startling observation: vampirism seemed remarkably similar to the behavior displayed by men infected with rabies. Here are some parallels he noted.

VAMPIRES	PEOPLE WITH RABIES
Bite humans	Have been known to bite others
Virile and sexy	Experience increased sex drive
Live by night	Often experience insomnia and wander at night
Affected by garlic, mirrors, light	Hypersensitive to stimuli including strong smells; bright lights can cause teeth baring, frothing at the mouth
Exhumed vampires exhibit blood flow	Exhumed corpses have blood flowing from mouth

THE VAMPIRE EVOLVES

THE MOST ENDURING OF ALL IMMORTALS HAS GONE FROM SCARY TO SYMPATHETIC.

Paul Wesley and Nina Dobrev in *The Vampire Diaries*, 2009.

THE VAMPIRE ECONOMY

Whether in print, on television, or on the big screen, vampires mean big bucks.

Author Stephanie Meyer received a $750,000 advance for the three-book Twilight series.

→ The first *Twilight* film grossed an impressive $69.6 million at the box office; together, all three grossed $1.8 billion.

→ In 2009, *The Vampire Diaries* television series premiered to a record-setting 4.9 million viewers.

→ Anne Rice, author of the *Vampire Chronicles* series, is said to be worth $50 million.

Stories of vampires circulated for hundreds of years in Europe, but it took 19th-century Gothic literature and an early-20th-century black-and-white movie for the charming, deathless blood-drinker to really seduce the public.

The Evolution of a Bloodsucker

Vampires traditionally were folkloric figures of terror and disgust, thought to haunt graveyards and stalk the living. But the Romantic movement in 19th-century literature changed all that. Noted for dramatic effects, an interest in the eerie and otherworldly, and for extremes of emotion, Romanticism generated thousands of terrifying tales. Two of the most famous emerged from a chalet in Switzerland, where the poet Lord Byron was vacationing in 1816 with his doctor, John William Polidori, his fellow poet Percy Shelley, and writer Mary Wollstonecraft. When the group was kept indoors by bad weather, Byron challenged his friends to write scary stories to pass the time. Wollstonecraft created Frankenstein, while Polidori fashioned a Casanova-type character he called "The Vampyre." The story was eventually published in a magazine, though falsely attributed to Lord Byron.

Other writers of the era were also enchanted with the idea of vampires. In 1897, Irish author Bram Stoker was inspired by a dream he had of a young woman trying to kiss a young man on the throat while a furious count protested, "This man belongs to me." The antihero of Stoker's 1897 novel *Dracula* was a nobleman, a centuries-old vampire, and a sorcerer. The book was popular when released, but Count Dracula didn't really become a sensation until Bela Lugosi immortalized Stoker's tale in a 1931 film based on the novel. Released by Universal Pictures, the film shocked viewers unused to horror on the screen. Some even collapsed at early screenings, and the movie became a box office smash.

Human Condition

Over time, the bloodthirsty noble embodied by Lugosi gave way to more sympathetic and varied portrayals of vampires. Writers began to embrace the human nature of the undead and imagine them in different settings. When horror writer Stephen King published his novel *Salem's Lot* in 1975, he featured the ancient vampire Danny Glick, who maintained eternal youth by biting the townspeople of a hamlet in rural Maine.

In 1976, Anne Rice published the first of her best-selling *Vampire Chronicles* novels, *Interview with the Vampire*. Her evil, beautiful antihero, Lestat de Lioncourt, has a foil in Louis de Pointe du Lac, a more compassionate and moral—more human—vampire. *The Vampire Diaries* television series, based on books by L.J. Smith, echoes this theme as well: One vampire brother is an old-school bloodsucker and brute, while the other is trying hard to be human. In the first of Stephenie Meyer's *Twilight* novels, the vampire Edward Cullen tries to wean himself off of human blood and is tempted by the comely human Bella Swan. Cullen winds up competing with a werewolf for her love.

Feeding Off Fears

If the vampires of old and the current incarnations have anything in common, it is that they both reflect the public's fears and concerns, according to Margot Adler, an NPR correspondent and the author of *Vampires Are Us*. The Whitley Strieber movie *The Hunger* and the Anne Rice series of books, for example, were both popular in the 1980s, when AIDS was at epidemic levels and fear of "tainted blood" raged through the public. Adler once spent nine months reading 75 vampire tales, and says she hungered for more. As the vampire myth evolves, says Adler, vampires are "struggling to be moral." It can be a lot trickier than just engaging in Dracula's old-fashioned blood sport.

Indra Ové and Tom Cruise in *Interview with the Vampire: The Vampire Chronicles*, 1994.

NEW SUCKER BORN EVERY MINUTE

Contemporary versions of the vampire add a twist to the traditional stories of forbidden love, ancient blood curses, and immortality

→ **Out for blood.** While the classic vampire has an insatiable appetite for blood, in the *True Blood* HBO series, non-vampires lust after the blood of vampire Bill Compton.

→ **In it for love.** Louis, the vampire with a heart in Anne Rice's *Vampire Chronicles*, turns an ailing young woman into a vampire so that she can be immortal.

→ **Battle of good and evil.** The vampire named Angel in the *Buffy the Vampire Slayer* series is more of a devil, though he repents of his misdeeds when he falls for Buffy.

WHO'S YOUR (BLOOD) TYPE?

Lugosi vs. Pattinson

Hungarian-American actor Bela Lugosi, who originally played Count Dracula in a Broadway production, went on to become the most famous star ever to portray a vampire—until Robert Pattison, the pale hero of the *Twilight* films, came along in 2008. Here is how they stack up, Dracula vs. Cullen. Who's the fairest?

Lugosi	Pattinson
49 years old in the 1931 film	22 years young in the 2008 film
Exaggerated accent	All-American
Heavy on the stage makeup	Unadorned but ethereal
Dressed to kill: white bow tie, white dress shirt, black cape	Casual chic: V-neck sweater over T-shirt, black cape
Avoids the sun at all costs	Skin sparkles in the sun
Aristocratic	Aloof
Old-world charm with a dash of menace	Drop-dead handsome

WHO KNEW?

Bela Lugosi not only lived the part of Dracula—he died it. Before he was buried at age 74, he was garbed in a Dracula cape and his hair and eyebrows were dyed black, according to his wishes.

THE ZOMBIE APOCALYPSE

IN THE VOODOO TRADITION, THE DEAD ARE MEANT TO SERVE THE LIVING. IT SEEMS SOME OF THEM ALMOST HAVE.

A voodoo ceremony being performed to the beat of a drum.

You may not believe in Hollywood-style zombies—those hungry, lurching, walking dead. But as with many supernatural tales, the zombie story has some truth at its center. In some cases, it is more horrifying than fiction.

Some research shows that in the 16th, 17th, and 18th centuries, there were West African voodoo priests who created compliant slaves—zombies, if you will—by administering a special neurotoxin that mimicked death. A victim might be zombified as punishment for unacceptable behavior, or as an act of revenge. Some of the victims were sent to work on the sugar plantations of what are now Haiti and Jamaica.

To turn someone into a zombie, a voodoo priest or shaman called a *bokor* forced the prisoner to ingest a powder derived from the venomous puffer fish. The poison, 100 times more deadly than potassium cyanide, caused paralysis, slowed the heart rate, and suppressed temperature and other vital functions.

Once under the poison's influence, the seemingly dead victim was buried. A short time later, the bokor would "resurrect" him. Sometimes, the victim would also be given a substance that caused hallucinations and increased suggestibility. From that point

on, the zombie would be under the bokor's power, convinced that the bokor had stolen his soul.

Zombies and Voodoo

In that era, people in West Africa, the Caribbean, and elsewhere believed in what we now call voodoo, a set of spiritual convictions about life, death, and rebirth. In voodoo, the boundary between earthly and spiritual realms can be crossed, and the living and the dead have a duty to serve each other.

Voodoo believers worship spirits using personal altars and a variety of ritual objects including candles, beads, flowers, religious symbols, and other items. Community ceremonies feature group drumming, music, and dance. During these rituals, the soul of a dead person displaces that of a living one—usually a voodoo shaman—thus "possessing" him or her briefly.

Westerners trivialize voodoo as witchcraft or black magic, when it is actually a "distillation of very profound religious ideas," according to Wade Davis, author of *The Serpent and the Rainbow: A Harvard Scientist's Astonishing Journey into the Secret Societies of Haitian Voodoo, Zombis[cq], and Magic.*

Clairvius Narcisse, declared dead, sits on the site where he was buried and rose again as a zombie.

BORN AGAIN

For 18 years, a real-life zombie walked the earth.

In 1980, a Haitian woman was shocked to see her brother in their village's open-air market. His name was Clairvius Narcisse, and for 18 years his sister and her family had believed he had passed away.

But Narcisse had been alive the whole time and had a grotesque tale to share: He had been turned into a zombie and sent to work as a slave on a sugar plantation.

As Narcisse told it, he had entered the hospital, apparently dying, not knowing he had secretly been given a dose of paralysis-causing poison. He was pronounced dead and was buried, though he remained awake in a dreamlike state throughout the ordeal.

After some time had passed—he was unsure how long—he was pulled out of the coffin, beaten, and sent to a sugar plantation. There he was regularly given drugs to keep him in the zombielike state.

It was only after Narcisse escaped that the effects of the medication wore off and he was able to function normally again. Doctors who examined Narcisse could find no apparent motive for him to lie. Later, Narcisse said in an interview that he believed his brother, with whom he had had a land dispute, had arranged for the zombification.

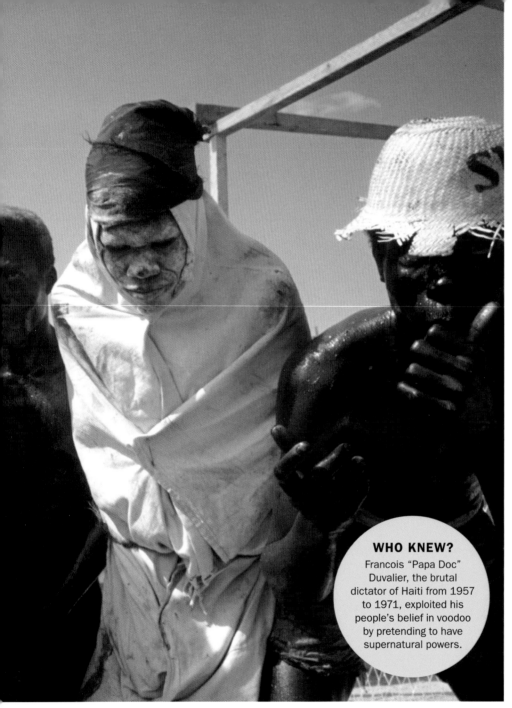

WHO KNEW?
Francois "Papa Doc" Duvalier, the brutal dictator of Haiti from 1957 to 1971, exploited his people's belief in voodoo by pretending to have supernatural powers.

A group of men dressed as zombies perform a symbolic ritual in Haiti.

Lives in Limbo

Today, voodoo is still one of Haiti's official religions, and Haiti is the country most closely associated with zombies. However, contemporary followers say the practice of zombification is a thing of the past. Nevertheless, the real-life zombies were hardly brain-eating pop culture icons. They were human beings rendered tragically passive or catatonic through systematic and ongoing poisoning. These poor souls were doomed to live out their lives, sometimes long ones, in a limbo state between life and death.

147

RETURN OF THE DEAD

WHAT'S SCARIER THAN A HOLLYWOOD ZOMBIE? REAL-LIFE FLESH-EATERS ON THE PROWL.

TEACHABLE MOMENT?

A hoaxer spreads fear about a zombie protein to warn people about abuses of social media.

In May 2012, after a drugged Florida man ate the face of a homeless person, rumors of a real-life zombie virus spread rapidly across the Internet. The reports were the work of Alfred Moya, a Web professional, who used Twitter, You-Tube, a website, and a faked news article to publicize a rogue protein he called Lysergic Quinine Protein (LQP-79). According to Moya's information, LQP-79 was dangerous and transforming people into zombies. It was a week before the episode was revealed as a hoax. Moya claimed his intention was simply to warn about the power of social media.

All the world loves a zombie, the flesh-eating corpses who star in blockbuster movies, survivalist websites, and sometimes highbrow fiction. Even the U.S. government's Centers for Disease Control and Prevention have gotten in on the zombie craze with a tongue-in-cheek campaign using a zombie apocalypse to educate about preparedness for hurricanes, pandemics, or terrorist attacks.

The idea that the dead can be reanimated —brought back to life—is not a new one. The species of zombie that permeates contemporary popular culture has its roots in Haitian voodoo.

But unlike Haitian zombies, current iterations of the undead wander around with lifeless stares, shuffling and groaning, in search of human flesh to devour. Could there be a grain of truth to today's zombie-mania? Is there actually a contagious virus out there that could turn people into zombies?

Real-Life Flesh Eaters

In recent years, a handful of unrelated incidents prompted a wave of Internet hysteria about an infectious zombie virus. In 2009, a Texas mother was accused of killing her newborn son and eating part of his brain and several toes. In 2012, a de-

ranged assailant ate the flesh of the face of a homeless man on the streets of Miami. The "zombie," a man high on drugs, had to be shot four times by police before he stopped the attack. Within days, a New Jersey man stabbed himself repeatedly and ate his own intestines before he was subdued by officials. While these episodes clearly involved serious mental illness, they set off wild talk of a real zombie apocalypse.

Speculation ran rampant that the attacks resulted from an actual rabies-like virus that infected brain tissue. The theory was that rabies, which is transmitted through biting and can cause a victim to bite others, was mutating into an airborne virus that could spread rapidly. Scientists dismissed the notion on the grounds that viruses do not mutate to take on characteristics of radically different viruses.

WHO KNEW?

Most of the zombies in *Night of the Living Dead* were nonprofessional actors, including local steel-workers, meatpackers, and ad executives who also supplied props, did their own makeup, and donated equipment.

COULD HAVE BEEN WORSE

Zombie movies are beloved for their gore and violence, but many have been toned down to get past the censors.

→ *Night of the Living Dead* **(1968)** Before this George Romero classic horror flick was released in the United Kingdom, the British Board of Film Classification (BBFC) insisted on the removal of scenes featuring flesh-eating.

→ *Dawn of the Dead* **(1978)** The BBFC strikes again. Before allowing this George Romero film into U.K. theaters, the censorship board ordered the removal of footage of an exploding head, a screwdriver killing, stabbings, and scenes of disembowelment.

→ *Zombie* **(1979)** During filming of this Italian scarefest, scenes were shot of a zombie coming out of the water in New York City, but they did not make it into the final cut. The film was considered so violent, moviegoers were given airline sick bags.

→ *Shaun of the Dead* **(2004)** This British zombie spoof originally contained longer garden scenes and featured a hanged-man zombie and a woman being eaten by her own dog.

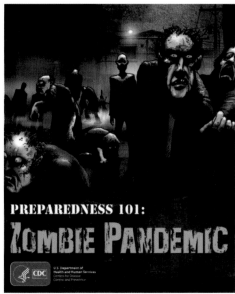

CDC poster playfully using zombies to urge emergency preparedness.

A scene from *White Zombie*, 1932. It is the story of a woman turned into a zombie by an evil voodoo master.

THE BIG BAD WEREWOLF

FROM ANCIENT MYTHS TO THE *TWILIGHT* SERIES, THESE HAIRY CREATURES HAVE PLAYED A STARRING ROLE IN THE STORIES WE TELL.

Afraid of werewolves? Blame it on the Greek gods. According to mythology, when King Lycaon wanted to see if Zeus really was all-knowing, he slaughtered a child and served the dismembered pieces to the Olympian ruler in a dish. Discovering the ruse, a furious Zeus turned Lycaon into a wolf and killed his 50 sons by lightning bolts. The werewolf, a shape-shifting and violent creature, has lurked ominously in the world's imagination ever since, a staple of folklore, fairy tales, novels, and movies.

MY MUSE HAS FANGS

Comedy duo Abbott and Costello found humor in werewolves. For novelist Guy Endore, the werewolf was an evil French soldier. Screenwriter Jeph Loeb imagined the beast as a high school basketball player. Here, a look at the werewolf on the small and big screen.

1913 *The Werewolf* The first werewolf movie ever made, this lost silent film was based on Native American legends.

1923 *Le Loup Garou* (France) This silent film portrays a man who becomes a werewolf after murdering a priest who cursed him.

1935 *The Werewolf of London* The first major Hollywood movie to feature a werewolf.

1941 *The Wolf Man* Stars Lon Chaney Jr. as the beast, along with Claude Rains and Bela Lugosi.

1943 *Frankenstein Meets the Wolf Man* The second film featuring Lon Chaney Jr. ends with a climactic battle with Frankenstein's monster.

1944 *House of Frankenstein* Chaney's third *Wolf Man* movie also stars Boris Karloff and brings in Dracula, a mad scientist, and a hunchback.

1948 *Abbott and Costello Meet Frankenstein* A parody of the previous *Wolf Man* movies with appearances by Bela Lugosi and Vincent Price.

1956 *The Werewolf* In this sci-fi movie, evil scientists inject an unsuspecting man with a serum that turns him into a werewolf.

1959 *El Hombre y el Monstruo* (Mexico) After making a deal with the devil, a pianist turns into a werewolf every time he plays.

1961 *The Curse of the Werewolf* This movie was based on Guy Endore's 1933 book *The Werewolf of Paris*, one of the most popular werewolf novels of the 20th century.

1965 *La Loba* (Mexico) A highly acclaimed film about a female werewolf.

1968 *La Marca del Hombre-lobo* (Spain) The first of the 14 werewolf movies in the Waldemar Daninsky saga about a cursed nobleman.

1970 *La Noche de Walpurgis* (Spain) The hugely successful fifth entry in the Waldemar Daninsky saga started the Spanish horror film boom of the 1970s.

1974 *The Beast Must Die* Guests at a country estate die one by one while trying to discover which of them is a werewolf.

1981 *An American Werewolf in London* This cult classic was one of the three Hollywood blockbusters that launched the werewolf movie craze of the 1980s.

1981 *The Howling* This film, set in a secluded resort where everyone turns out to be a werewolf, spawned seven sequels.

From *The Company of Wolves*, 1984.

Laura Vandervoort as Elena Michaels.

Zeus might not recognize Lycaon's descendants, who might be anthropomorphic wolf-human hybrids or a cross with another animal species or supernatural beings. Some werewolves in contemporary literature are immune to conventional weapons but vulnerable to silver. Others have become heroes as well as villains, facing off against vampires. In the popular *Twilight* series of movies and books, the werewolf has a role that would once have been unthinkable—a heart-throb seeking to win the heroine's love.

1981 *Wolfen* This crime-horror film, starring Albert Finney and Gregory Hines, was based on the 1978 novel of the same name by Whitley Strieber.

1981 *Returno del Hombre Lobo* (Spain) One of the top Waldemar Daninsky films, this movie features a showdown between the Wolf Man and the sadistic Blood Countess.

1984 *The Company of Wolves* (U.K.) This film, based on a 1979 Angela Carter short story of the same name, turns the *Little Red Riding Hood* fable into a werewolf story.

1985 *Silver Bullet* Stephen King wrote the screen adaptation of his 1985 illustrated novella *Cycle of the Werewolf*, set in a small Maine town.

1985 *Teen Wolf* A film starring Michael J. Fox as a werewolf in a human high school.

1987–1988 *Werewolf* The Fox network's one-season horror series features a college student seeking a cure for his condition.

1989 *Howling V: The Rebirth* From the popular *Howling* franchise, this direct-to-video movie features an unknown werewolf among the guests at a creepy Romanian castle.

1994 *Wolf* Jack Nicholson plays an unlucky book editor who gradually turns into a werewolf.

1997 *An American Werewolf in Paris* Sequel to *An American Werewolf in London.*

2000 *Ginger Snaps* (Canada) Teenage sisters, one of them a werewolf, are the protagonists in this first film of a trilogy that presents lycanthropy as a metaphor for puberty.

2002 *Dog Soldiers* (U.K.) An action-packed thriller focusing on British soldiers who encounter a family of werewolves.

2003 *Underworld* In the first of a series of four films, the vampire warrior Selene fights in the vampires-versus-werewolves wars.

2008 *Twilight* A tribe of werewolves figures prominently in this movie, based on the bestselling *Twilight* novels by Stephenie Meyer.

2011–2014 *Being Human* This horror/comedy TV series centers on three supernatural creatures, including a werewolf, who share an apartment and try to live as humans.

2010 *The Wolfman* This remake of Lon Chaney Jr.'s 1941 classic stars Benicio del Toro, supposedly cast because he looks like Chaney.

2011–present *Teen Wolf* A TV series about a high school werewolf who tries to hide his identity to fit in.

2014 *Bitten* (Canada) This TV series introduced Elena Michaels, a young werewolf woman, her human boyfriend, and her pack.

ALPHA GIRLS

The earliest werewolves were often portrayed as male, but some of the most memorable vulpine characters have been female.

Elena Michaels
The heroine of the *Women of the Otherworld* series of fantasy books is the werewolf Elena, who tries to live as a human. She is also the central character of the television show *Bitten*.

Kalix
In this series of novels about Kalix, a troubled teenage werewolf, the heroine hides out in London to avoid her Scottish pack and ruthless werewolf hunters.

Mercy Thompson
Raised by werewolves, auto mechanic Mercy can turn into a coyote at will in this urban fantasy book series.

Mags
In the *Seventh Doctor* books and BBC television series, the character Mags, a young punk from the planet Vulpana, is a werewolf.

Kitty Norville
Her name may be feline, but Kitty in this popular book series is a werewolf who hosts a talk-radio show about the supernatural. She becomes a target for brutal bounty hunters, hateful humans, and wrathful paranormals.

151

HOWLERS
IN THE NIGHT

WHEN THE FULL MOON GLOWS, CURSED MEN TRANSFORM INTO SAVAGE, WOLF-LIKE BEASTS—OR SO THE LEGEND GOES.

Actor David Naughton on the set of *An American Werewolf in London.*

IN WOLF'S CLOTHING

According to myth, werewolves revert to human form during the day—but there were ways to distinguish them from average citizens.

→ Eyebrows meet at the bridge of the nose

→ Glowing eyes

→ Pale skin

→ Broad hands

→ Elongated index and/or middle fingers

→ Small, pointed ears

→ Pentagram somewhere on the body, usually on the chest or hand

→ Hairy palms that might be shaved, leaving behind stubble or rough skin

Half-human, half beast, and completely terrifying, werewolves have haunted man's imagination from the earliest recorded time. Images of werewolf-like creatures have been found in Turkish cave paintings that date to 8000 BC. In the Mesopotamian era, the poem *The Epic of Gilgamesh* featured a shepherd who was turned into a wolf by the goddess Ishtar, and even the abandoned twins Romulus and Remus of ancient Roman myth were saved and suckled by a she-wolf.

Yet it was real-life Norse warriors who may have stoked belief in werewolves during the Middle Ages. In that period, bloodthirsty soldiers called berserkers dressed in coats made of wolf hide. During battles, the berserkers worked themselves into frenzies that reminded their targets of a pack of wolves. Some scholars believe the behavior was triggered by drugged foods the warriors ate before battle in order to feel invincible. Today going berserk, of course, means flying into a crazed rage.

Executed Like Witches

Fear of werewolves grew in tandem with the hysteria surrounding witchcraft in the later Middle Ages, and by the early 15th century, accused werewolves were tried and executed just like sorceresses. One of the first such proceedings took place in 1407 in Basel, Switzerland, kicking off a long period referred to by scholars as the Werewolf Witch Trials.

The most notorious and gruesome of these persecutions took place in 1589 in Redburg, Germany. While the facts of the case are difficult to ascertain, it is said that a middle-aged farmer named Peter Stumpp murdered 12 children, two pregnant women, and livestock. His punishment was death by torture in front of a crowd. Stumpp was first strapped spread-eagle to a wheel to allow his executioners to tear his flesh from his body with red-hot steel pincers. The executioners then broke his arms and legs with the blunt side of an ax, beheaded him, and threw his corpse onto a burning pyre. The farmer's head was placed atop a spike; beneath it hung a framed likeness of a wolf.

Stumpp was most likely a serial killer and cannibal who murdered his victims while wearing a wolf hide. Some historians believe he was also a converted Protestant and that the trial and execution were part of a political battle between the Catholics and Protestants. Stumpp's daughter and his mistress, found guilty by association, were also tortured and killed.

Word of the case spread quickly across Europe, touching off a mass hysteria and many more such executions. The last recorded case of a werewolf trial and killing occurred in Austria in the early 1800s.

Actor Lon Chaney Jr. on the set of the 1941 film *The Wolf Man*.

HAIR OF THE WOLF

A rare medical disorder, hypertrichosis is sometimes called the werewolf syndrome.

In March 2011, Supatra "Nat" Sasuphan entered the Guinness Book of World Records as "World's Hairiest Child." The 11-year-old Thai girl (who said she was "very happy" to be in the book) is one of only 50 people in the world known to have hypertrichosis, a condition that causes an abnormal amount of hair growth all over the body. Also known as Ambras syndrome, hypertrichosis runs in families and can be present at birth or appear later in life. Temporary hair removal is most often employed to manage the condition, as anything permanent involves chemicals that can result in scarring, hypersensitivity, and other skin problems.

Historically, people with hypertrichosis were often employed in traveling carnivals as "freaks" for display. In 2007, ABC News ran a story about Danny and Larry Gomez, brothers in Mexico with the disease who were put in cages at a circus and labeled "wolf children." Ultimately, the son of the circus owner convinced his father to train the boys as performers, and Danny, now in his 20s, is a trapeze artist. He claims ladies love his extra hair.

Jesus Fajardo, who has been diagnosed with hypertrichosis (right); and Maria Jose Cristerna, renowned as "the vampire woman" (left).

Unbound by gravity, a ghost can pass through solid objects such as
the walls of buildings where it spent its life.

CHAPTER 9
GHOSTS
AND
HAUNTINGS

ANNE BOLEYN, THE QUEEN OF ENGLAND, WAS FAMOUSLY BEHEADED AT THE TOWER OF LONDON IN 1536. TODAY, HER SPECTER IS SAID TO WANDER ABOUT, ITS HEAD TUCKED UNDER ITS ARM. WHAT OTHER OLD SPIRITS LURK IN THE SHADOWS?

VISITORS FROM BEYOND

APPARITIONS, BOGEYS, HAINTS, PHANTOMS: THEY'RE ALL A LITTLE SCARY. SO WHY WON'T THEY GO AWAY?

Almost every society and culture has ghosts and an explanation for them—whether it is the deceased seeking vengeance for a great wrong done during life or an omen of impending death.

Typically, ghosts are described as hostile to humans, seeking to harm them out of spite, cruelty, or for their own amusement. Some bring trouble, sickness, or catastrophe, while others try to invade the bodies of the living and possess their souls.

Often, ghosts are simply the spirits of women with unhappy stories. Brazil's Dama Branca, or White Lady, represents a young woman who died in childbirth or was an adulterer and murdered. Mute and pale, she haunts the countryside and remote roads in a long wispy dress. In Mexico, La Llorona, The Weeping Woman, is the ghost of Maria, a mother who drowned her children and then herself for the love of a man. Most luridly, Thailand's Phi Krasue, or Demonic Beauty, is the soul of an adulterous Khmer princess who was incompletely burned at the stake. She flies through the night air to feed on pus and other foul matter, killing people in the process.

These tortured souls who haunt the living can also be children or men who have died violently or tragically or are not yet ready to leave the earth or may be seeking revenge.

In England, the Black Dog is the spirit of a cursed or executed person or of an unbaptized child. It is black, large, and monstrous, with blazing red eyes, and is sometimes headless. While the Black Dog may portend death, it is also thought to sometimes be a benevolent protector. In China, a *jiangshi*, or "stiff corpse," feeds off the *chi* (life force) of the living or sucks their blood.

How are ghosts able to wreak havoc? Unbound by gravity, they can pass through solid objects. They usually appear at night, often in the buildings or cemeteries associated with their life. Some, called poltergeists, can make noises or move physical objects. A ghost might appear only to one person, even if others are nearby, and might convey visual or verbal messages to people through mediums who are able to communicate with the dead.

Mexican actors perform "La Llorona" (The Weeping Woman), as part of the Day of the Dead celebrations in 2009 in Xochimilco, Mexico.

A GHOST BY ANY OTHER NAME

Just about every society and religion claims at least a few ghosts. Here are some especially intriguing ones.

Where does it come from?	What is its name and what does it mean?	Who is it?	What does it look like?	What does it do?
India	**PRETA** hungry ghost	Spirit of a corrupt, devious, bitter, or greedy person	Usually invisible; sometimes seen as a mummified humanoid with skinny limbs and distended belly	Afflicted with acute hunger and thirst, it eats corpses and other foul substances but is never satisfied.
Jamaica	**DUPPY** ghost	"Shadow" of a dead person that remains on earth after the spirit has passed on, especially in the absence of a proper funeral	Invisible but often exudes a strong, sweet scent	Harasses with mischief; may terrify people in the form of a calf with burning eyes or do harm to someone at the behest of an enemy.
Japan	**KUCHISAKE-ONNA** slit-mouthed woman	Spirit of the concubine of an ancient samurai who slashed her mouth after she cheated on him	A beautiful woman in a surgical mask	Appears at night and asks men if they find her beautiful. If they answer "yes," she pulls off her mask to reveal her mutilated face.
Malaysia	**PONTIANAK** dead child	Soul of a stillborn girl	A hideous woman with sharp nails, a lovely young woman, or a bird; all having a strong frangipani scent	Lingers along roadsides or under trees, attacking men, disemboweling them, and drinking their blood.
Spain	**SANTA COMPAÑA** holy company	Tormented spirits	A procession of dead souls wearing hooded white robes and carrying candles, headed by a living person carrying a cross	Visits the homes of those who will soon die.
Sweden	**GAST** ghost	Soul of a murderer, a murdered person, a suicide, or someone with unfinished business	Translucent or skeletal, with sharp claws and fangs	Causes disease and accidents and enjoys frightening the living.
United States	**BLOODY MARY** sometimes called Mary Worth	Spirit of Mary Worth, who was either a witch, a child-murderer, or a beautiful young girl whose face was disfigured in an accident	A reanimated corpse, a witch, or a ghost, sometimes covered in blood	Appears in a mirror when summoned, usually by a preteen or teenaged girl. May tell the future, assault the girl, or gush blood.

HISTORY LESSONS

SINCE ANCIENT TIMES, HUMANS HAVE BELIEVED IN AND TOLD TALES ABOUT DISEMBODIED SPIRITS.

Macbeth Seeing the Ghost of Banquo (1854) by Theodore Chasseriau.

It didn't start with Shakespeare. It didn't start with Edgar Allen Poe, and it definitely didn't begin with *Poltergeist*. The idea of ghosts—restless specters who haunt people and places—originated millennia ago. To find the earliest apparitions, we must travel at least as far back as 4,000 years, to cultures in which the soul was first considered separate from the body and funeral rituals evolved to assist the spirits of the dead with their transition to the afterlife. If these rituals were not performed, or if they were done incorrectly, the person's spirit could not cross over. In ancient Egypt, ghostly visions were recorded in inscriptions, on papyrus scrolls, and in tomb paintings. The spectral sightings continued in ancient Greece and in Rome, where the author and statesman Pliny the Younger complained of a bearded, chain-rattling specter haunting his home.

"Middle-Aged" Spirits

Supernatural belief was widespread in Medieval and Renaissance Europe. In 856 AD, a poltergeist was reported to be tormenting a German farm family, throwing stones and starting fires. More than 1,000 years later, a monk in North Yorkshire, England, compiled eerie local occurrences of restless howling spirits. In one unsettling tale, the coffin of a deceased rector who was haunting the countryside was exhumed. As townspeople threw the coffin into a local river, the oxen drawing the wagon became severely agitated, plunged into the water, and almost drowned. Ever since the second wife of Henry the VIII, Anne Boleyn, was beheaded, she has reportedly haunted the Tower of London as well as her ancestral home, Hever Castle, in Kent.

High-Profile Ghosts

In fact, history is full of the ghosts of notable figures, including royalty, clergy, military leaders, revolutionaries, and criminals. Legend has it that Benjamin Franklin's toga-clad statue sometimes steps down off its pedestal at the American Philosophical Society's library, in Philadelphia, and dances a jig. Abraham Lincoln is a popular White House apparition. Ghostly battalions abound, too. Civil War spirits have been spotted at the battle site in Gettysburg, Pennsylvania, and World War I ghosts haunt sites at Gallipoli, near Turkey, and Verdun, in northeastern France.

THE PHANTOMS OF FICTION

There are "real" ghosts, and then there are ghost stories. These are some great ones:

→ *The Legend of Sleepy Hollow*, 1820
Washington Irving's tale, based on German folklore, features a terrifying headless horseman.

→ *The Turn of the Screw*, 1898
In this Henry James novella, a governess at a haunted estate struggles to save her charges from malicious phantoms.

→ *A Christmas Carol*, 1843
Charles Dickens's novella introduced some of literature's most memorable chain-rattling holiday spirits.

→ *The Haunting of Hill House*, 1959
Shirley Jackson's novel is considered one of the best literary ghost stories ever written.

→ *The Shining*, 1977
Thanks to Stephen King's novel set in a haunted hotel, nobody wants to stay in room 217.

"SOMETHING WICKED THIS WAY COMES..."

William Shakespeare's many ghostly characters reflected the beliefs and superstitions of his time.

GHOST of the dead king in *Hamlet*, Act 1, Scene 5:
I am thy father's spirit,
Doomed for a certain term to walk the night,
And for the day confined to fast in fires,
'Til the foul crimes done in my days of nature
Are burnt and purged away. But that I am forbid
To tell the secrets of my prison house,
I could a tale unfold whose lightest word
Would harrow up thy soul, freeze thy young blood,
Make thy two eyes like stars start from their spheres,
Thy knotted and combined locks to part
And each particular hair to stand an end,
Like quills upon the fretful porpentine.

Back in Elizabethan times, ghosts were considered real, and those who didn't believe in them were asking for trouble. So it makes sense that Shakespeare's plays would be full of malevolent spirits. *Richard III*, *Julius Caesar*, *Macbeth*, and *Hamlet* all feature terrifying phantoms who come back from the dead to deliver prophesies or warnings. These ghosts didn't just keep Elizabethan-era audiences tossing and turning at night; they also moved the plot along. Hamlet, for example, is visited by the ghost of his murdered father, the former King of Denmark. The apparition tells Hamlet that he was poisoned by his brother Claudius, who has assumed his throne, and asks Hamlet to avenge his death—which begins the play's tragic chain of events.

AMERICA'S MOST HAUNTED

THOUSANDS OF HOMES ARE RUMORED TO HARBOR GHOSTS. SOME ARE BENEVOLENT; MANY ARE NOT.

The Myrtles Plantation.

WHO KNEW?

In 1985, Mickey Deans, the last husband of singer and actress Judy Garland, purchased Franklin Castle and lived there for more than a decade.

The Hannes Tiedemann House, known as Franklin Castle.

Apparitions, mysterious sounds, strange odors, cold spots, distraught pets. These are the signs of America's 3,500 to 5,000 haunted houses, which are as different as they are alike. In Chicago, there's the Hull House, once a refuge for new immigrants and now a museum said to be haunted by a child born with pointed ears, horns, scale-covered skin, and a tail. In tony Palm Beach, Florida, occupants of the Riddle House, a onetime funeral parlor, have reported hearing rattling chains and soft voices. And then there's the Latta Plantation in Huntersville, North Carolina, where hordes of ladybugs can suddenly swarm or the smell of baking apple pie can mysteriously fill the air.

Is there anything to the strange tales, or are they self-perpetuating hoaxes? More than a third of Americans polled by Gallup believe in haunted houses, but even paranormal investigators caution that haunting is often the power of suggestion.

Here, peek inside some of the country's most highly rated haunted houses.

Franklin Castle: Where Did the Baby Skeletons Come From?

In 1881, German banker Hannes Tiedemann commissioned the construction of a stately 30-room mansion for his family on Franklin Boulevard in Cleveland, Ohio. With a carriage house and tower, the handsome sandstone residence was noted as a fine example of Queen Anne–style architecture.

Inside the walls of Franklin Castle, however, tragedy lurked. Tiedemann was rumored to be abusive; local lore has it that his mother, wife, children, and a servant girl had all died under mysterious circumstances within a short period of time. Today many believe the castle is cursed, and there are reports of sobbing, voices behind walls, and faces rising out of the woodwork.

The Romano family, which owned the home from 1968 to 1976, reportedly moved out after being warned by a ghost-child of an impending death. Passersby claim to have seen a woman dressed in black—be-

Saint Michael the Archangel.

lieved to be the ghost of the Tiedemanns' servant—in the turret windows. Some say that is the spot where Tiedemann hacked the young girl to death with an ax. A small figure, thought to be the ghost of one of the Tiedemann children, has been spotted wandering around the ballroom.

In the 1970s, skeletons of several babies were found in a sealed room in Franklin Castle. The county coroner determined the bones to be very old and concluded that they might have been medical specimens. More suspicious Clevelandites said they were the bones of the deceased Tiedemann children.

The Plantation of Terror

Just outside Baton Rouge, Louisiana, is the infamous Myrtles Plantation, built in 1796 and believed to be haunted by 12 ghosts. Some are said to leave handprints on mirrors, others to practice voodoo. The footsteps of one supposedly can be heard on a Myrtles staircase.

What awful past has created so many turbulent souls? The unrest is often traced to a slave, Chloe, who allegedly was forced into an affair by onetime Myrtles owner Mark Woodruff. According to legend, Woodruff caught Chloe listening at a keyhole and ordered her ear cut off. Ever after, she wore a green turban.

In revenge, Chloe fed the family poisoned cake, killing Woodruff's wife and two daughters. Other slaves supposedly hanged Chloe and threw her body in the Mississippi River.

The murders, and even Chloe's existence, are in question, but visitors swear they've seen an apparition in a green turban, along with ghosts of other slaves. One occupant who did meet an untimely end at the Myrtles was William Drew Winter, an attorney who lived there from 1860 to 1871. Winter was shot by a stranger and died staggering up the stairs, where his footsteps are sometimes heard today.

Stacey Jones, founder of Central New York Ghost Hunters, has said that she visited the Myrtles Plantation, now a bed and breakfast, with a friend. During the stay, Jones's companion was supposedly held down in the bed all night by a mysterious force. "We slept in the children's bedroom," Jones says. "She was unable to move or cry out for help."

Willard Library, Evansville, Indiana.

UNEXPECTED FAVORITES

It isn't just houses. Spirits like to hang out in stores and other public places, too.

THE PLACE **Toys "R" Us,** Sunnyvale, California.

THE GHOST **Johan Johnson,** a farmhand from the 1880s who worked at the former ranch where the toy store now sits.

SCARINESS FACTOR **Low:** Johnson is a fun ghost who likes to pull pranks and move toys around.

THE PLACE **Willard Library,** Evansville, Indiana.

THE GHOST **The Grey Lady,** a veiled woman.

SCARINESS FACTOR **Medium:** The Grey Lady is not malevolent, employees say. But she makes her presence known— a lot—by touching people's hair, moving furniture around, and leaving a waft of perfume in the air.

THE PLACE **Bobby Mackey's Music World,** Wilder, Kentucky

THE GHOST **Pearl Bryan,** a young woman found murdered in the area in 1896, as well as others.

SCARINESS FACTOR **High:** The nightclub is said to have a gateway to Hell in its basement.

WHO KNEW?
Kathy Bates plays Madame Delphine LaLaurie, based on the real woman, in the television series *American Horror Story: Coven.*

The LaLaurie residence on Royal Street in New Orleans is said to be haunted by slaves who were tortured there.

New Orleans Torture House

It was just another grand old home in New Orleans' French Quarter, until a fire in 1834 led to a horrible discovery. The imposing stucco mansion on Royal Street, owned by a wealthy couple, Dr. Louis LaLaurie and Delphine Macarty LaLaurie, hid a secret: Madame LaLaurie was a monstrous woman who tortured her household slaves. When the fire broke out and neighbors rushed in to help, they came upon "atrocities the details of which seem to be too incredible for human belief," according to a newspaper report at the time. Seven slaves were found restrained by their necks, "with their limbs apparently stretched and torn from one extremity to

another." New Orleans residents were so furious, they stormed the house, nearly demolishing it.

The LaLauries left New Orleans, but their mansion remained the city's most infamous haunted house. Over the years the building was used for a variety of purposes, including a girls' school and apartments, but reports of strange goings-on continued. People claimed to see ghosts of a slave in chains and Madame LaLaurie herself, and to hear screaming.

These days, the Royal Street mansion seems relatively peaceful. When the actor Nicolas Cage owned it for a while in the early 2000s, he told the *New York Daily News* that he had never experienced anything su-

The haunted Chambers mansion, on Nob Hill in San Francisco, less than ten years after it was built.

Pennsylvania College, Gettysburg, postcard, 1903. View of Pennsylvania College, renamed Gettysburg College in 1921.

HAUNTED U.

The most frightening things about college are weird roommates and whatever is left in the fridge at the end of the semester—right? Well, maybe not.

→ At **Keene State College** in New Hampshire, a former all-women's residence hall is said to be haunted by the ghost of a school superinten-dent who doesn't like that the dorm is now coed.

→ At **Fordham University** in Bronx, New York, built where an old hospital used to be, students report numerous ghostly sightings.

→ At **Gettysburg College** in Pennsylvania, the site of the Civil War's bloodiest battle, a campus theater is home to an apparition that students say likes to sit in on rehearsals.

pernatural. In 2010 the mansion sold for $2.1 million; it is now owned by a Texas energy trader, who renovated and redecorated it.

Chambers of Horror

Located in a historic neighborhood in San Francisco, California, the elegant Chambers mansion sold for over $4 million in 2013. That's a lot of money for a house, but this one came with five bedrooms, a media room, and the ghost of Claudia Chambers. According to local lore, the 1887 Queen Anne Victorian was built by a wealthy man who lived there with his two nieces, to whom he willed the place when he died. The women despised each other. One of them, Claudia, is said to have died mysteri-

ously in an awful accident involving a farm implement. Some say she was murdered by an insane relative who lived in the attic.

The house passed from buyer to buyer after that, and for a while in the 1970s, it was a hotel whose guests included Barbra Streisand and Robin Williams. People who have visited or stayed in the house report lots of strange incidents, including flashing lights, sudden cold, and windows opening and closing mysteriously. Even the former hotel owner told the *Wall Street Journal* that the place was haunted.

These days the residence is in private hands, so what goes on behind the walls is officially between the new owner and Claudia Chambers.

BRITISH INVASION

THE GHOSTS THAT HAUNT THE CASTLES AND INNS OF THE UNITED KINGDOM MIGHT BE ROYAL OR DISLOYAL.

Britain's most haunted house, the Ancient Ram Inn, in Wotton-under-Edge, Gloucestershire.

A LUCRATIVE SPECTER

British phantasms have spurred a boom for the travel industry.

→ **Tours of Excellence** brings visitors to a variety of reportedly haunted locales, including Chillingham Castle, Northumberland, where the ghost of Lady Berkeley roams the hallways looking for her unfaithful husband; and Castell Coch in Bath, where Dame Griffiths mourns for her drowned young son.

→ **Fright Nights** offers weekend trips guided by mediums and ghost-hunting experts to visit haunted caves, a women's prison, and Armley Mills in Leeds, a former textile mill where children's laughter echoes and a ghost named Harold whispers secrets.

Britain's castles and inns, many of which date to medieval times, have witnessed centuries of murder, suicide, and treachery. Today, otherworldly apparitions are said to offer testimony to this turbulent past, wandering the rooms and gardens where they died. Want to be spooked? Time for a ghost-hunting trip to these most intriguing isles.

A Beheaded Queen

The Tower of London, which dates to the 11th century and has served as a royal residence, a prison, and an armory, has one of the most treacherous histories of any edifice in the United Kingdom. It is the site where Anne Boleyn, King Henry VIII's second wife, was famously beheaded in 1536 on various false charges, and the wronged queen is said to wander the place with her head tucked under her arm.

Anne is in good company. Lady Margaret Pole, the 8th Countess of Salisbury, was brutally executed at the tower five years later, also at the behest of Henry VIII. According to legend, Lady Margaret refused to lay her head on the chopping block and was forced down by the executioner. When his first stroke hit Margaret on the shoulder instead of the neck, she sprang up and tried to escape. It took the executioner ten more blows to finally kill Lady Margaret. Her ghost has been spied on the anniversary of her execution, frantically running around the tower with blood pouring from her wounds.

Galloping Through Walls

West of London, in Gloucestershire, sits the Ancient Ram Inn in Wotton-under-Edge, another of England's famously haunted sites. Dating to 1145, the former pub at one point was used to house slaves and workers who helped build a local church. Today, 20 ghosts and apparitions are reported to occupy the Ancient Ram, including a 16th-century witch who was supposed to be burned at the stake but took refuge at the inn; the ghost of her cat, who is said to urinate on the beds; a monk who haunts the bishop's room; a Roman centurion on horseback who gallops through walls; and a pagan high priestess. Eight former guests of the inn reportedly have undergone exorcisms after visiting, and the owner carries a Bible at all times. Perhaps the ghostly crowd can be explained by the fact that the hotel was built on a pagan site once used for ritual sacrifice.

Phantom Ropes

Wales, where humans have lived for at least 29,000 years, also has its fair share of apparitions. Destination number one for many ghost-hunters is the Skirrid Mountain Inn

Tulloch Castle in Dingwall, Ross-Shire, Scotland.

Anne Boleyn.

THE TRAVELING GHOST QUEEN

The specter of Anne Boleyn has been seen all across England, particularly near landmarks of her brief but eventful life.

→ **Blickling Hall, Norfolk**

Anne's birthplace. She is said to visit in a black funeral coach on the anniversary of her execution, May 19, 1536. Dressed in white and holding her severed head, Anne is driven by a headless horseman and four black, headless horses.

→ **Hever Castle, Kent**

Where Anne grew up. She has been spied in the garden where she was courted by Henry VIII.

→ **Hampton Court Palace and Windsor Castle, London**

The homes of Anne and Henry VIII, where she is often seen at a window.

→ **The Tower of London**

Where she was executed. Salle Church, Norfolk: Where some believe Anne's body was moved after her original burial in the Chapel of St. Peter ad Vincula in the Tower of London.

in Llanfihangel, which long ago doubled as a courthouse. One ghost said to lurk there belongs to John Crowther, a 12th-century sheep thief who was convicted in the courthouse and hanged by a rope from one of the ceiling beams. Contemporary guests have reported feeling phantom ropes winding around their necks and tightening, with telltale marks on their flesh for days afterward.

Next stop: Ireland's Kinnitty Castle in County Offaly, a luxurious inn with a turbulent history dating to the ancient druids. Kinnitty Castle's resident specter is known as the Phantom Monk of Kinnitty, who has told at least one hotel staffer that he haunts the hotel to remind guests of the monks who once lived there.

Then there is Tulloch Castle Hotel in Scotland. This resort can trace its history to the 12th century and is thought to be haunted by Elizabeth Davidson, a former owner's wife, also known as the Green Lady. During World War II, after the evacuation of Allied soldiers from Dunkirk, France, Tulloch Castle became a war hospital, which seems to have added to its ghostly population. Visitors, including many paranormal investigative teams, have reported seeing orbs of light, feeling patches of cold air, and hearing sounds from clicks to thuds.

THE ASIAN CONNECTION

WHY SHOULD THE WEST HAVE ALL THE FUN? CHINA, JAPAN AND INDIA HAVE THEIR OWN SPOOKY SUPERNATURAL BEINGS.

A sandstorm rising off the desert. Could it be a jinn?

SPIRITS IN THE MIDDLE EAST

A diabolical apparition was said to haunt the desert.

In ancient Islamic tradition, there exist both angels and a type of supernatural being called *jinn*, intelligent form-changing spirits of lower rank than angels. Like humans, jinn can be good or evil. According to Arabic mythology, a particularly diabolical type of jinn known as *ghuls* were believed to haunt the desert, attempting to lure, murder, and eat travelers. Legend cautioned to strike a ghul dead with one blow, as a second blow would resurrect it.

Modern Muslims sometimes use "ghul" to mean a human or demonic cannibal, and the term is often used to caution misbehaving children.

"Lui Ken Conjures Ghosts of Parents." "Kuan Lu and the Complaining Ghost." "The Poltergeist." These titles might sound like the creation of modern-day Hollywood, but they are centuries-old stories found in *In Search of the Supernatural: The Written Record,* a compilation of over 400 Chinese legends about the supernatural, attributed to Bao Gan, a 4th-century historian.

Spirits have long played a part in Chinese culture. Buddhism, which spread through China in the first and second centuries, taught that the dead crossed a bridge over an abyss, endured numerous trials in the underworld, and passed through six suffering cycles before reincarnation. The afterlife was depicted as an imperial bureaucracy in which the departed person's fate depended on how generous his family members were in making offerings. Similarly, followers of the philosopher Confucius in ancient times believed in *gui* (ghosts), which are still celebrated today. There's a yearly ghost festival, held in late summer, when the spirits of dead ancestors are said to return to Earth for a visit. Relatives prepare celebratory feasts, leaving an empty chair at the table for each deceased member of the family.

Beware of Faint Souls

In Japan, the traditions of Buddhism, Taoism, and Shinto, the indigenous religion, all incorporate spirits. One ancient belief holds that after death, the *reikon* (spirit) departs the body and enters purgatory. There it awaits funeral and post-funeral rites before joining its ancestors in a peaceful afterlife. Eventually the reikon becomes the family guardian, returning each summer during the country's traditional Obon Festival, which is similar to the Chinese ghost festival.

But if before death, the departed experienced revenge, jealousy, hatred, or sorrow, or died suddenly or violently, his or her reikon transforms into a *yurei* (faint soul), doomed to haunt the living. Like their Chinese and Western counterparts, yurei are troubled wandering spirits, often depicted wearing white shrouds, with long, tangled hair. There are different categories of yurei: *onryo* seek revenge; *goryo* died as martyrs, *ubame* are women who died in

Japanese worshippers place one thousand floating paper lanterns in a river in Japan for the Buddhist festival of the dead.

childbirth, *zashiki-warashi* died as children, and *funayurei* died at sea.

A Dead Giveaway

In the culture of India, a *bhoot* is a ghost, usually of someone who can't rest because he or she has unresolved earthly business or died violently. Bhoots are said to haunt abandoned homes, hearths, rooftops, crossroads, trees, and deserts. Because the earth is sacred, though, they never touch it, instead hovering above it. They can take the form of animals, but they usually appear as humans. There's one sure way to tell if you've encountered a bhoot: Its feet point backward.

SUPERNATURAL SITES
Where the dead and undead like to visit.

→ **Kuldhara, Rajasthan, India.** According to folklore, one night in 1825, inhabitants of this village vanished rather than allow the state's minister to marry the chieftain's beautiful daughter. Their spirits can still be seen, heard, and felt.

→ **Bengal Swamps, West Bengal, India.** Locals believe these marshes to be haunted by dead fishermen who can cause sailors to lose their bearings and drown.

→ **Jing'an Park, Shanghai, China.** This urban oasis near the city's oldest temple was once a cemetery. Vengeful lurking water ghosts in its pond are said to try to drown unsuspecting visitors.

167

ISLANDS OF TERROR

THE SPIRITS OF THE DEAD ARE SAID TO LINGER AMONG US IN PUBLIC AS WELL AS PRIVATE SPACES.

ACCIDENT PRONE

Ghosts are blamed for the high number of crashes on a Hong Kong thoroughfare.

Tuen Mun Road is one of the main arteries of Hong Kong, China—and may be as heavily traveled by the dead as by the living. Constructed in 1977, Tuen Mun was one of Hong Kong's first high-speed roads, and has been the site of an extremely high number of accidents. Hundreds of local witnesses have claimed that the road is haunted by the ghosts of those who have died on it. Some blame these apparitions for causing more accidents by appearing in the middle of the road and forcing drivers to swerve, lose control of their vehicles, and crash. A major road reconstruction was scheduled for completion in 2014.

Small islands, cut off from the mainland, can provide refuge to spooky characters, whether former prison inmates, victims of the Bubonic Plague, or the spirit of a drowned child.

A Chilling Cellblock

Alcatraz, the former a maximum-security facility on an island in the San Francisco Bay, California, has long been rumored to be haunted by inmates who died or were murdered there. One of their favorite spots is the isolation area known as the Hole, and the Hole's cell 14D. According to one tale, an inmate consigned to the room in the 1940s died after screaming in terror throughout the night. At roll call the next morning, some guards reported seeing the dead man reappear among his fellow prisoners, only to vanish immediately. There's also a utility hall where the ghosts of three inmates who were gunned down trying to escape have been heard to make clanging sounds. And then there's Cellblock C: Here lurks the spirit of Abie Maldowitz, a hit man known as the Butcher who was murdered while serving time.

Although Alcatraz was decommissioned in 1963, the National Park Service continues to run tours there, and nighttime tours are among the most popular. Perhaps visitors hope to hear the plaintive sounds of Al Capone's banjo, which he took up in his last years at Alcatraz as he slowly died of syphilis; rangers, employees, and visitors have all reported hearing the mob boss's music.

Torture, Murder, and More

Halfway around the world, the Pacific Ocean prison colony of Norfolk Island was once home to violent convicts shipped there from around the British empire during the mid-1800s.

Inmates on the isolated island, nearly 900 miles from the Australian mainland, were tortured and even murdered by guards and fellow prisoners. Many referred to the penal colony as hell on earth. The prison has been closed for more than a century though, and starting in the early 20th century, Norfolk became a residential area. Today, it is described as haunted. When Colleen McCullough, author of *The Thornbirds*, was living on Norfolk Island, she reported numerous ghostly encounters, some in her own home. An Australian documentary series, *The Extraordinary*, has

Dolls hang on the Island of the Dolls in Xochimilco, Mexico City.

been filmed there, as well as several ghost-hunting shows.

Dumping Ground for the Dead

Poveglia Island, just minutes from Venice by boat, could be described as the spookiest island in the world. Over the centuries it has served the most morbid of purposes, from a quarantine area for plague victims to a dumping ground for the dead, to an asylum for the mentally ill who reportedly were the subject of bizarre experiments. According to one estimate, nearly 50 percent of the island's soil consists of human ash and remains. The island was abandoned in the 1960s, but today is considered haunted by the tortured souls of those who were buried there. The Italian tourism board prohibits visitation.

Hello, Dolly

There's only one dead man on the eerie Mexican Isla de Las Munecas, also known as the Island of the Dolls, but the fear factor may be as great as on Poveglia. According to legend, Don Julian Santana Barrera, the only resident of this tiny isle in a canal south of Mexico City, reported hearing the voice of a little girl who was said to have drowned there. To appease the unhappy soul, Don Julian began gathering dolls and hanging them in the trees. Don Julian himself drowned in the canal in 2001, and since then, the collection of dolls has grown to the thousands. Their detached limbs, decapitated heads, and blank faces festoon hundreds of trees in a display that can seem threatening in broad daylight and downright terrifying at night. Locals claim that the supernatural energy of the drowned child has come to possess the dolls and that they can now move their heads and arms and even open their eyes. Some witnesses claim to have heard the dolls whispering to each other in the quiet of the Mexican night.

THE HUNT IS ON

MODERN GHOSTBUSTERS MEASURE ELECTROMAGNETIC ENERGY AND SOUNDS HUMANS CAN'T DETECT. BUT CAN THEY BE TRUSTED?

A computer-generated image of a ghostly figure.

GHOSTOLOGY

The term *ghost* generally applies to any spirit that continues to exist in some form after death, but they come in many forms. Here's a guide.

→ A "crisis apparition" occurs as the spirit of a dying person visits to say good-bye to loved one.

→ "Residual ghosts" are imprints of a person's energy. They lack conscious awareness and re-experience their final moments as humans in a never-ending loop.

→ A "living ghost" leaves the body of someone who is still alive but who is having a near-death experience.

→ "Earthbound ghosts" are said to be trapped in the dimension of the living indefinitely, unaware that they are dead.

How is it possible to prove the existence of a ghost? Researchers have been chasing this elusive goal since the 19th century, when paranormal experts dug into the history of a haunted site and interviewed witnesses, police-style, while collecting purported evidence.

Methods today are decidedly more high-tech, with serious ghost hunters using digital meters, special audio and video recorders, and computers to track their quarry. But the investigator's work is no less controversial than in the past.

Skeptics refer to even the most sophisticated operations as pseudoscience. They criticize ghost hunters for flawed logic and mystical trappings. The ghost hunter who claims to have detected an apparition because of a cool temperature in one area of a home is belittled for overlooking other, more logical explanations. His tools and practices are dismissed as "techno-mysticism," a fusion of scientific method with spiritual belief.

Harry Price: Pioneer

Englishman Harry Price (1881–1948) was one of the earliest and most influential ghost hunters, best remembered for his 19-year investigation of Borley Rectory, a supposedly haunted Victorian mansion in Essex, England.

In addition to writing two books about the Borley case, Price used his findings to produce some of the earliest professional tools of the trade. He created the first ghost hunter's kit, containing still cameras for indoor and outdoor photography, a remote-control motion-picture camera, and a fingerprinting kit. He also put together the first ghost-hunting handbook.

Such aids were essential to Price's investigation of Borley Rectory. Built in 1862, the house was rumored to be haunted from the beginning. Residents reported seeing a nun's ghost in the garden, a phantom coach and horses, a ghostly dog, and even a headless man. Over the years, an organ was heard playing on its own and visitors said that they'd been thrown out of bed or locked out of rooms.

Price, who immersed himself in his rectory sleuthing in the 1930s, ended up debunking most of the phenomena. Yet he said he witnessed many occurrences that he was unable to explain, such as wine turning into ink, doors that locked on their own, and bottles that flew willy-nilly across rooms. During one séance, Price, said a spirit "manifested" and made a bar of soap appear out of nowhere.

Borley Rectory, Suffolk, England.

Electromagnetic field meter.

Although Borley burned to the ground in 1944, there have been reports of supernatural happenings where the house once stood and in the nearby churchyard. It is still referred to as "the most haunted house in England."

Paranormal Superstars

Generations of ghostbusters have followed in Price's wake, but few have become as renowned as Jason Hawes and Grant Wilson, stars of the Syfy channel's series *Ghost Hunters*. The two men have pioneered the use of electronic equipment in investigations and inspired a new generation of ghost hunters.

Jason Hawes and Grant Wilson.

On the program, which has been airing since 2004, Hawes, Wilson, and their team first interview witnesses and do historical research. They then occupy the site, sometimes for several days. Using equipment developed or adapted for the purpose, the investigators measure fluctuations in temperature and electromagnetic energy and record hours of video and audio. After logging their results, Hawes and Wilson review the recordings, searching for images and sounds.

Most often, they find ordinary causes for the unexplained events. But occasionally, the two ghost hunters come across phenomena that defy conventional explanation. During their 2007 investigation of the St. Augustine, Florida, lighthouse—reportedly haunted by the ghost of a girl in a red dress—Hawes and Wilson observed a shadowy figure and heard a woman's cry. In their report, they stated that they'd captured video footage "clearly showing a shadow. A moment later, [viewers] heard a female voice crying for help, and saw the shadow dart to the right." In the absence of other evidence to explain the incidents, Hawes and Wilson diagnosed St. Augustine Lighthouse as haunted.

POLTERGEISTS
AND OTHER
TROUBLEMAKERS

A FAMILY FROM WEST PITTON, PENNSYLVANIA, IS HAUNTED BY A HOST OF FRIGHTENING, NOISY GHOSTS.

One of the most famous incidents of alleged poltergeist activity occurred in West Pitton, Pennsylvania. In the summer of 1973, Jack Smurl, his wife, Janet, and their two daughters, Dawn and Heather, moved into one half of a duplex owned by Jack's parents. At first, the new residence seemed normal.

Then, in January 1974, a mysterious stain, impossible to remove, appeared on the Smurls' ceiling. The couple found deep scratches on recently refurbished bathroom woodwork, and the television burst into flames. In one instance, Dawn thought she saw spirits floating in her room, alarming her parents and sister.

After the birth of the Smurls' twin daughters, Shannon and Carlin, occurrences worsened. Toilets supposedly flushed themselves, unplugged radios turned on, and horrible odors filled the house. Family and neighbors said they heard screams and cursing when no one was speaking.

Then things became violent. Janet claimed she was levitated and hurled into walls, as was the family dog. A ceiling fan nearly fell on Shannon, who was later tossed down the stairs. Jack claimed he was sexually assaulted twice: first by a scale-covered succubus with an old woman's head on a young woman's body, and again by a half-man, half-pig.

In 1986, the Smurls sought help from Ed and Lorraine Warren, paranormal investigators and

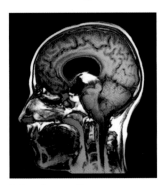

Colored magnetic resonance imaging (MRI) scan showing water on the brain.

self-proclaimed "demonologists."

After an investigation, the Warrens concluded that the Smurl family was being haunted by three "minor" spirits and one demon who seemed to be particularly focused on Jack.

The Smurls finally moved out of the duplex in 1988. Robert Curran covered the case in a book, *The Haunted: One Family's Nightmare*, and a television movie based on the book aired in 1991.

Was the Smurl Case a Hoax?

There were a variety of nonparanormal explanations for the Smurls' experiences, said skeptics at the time. Paul Kurtz, the founder of the Committee for the Scientific Investigation of Claims of the Paranormal, part of a nonprofit that investigated fringe-science claims, pointed to three possibilities.

TEENAGE PRANKS. Young people are often discovered to be behind poltergeist ac-

tivity, and the Smurls' eldest daughter, Dawn, who was 17 in 1986, gave many different accounts of what occurred.

PSYCHOLOGICAL AND PHYSIOLOGICAL DISORDERS. Three years before the occurrences began, Jack Smurl had brain surgery to relieve water on the brain. He could have been experiencing hallucinations or delusions.

FINANCIAL GAIN. Days before the story broke, Jack reportedly was seen negotiating with a Hollywood production company.

Kurtz also said the Warrens could not be viewed as impartial investigators in the case. He claimed that the Warrens, who were acting as spokespeople for the family, were blocking his access to the house, even though the Smurls had allegedly given Kurtz and his team permission to investigate. Ed Warren also claimed to have audio and video recordings of supernatural events, yet he refused to release them.

Heather O'Rourke in *Poltergeist*.

THE CASE OF THE CURSED CASTS

Four actors in the *Poltergeist* films died unusual, unexpected deaths.

In the summer of 1982, *Poltergeist*, a film directed by Tobe Hooper, was released and raked in more than $100 million at the box office. Depicting the fictional Freeling family's battle with malicious spirits, the film would go on to spawn two sequels.

Success, however, came with a price. The 1982 *Poltergeist* gained notoriety as a "cursed" production as tragedy seemed to plague the young actors portraying the Freeling children.

A mechanical clown malfunctioned while shooting a scene, almost choking Oliver Robins, the actor who played Robbie Freeling, to death.

On the eve of Halloween 1982, actress Dominique Dunn, 22, who played eldest Freeling daughter, Dana, was strangled by her ex-boyfriend, John Sweeney, and died four days later.

Actors in *Poltergeist II*, released in 1986, also seemed to be cursed. Julian Beck, who played the sinister preacher Kane, died of cancer shortly after the film wrapped. Will Sampson, who played the shaman, died about the same time of kidney failure. A practicing medicine man, Sampson had exorcised the *Poltergeist II* set, claiming it to be haunted by "alien spirits."

Actress Heather O'Rourke, 12, who portrayed Carol Anne Freeling, died during surgery to repair a bowel obstruction at a San Diego hospital in 1988, four months before the release of *Poltergeist III* and the day after the Super Bowl, also in San Diego. In the first *Poltergeist* film, a poster for the 1988 Super Bowl in San Diego is seen on the wall of Robbie Freeling's bedroom's right before the clown doll comes to life.

WHO KNEW?

Real skeletons were used on the *Poltergeist* set because they were cheaper than plastic ones.

CHILDREN OF THE DEVIL?

THIS GROUP OF TROUBLED TEENAGERS SEEMED TO BE UNDER THE THRALL OF DEMONS.

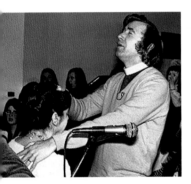

Reverend Trevor Dearing exorcises a member of his congregation during a service.

Generations of Americans learned about the murky world of exorcism from the 1973 movie *The Exorcist*. While the film may have seemed like the fantasy of a director looking for a horror hit, it was actually inspired by a real event.

In 1949, the *Washington Post* ran a story about a 14-year-old boy who had reportedly become possessed by the devil. According to the article, it was only after multiple exorcisms that the demon was cast out of the unnamed Maryland teenager. The possession was diagnosed after numerous bizarre incidents took place in the boy's presence: Chairs, beds, and even fruit moved of its own accord, and ominous words appeared scratched into his skin.

Teen Troubles

After an attempted exorcism at the Jesuit-run Georgetown University Hospital failed, the boy was eventually taken to another hospital, in St. Louis, Missouri, where priests again tried to carry out an exorcism. As they performed the rites, the teen cursed, vomited, urinated, and spewed various phrases in Latin, a language he hadn't learned. At one point he managed to wriggle free, and allegedly broke the nose of a Jesuit student who had been called in to assist. Witnesses reported that the bed jumped up and down and that a bottle of holy water flew across the room.

Eventually the ritual was successful, and the boy is said to have gone on to live a normal, happy life. Today it is theorized that he was suffering from schizophrenia or Tourette's syndrome, or had been a victim of sexual abuse. Still, the demonic-possession story continues to fascinate.

A Tragic Misdiagnosis

Another infamous attempt at exorcism (and the inspiration for the 2005 movie *The Exorcism of Emily Rose*) took place in Germany in the 1970s. Sixteen-year-old Anneliese Michel was diagnosed with epilepsy after having a seizure. The anti-convulsants she was prescribed did little to quell her condition, and as time went on Michel claimed to see "devil faces on the walls," with "seven crowns and seven horns." She also said she heard demonic voices.

By 1973, Michel was suffering speech problems and fits of rage. She ate spiders, lapped at puddles of her own urine, and hurled herself into walls. Even when she was relatively composed, she exhibited signs of severe mental illness and talked about suicide.

In 1975, Michel's mother sought help from two Roman Catholic priests, who began performing exorcism rites once or twice a week. The priests would later recount that Michel was possessed by six demons, including Judas Iscariot and Adolf

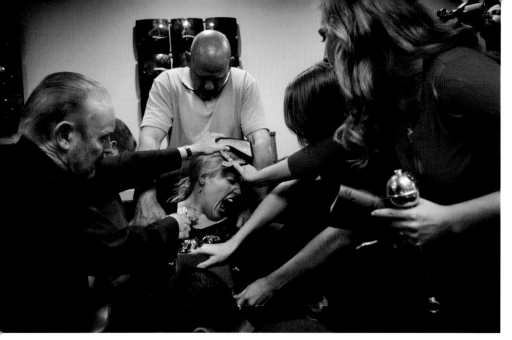

Radio and television evangelist and exorcist Bob Larson with his daughters during an exorcism session.

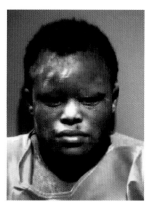

Monifa Denise Sanford was accused of killing two children. Sanford said she was performing an exorcism.

Hitler. The attempts at exorcism continued, even after Michel refused to eat and suffered two broken kneecaps from constant genuflecting. Her weight dropped to 68 pounds, and she died on July 1, 1976, from severe malnutrition and dehydration. She was 23 years old.

Although Michel's parents seemed to believe wholeheartedly that their daughter had been possessed and not conventionally ill, they, and the two priests, were eventually found guilty of negligent homicide. Michel is considered a tragic victim of abuse and religious hysteria.

A MIDWESTERN MYSTERY

One of the most remarkable examples of alleged possession in recent memory happened in Indiana.

The strange events began in March 2012. One night, Latoya Ammons, a mother of three, saw her 12-year-old daughter levitating above a bed in the family's Gary, Indiana, home. Soon, the other children and Ammons herself felt they were being choked, thrown, and held down. Certain that the family was in the thrall of the supernatural, Ammons contacted her church and invited psychics to visit. She was told the house was occupied by demons.

What followed, according to a 2014 report in the *Indianapolis Star*, were months of psychological evaluations, an intervention by the Department of Child Services, and a police investigation. Eventually, the family called in a priest,

who performed three exorcisms—the last one in June 2012. Since then, the family has been demon-free. They now live in a different house.

You could chalk all of this up to mental illness or a hoax. But what makes the Ammons case unique is that some of the bizarre happenings were reportedly witnessed by officials sent in to help. One Department of Child Services case manager saw Ammons's nine-year-old boy glide backward up the wall of a medical examination room. Police who visited the Ammons house reported malfunctioning equipment, mysterious voices, and ghostly images in photos. Was it a mass delusion, or a true case of demonic possession?

AMITYVILLE'S INVESTIGATORS

DEMON-BATTLERS EDWARD AND LORRAINE WARREN CAPTIVATED THE PRESS AND HOLLYWOOD.

THE REAL-LIFE *CONJURING*

The 2013 film *The Conjuring* is based on the 1971 experiences of Carolyn and Roger Perron, a Rhode Island family. Terrorized by such bizarre phenomena as blood oozing from an orange and visions of the floating, disembodied head of an old woman, the Perrons turned to Edward and Lorraine Warren.

The Warrens concluded that the Perrons' house was haunted by a 19th-century occupant, Bathsheba Sheran, who had been implicated in a child's disappearance. Though Sheran was found not guilty, she was accused by her contemporaries of witchcraft, and the Warrens believed she had cursed the house. They "de-demonized" Carolyn Perron, and the Perrons decided to remain in the house. "Eventually," Carolyn said, "[we] accepted the fact that we were not living there alone."

Ghost-hunters Edward and Lorraine Warren have consulted on some of America's most notorious paranormal cases, from the incident that spawned the *Amityville Horror* films to the trial of Arne Johnson, a convicted murderer whose lawyers claimed he was possessed by the devil. Edward, who died in 2006, described himself as a "religious demonologist"—an expert in malevolent supernatural beings. Lorraine, a clairvoyant and trance medium, still consults on cases and runs a private occult museum in Connecticut.

From the 1970s when the Warrens first rose to prominence, until Edward's death, the couple claimed to have investigated more than 10,000 cases. But critics have poked holes in many of the Warrens' best-known inquiries, labeling them hoaxes or publicity stunts. Steven Novella, a neurologist and president of the New England Skeptical Society, has described the couple as talented storytellers.

The Amityville Horror Case

The most infamous of the Warrens' consultations unfolded in Amityville, New York, at the behest of a family who believed their home was haunted by a violent, demonic presence. Their fears were rooted in the

Lorraine Warren at the premiere of the film *The Conjuring*.

A Suffolk County policeman uses a mine detector on the lawn of Ronald DeFeo's home in Amityville, New York.

horrific 1974 murders of six members of the DeFeo family by the eldest son, Ronald DeFeo Jr. Thirteen months later, George and Kathy Lutz bought the DeFeo home and moved in. Soon they complained of murderous nightmares, strange odors, cloven hoofprints, demons, voices, and other phenomena. The Lutzes met with parapsychologists, including the Warrens, who assembled a team of investigators and attracted reporters.

Lorraine believed that the same demons terrifying the Lutz family had possessed Ron DeFeo Jr. She suspected that prior suffering on the property and occupation by a practicing black magician in the 1920s had invited dark spirits into the home. To uproot the demons, the Warrens "invited God" into the house, relying on their Catholic faith. Lorraine claimed to have had a vision of a saint, and the Warren team captured a photograph of what they believed was a spirit.

The Amityville story inspired many books, movies, television accounts, and even lawsuits, but the facts around the case remain controversial.

Werewolf Demon

In 1983, the Warrens attracted more publicity thanks to Bill Ramsey, a Londoner who supposedly believed himself a werewolf. Ramsey had flown into periodic rages, snarling and attempting to bite people, since he was nine years old. A policeman in the case claimed Ramsey had almost choked him to death. "He had mad staring eyes," Sgt. Terry Fisher told Susan Michaels, author of the 1996 book *Sightings.* "He said, 'the Devil is in me. You are going to die.' "

Ramsey was committed to a psychiatric institution, but no sign of mental illness was found. The Warrens saw a television program about him and, believing he was possessed by a wolf's demonic spirit, they brought Ramsey to the United States for an exorcism. They engaged a Catholic priest, Richard McKenna, to perform the rite at their church in Connecticut. With guards standing by, McKenna made the sign of the cross and chanted in Latin. "Bill's lips curled up and his teeth protruded. He howled and tried to bite the priest," said Lorraine, who, with her husband, published an account of the episode, *Werewolf: A True Story of Demonic Possession,* in 1991.

Ed Warren spotted the White Lady at Union Cemetery (pictured here) in Easton, Connecticut, in 1992. The ghost is said to travel between Union and nearby Stepney Cemetery, where Warren was buried in 2006.

Texts dating to biblical times give instructions
on how to harness the power of demons.

CHAPTER 10

MORE OR LESS THAN HUMAN

THE DEVIL MADE ME DO IT. SAVED BY AN ANGEL. OTHERWORLDLY BEINGS ARE THOUGHT TO INTERFERE IN OUR DAILY LIVES ON A REGULAR BASIS—OR SOMETIMES IT JUST FEELS THAT WAY.

A biblical demon from the bronze door of Duomo di Santa Maria Assunta, Pisa, Italy.

THE MADNESS OF CROWDS

Even in modern America, mass hysteria remains surprisingly common.

Periodically, crowds of people can fall prey to mysterious sicknesses or symptoms. These illnesses were once believed to be possession or witchcraft, but the modern diagnosis is mass sociogenic illness. In the examples below, the groups of victims were at first thought to be affected by the environment or an infectious organism; each later turned out to be a case of mass hysteria.

→ **The bizarre event:** About 20 high school students began regularly twitching and suffering seizures.
Where and when: Le Roy, New York, 2011
First assumption: Environmental contamination

→ **The bizarre event:** Soon after 9/11, schoolchildren broke out in unexplained rashes.
Where and when: Indiana, Virginia, Pennsylvania, Oregon, 2001
First assumption: Bioterrorism

→ **The bizarre event:** 23 emergency-room staff fell ill after treating a cancer patient, who later died
Where and when: Riverside, California, 1994
First assumption: Exposure to toxic fumes in the patient's blood

THE DEVIL MADE THEM DO IT

TO BELIEVERS IN BIBLICAL TIMES, DEMONS WERE RESPONSIBLE FOR THE EVIL DONE ON EARTH.

Satan, of course, is the worst of the biblical demons—the fallen angel who turns his back on God, persuades Eve to eat the forbidden fruit, and is responsible for all human evil and suffering. Nobody, not even Jesus, is immune to Satan's diabolical pressure.

In the New Testament, Satan tempts Jesus three times. The first: After being baptized by John, Jesus journeys into the desert and fasts for 40 days. Satan appears, suggesting that the ravenous Jesus use his power to make bread out of stones. In a second attempt, Satan encourages Jesus to jump from the pinnacle of the Temple in Jerusalem because God will keep Jesus from harm. Finally, Satan promises Jesus all of the kingdoms of the world to switch allegiance from God to Satan. In refusing each of these temptations, Jesus proves himself the Messiah.

But while Satan is "the" Devil, there are also numerous lesser demons in the Bible. In fact, the Good Book is full of references to people and even livestock possessed and tormented by spirits.

In one of the miracles of Jesus described in the gospels of Mark, Matthew, and Luke, Jesus meets a man possessed by a legion of demons. After Jesus commands the evil spirits to leave the man's body, they possess a nearby herd of two thousand pigs, who rush down a hill into a lake and drown themselves. The man is restored to his right mind.

Deal With the Devil

Alarmingly, one can invite a demon's presence. Texts dating to biblical times give instructions on how to harness the power and knowledge of demons. *The Testament of Solomon,* written in Greek around the time of Christ, describes the Hebrew King Solomon besting a host of demons who were interfering with the building of the First Temple of Jerusalem. The episode did not end well for Solomon, however. In turning away from God to dabble with demons, the ruler helped bring about the destruction of his kingdom, according to the Old Testament. More recently, *The Grand Grimoire,* a compilation of works on black magic believed to date from the 13th to 18th centuries, details how to summon Lucifer.

While skeptics tend to interpret supposed demonic possession as a primitive way to explain mental illness or misbehavior, the concept of evil beings lives on today in religion, folklore, and popular culture. For believers, demons are the under-

The Temptation of Adam, c. 1520.

world creatures and forces that manipulate us to behave badly, and the symptoms are different from mental illness. According to the Vatican, a person claiming to be possessed should be evaluated to rule out physical and emotional causes first. If that person can suddenly speak or understand a foreign language he or she has never learned, for example, it might just be the devil's work.

THE
MAGICK MAN

CONTROVERSIAL OCCULTIST ALEISTER CROWLEY REVELED IN HIS NOTORIETY AND CALLED HIMSELF "THE GREAT BEAST."

Lucifer, as portrayed in a 1522 illustration.

DEMONOLOGY VS. DEMONOLATRY

In Ancient Greece, *daemones* were simply intermediaries between divine and mortal realms. Judeo-Christian theology redefined "demons" as malevolent spirits cast out of heaven.

While *demonologists* simply study these unworldly entities, *demonolatry* is the religious worship of a pantheon of entities, including the supreme beings Lucifer and Beelzebub and a variety of lower-level demons. Various rituals have been devised to communicate with them, summon them, tap into their power, and praise them. Believe it or not, most demonolatrists do not pursue harmful agendas—though some do attempt to use their powers to hurt others.

One of the most influential counter-culture figures in 20th-century Great Britain, Aleister Crowley (1875–1947), called himself the Great Beast, and for good reason. Crowley's lavish lifestyle included far-flung travel and mountaineering, wild spending, dozens of affairs with men and women, and heavy drug use. He was also a spiritual leader who embraced seemingly dark arts such as tarot and alchemy and was a key figure in two secret societies. His guiding principle, "Do what thou wilt," seemed to endorse a life of purely physical pleasure.

While some considered Crowley a prophet, others called him a Satanist who promoted immoral behavior. For his anti-Christian pronouncements and promiscuity, he was named "the wickedest man in the world" by the British press. Crowley today remains a divisive figure. Though his lifestyle was decadent and rooted in the occult, he is also remembered as pioneering a third way between religion and science: In a 2002 BBC poll, Crowley was proclaimed one of the 100 greatest Britons of all time.

Secret Societies

Educated at Cambridge University, Crowley started dabbling in the occult in 1898 when he joined the Hermetic Order of the Golden Dawn, a secret society devoted to the study and practice of metaphysics and paranormal activities. William Butler Yeats, the poet, and Bram Stoker, author of the novel *Dracula,* were among its early members.

For the next few years, Crowley studied Buddhist and Hindu philosophy and spent time in both Mexico and India. In 1904, he traveled to Egypt for his honeymoon, a voyage that proved a turning point in Crowley's life. During the trip, he claimed to have received dictation of *The Book of the Law,* a sacred text that Crowley later said was the word of the Egyptian god Horus, who had chosen him as a prophet. He used the text as the basis for a new, polytheistic faith called Thelema, which guided followers to "be free of all standard ways and codes of conduct."

A Special "K"

Crowley did not want Thelema to be dismissed as sleight-of-hand occult entertainment, and sought to differentiate the faith from ceremonial magic. To signify the difference between the two, Crowley restored the archaic letter "k" to the word *magick* when writing about Thelema's physical, mental, and spiritual exercises. He became involved with the secret society Ordo Templi Orientis, eventually assuming control of the group's British branch and encouraging members to follow Thelema.

> ## "Remember all ye that existence is pure joy."
> —Aleister Crowley, from *The Book of the Law*, basis of his religion Thelema

Crowley's looks—thin, bald, faintly menacing—probably contributed to his fearsome reputation.

ALEISTER ROCKS

The Beatles and Led Zeppelin had a particular fondness for Crowley.

→ Crowley is depicted on the cover of *Sergeant Pepper's Lonely Hearts Club Band* (1967) next to Mae West.

→ Crowley's motto, "Do what thou wilt," is inscribed into the vinyl record of *Led Zeppelin III* (1970). And in 1971, guitarist Jimmy Page bought Boleskine House, Crowley's former home in Scotland, on Loch Ness—the lake famous for its "monster." Page owned the property until 1991 and claims a severed head haunts the house.

Crowley today is remembered as the founder of Thelema and as a hedonist. Yet some believe that his libertine ways were misunderstood and that Crowley was mentally and spiritually damaged by demons he underestimated. They point to a six-month-long evil spirit–conjuring episode known as the Abramelin ritual, in which Crowley was required to evoke figures, including Lucifer, in order to remove their negative influences from his life. According to his supporters, Crowley aborted the spell prior to its completion and instead of banning the evil entities became possessed by them.

Shortly before his death in 1947, Crowley supposedly put a curse on his doctor because he refused to refill Crowley's prescription for morphine. The doctor died within 24 hours of Crowley himself.

HEAVENLY CREATURES

ANGELS SERVE AS CELESTIAL MESSENGERS AND PROTECTORS IN MANY WORLD RELIGIONS.

Gabriel, who alerts the Virgin Mary that she has been chosen by God as the mother of Jesus, is one of the best-known angels in Western culture, but he is hardly the only heavenly being out there. Numerous world religions and traditions refer to angelic figures who emanate goodness, deliver messages from God, and keep humans safe. Images of these heavenly creatures, whether Renaissance paintings or Victoria's Secret ads, tend to portray angels as cherubic baby boys or graceful girls. Theologians have objected to the interpretation, saying that angels are genderless spirits, not physical beings, and above human activities. They can, however, take a human form when they need to.

Holy Go-Betweens

Angels' roles vary depending on the tradition. In Islam, the angel Jabra'il (Gabriel) brings the word of Allah to the prophet Mohammed. In Mormonism, the angel Moroni is the messenger who reveals the Book of Mormon to the prophet Joseph Smith.

Judaism also features angels: In the Old Testament, an angel appears to Abraham to tell him he and Sarah will finally have a child; another later intervenes to stop Abraham from sacrificing his beloved son Isaac. Some scholars have suggested that such angels, called *malachim* in Hebrew, were incorporated into ancient teachings because they were easier for humans to visualize than an amorphous, omnipotent deity.

Eleven Heads, a Thousand Arms

Angels of a kind can be found in Eastern religions as well. Buddhists have *bodhisattvas*, enlightened beings who inhabit the celestial realm. In Tibetan Buddhism, the beloved bodhisattva Chenrezig embodies loving-kindness and compassion. According to lore, Chenrezig has multiple limbs—as many as eleven heads and a thousand arms—in order to help numerous suffering creatures at once. In Chinese Buddhism, Chenrezig takes on a female form as Kwan Yin, the goddess of mercy, who helps the dead make their transition into paradise.

In Hinduism and Buddhism, *apsaras* function somewhat like Western angels do: These heavenly, graceful female beings wear flowing garments, play musical instruments, and can stand on clouds. Though they can fly, they aren't usually depicted with wings. However, they are always shapely and alluring and frequently are depicted with bare breasts.

Tobias and the Archangel Raphael, attributed to Titian (Tiziano Vecellio), c. 16th century.

THINGS WITH WINGS

Angels and other flying deities have long been subjects in art and in popular culture.

→ In Norse mythology, Valkyries appeared at battles to decide which soldiers would be victorious and which would not. Then they escorted the dead to Valhalla, or paradise.

→ This image of Jabra'il (Gabriel) appears in a 13th-century manuscript called *The Wonders of Creation and the Oddities of Existence*. Written by a judge living in what is now Iraq, it covers a variety of topics, including astrology, natural history, and superstition.

→ The artist Marc Chagall once had a vision of an angel bathed in brilliant blue light. Throughout the rest of his career, he depicted many angels in his work.

This statuette of the Golem of Prague depicts the straps that reportedly held the figure together. One patches a crack in his chest.

CREATION THEORY

Actress Natasha Calis carrying a dybbuk box in a scene from *The Possession*.

JEWS OF THE MIDDLE AGES ARE SAID TO HAVE SHAPED MEN OF CLAY AND USED MAGIC TO BREATHE LIFE INTO THEM.

You can travel to the beautiful city of Prague in the Czech Republic, and visit its famous 13th-century Old New Synagogue. But don't set your heart on visiting the building's attic. The room has been closed off for decades to protect people, or so it is said. Inside lives the remains of a golem, an artificial human being made out of clay and brought to life by Jewish magic.

Jews, like Christians, have a long history of superstitions, and their interest in demons, spirits, and magic was especially strong during the Middle Ages. Jews wore special charms to ward off the evil eye, and for good luck many would touch a mezuzah, a sacred door decoration that contains a verse from the Torah. For a Jewish magician of the era, there was no greater feat than bringing inanimate matter to life. The *Sefer Yezirah* (Book of Creation), considered a guide to magic by some European Jews, even contained vague instructions on how to make a golem.

Creating a Protector

The most famous golem of legend involves Judah Loew ben Bezalel, a 16th-century rabbi in Prague who supposedly created such a clay man to defend the Jewish ghetto from anti-Semitic attacks. According to the story, the Jews in Prague were to be killed by order of the Holy Roman Emperor. To protect his community, the rabbi fashioned a man from the clay of the Vltava River. Using the mystical teachings of kabbalah, Rabbi Loew brought the figure to life and inscribed the Hebrew word *emet* (truth) on the creature's forehead.

The golem fulfilled its purpose, but eventually it went on a destructive rampage. Rabbi Loew feared losing control of the creature and smeared clay on its forehead, turning the word *emet* into *met*, the Hebrew word for death. The monster crumbled into lifeless lumps of clay that Rabbi Loew placed in the synagogue's attic. They are said to be there still, waiting in case it is ever necessary to bring the golem back.

Is it just a story? When the Old New Synagogue was renovated in 1883, the workers could find no evidence of the golem's remains. Czech lore tells of a Nazi soldier who climbed to the synagogue attic during World War II and attempted to stab the golem, only to die on the spot. The Old New Synagogue was miraculously spared during World War II, while most others in the area were destroyed. Today, the lowest ten feet of the stairs leading to the synagogue's attic have been removed and the room is closed to the public.

Skeptics dismiss the story of Rabbi Loew's golem as the creation of 19th-century writers, but many orthodox Jews believe the tale.

CHASING SPIRITS

Spooky dybbuks can enter a person's body.

According to Jewish tradition, a dybbuk is a restless ghost or disturbed spirit. A dybbuk can be exorcised by invoking the name of God, reading Biblical verses, or reciting magical numbers.

→ In April 1999 in Dimona, Israel, a widow claimed that her deceased husband had entered her body and that the voice of a man was coming from her throat. Over the objections of his peers, Rabbi David Batzri performed an exorcism and the dybbuk fled.

→ The "dybbuk box" is a small wooden wine cabinet that is supposedly haunted by a dybbuk. In 2003, the owner of one such box put it up for sale on eBay. The seller claimed that the box had plagued several owners with disastrous luck; one said the box caused lights in his house to burn out, and his hair to fall out. The online auction page logged more than 120,000 hits, and the box was the inspiration for the 2012 film *The Possession*.

Each year, millions of people report near-death
experiences at the moment of clinical death.

CHAPTER 11
NEAR-DEATH EXPERIENCES

RELIGIONS HAVE LONG ATTEMPTED TO EXPLAIN DEATH, BUT SERIOUS-MINDED INVESTIGATORS HAVE ONLY RECENTLY BEGUN EXPLORING WHETHER THE HUMAN SOUL SURVIVES WHEN PHYSICAL LIFE ENDS.

BETTER LIFE NEXT TIME

BILLIONS OF PEOPLE BELIEVE IN REINCARNATION. A FEW EVEN CLAIM TO REMEMBER WHO AND WHERE THEY'VE BEEN.

CHILDREN WITH A PAST

They said they could remember previous lives, and one academic worked to prove it.

After studying thousands of two- to four-year-olds from around the world from the 1970s to 1990s, Dr. Ian Stevenson, an academic psychiatrist and head of the University of Virginia's Division of Perceptual Studies, concluded that the children's memories of past lives were real. Dr. Stevenson verified the personal circumstances and history of the people the children had said were their previous selves. Skeptics chalk up the children's reports to selective thinking, false memories, and pure imagination. But the stories are extraordinary:

➜ A three-year-old English girl, walking through a cemetery with her mother, said, "There is where I sleep." She was pointing at her grandmother's grave. At home, she said she was afraid of the hallway. It was where her grandmother had died, before the girl's birth.

➜ An American boy who often dreamed he was a French trapper in 18th-century America spoke French in his sleep. He knew no French when awake.

➜ A three-year-old Israeli boy recalled being killed with an ax in a previous life, and showed police where a man's body and an ax were buried.

The survival of the soul after death is a central tenet of many faiths. But the majority of Eastern religions teach that rather than going on to heaven, the soul is reborn into a new body. In some belief systems, reincarnated souls pass from human to human, often within castes, tribes, or families. Other systems assign the soul a better or worse next life based on one's behavior in the present life. Some spiritual practices teach that the cycle of reincarnation is endless, but most see it as a process of growth that ultimately leads to spiritual enlightenment. Along the way, a soul may or may not remember its previous lives.

The Spiritual Cycle

At the heart of reincarnation, which means, literally, "entering the flesh again," is the Hindu concept of *samsara,* a Sanskrit word meaning the cycle or wheel of life. A person's present existence is but one of many incarnations of his or her soul. The good or bad intentions and deeds, or *karma,* of this life determine whether one is reincarnated into a human, animal, or divine being in the next. A life of meditation, self-denial, and service results in good karma and a better next life. From life to life, the goal is to overcome ignorance, egotism, and worldly desire in order to achieve a state in which suffering is replaced by bliss, peace, and perfection.

Most schools of Buddhism share the Hindu principles of reincarnation, with important distinctions. For Buddhists, samsara translates as "wandering about" or "continuous movement," a state of frustration arising from a preoccupation with the self and its experiences. Buddhism rejects the notion of a singular soul or consciousness that travels from one body to the next. Rather, the personality dies and its energy flows between lives in a "stream of consciousness." In its new body, this consciousness has a personality that is based on, but also different from, the old one. A special form of particularly intensive meditation can give Buddhists a glimpse of their previous lives.

Death and Life in the West

Reincarnation plays a lesser role in the history of Western religion. It was, however, quite important to the ancient Greeks. In the 5th century BC, the philosopher Pythagoras wrote that the immortal soul visits the underworld for rest and purification before being reincarnated; when the soul has been cleansed by repeated passes through the cycle, it is released. A century and a half later, Plato added that a person must do good works to purify and release the soul. A soul that sins repeatedly degenerates with each life and will be eternally damned.

In the year 533 AD, an assembly of Christian bishops declared reincarnation a heresy: Christians had only one life in which to earn entry into heaven. Jews historically rejected reincarnation as well, but Kabbalah,

Wheel of Samsara at the Temple of the Thousand Buddhas in Saône et Loire, France.

The 14th Dalai Lama, 1939.

When a Tibetan Buddhist Dalai Lama dies, the search begins for his reincarnation.

Tenzin Gyatso was three years old when he was identified as the reincarnation of the Dalai Lama. It was 1937, and Tibet's 13th spiritual leader had died. The little boy became a novice monk, and in 1940 was named the 14th Dalai Lama.

In Tibetan Buddhism, the Dalai Lama is the reincarnation of an especially enlightened type of being called a *bodhisattva.* Most Dalai Lamas have been found as children or teenagers.

Clues to the identity of the new Dalai Lama may be found in prophesies or in the writings of his immediate predecessor, which might include descriptions of the reincarnate's parents or home. The High Lamas look for signs in holy places and may consult an astrologer monk. When they locate a potential Dalai Lama, they test him by asking him to recognize people or possessions from the previous Dalai Lama's life.

a mystical sect that arose in the 12th century and still exists today, embraced the concept.

These days, some spiritually minded Westerners continue to believe. European and American interest in reincarnation was renewed with Madame Helena Blavatsky's revival in the 1870s of the centuries-old esoteric religion Theosophy, which included the Eastern notion that the soul perfects itself while passing through multiple lifetimes. Occultists carried the mystical approach to reincarnation into the 20th century, and New Agers, Neo-Pagans, and Wiccans have brought it into this one.

RETURNING FROM THE LAND OF THE DEAD

FOR HUNDREDS OF YEARS, PEOPLE HAVE REPORTED VISITING "THE OTHER SIDE."

Elisabeth Kübler-Ross.

ELISABETH KÜBLER-ROSS

The Doyenne of Death

Psychiatrist Elisabeth Kübler-Ross is most famous as the author of the 1969 book *On Death and Dying*, which laid out her concept of the five stages of grief: denial, anger, bargaining, depression, and acceptance.

Kübler-Ross claimed that near-death experiences are proof there is life after death. The fact that people have psychological and emotional experiences when they're brain-dead shows that consciousness survives after the body dies, she wrote. Does this prove the existence of a soul? Kübler-Ross thought so. "Dying is nothing to fear," she said. "It can be the most wonderful experience of your life."

You're floating above your body, watching doctors and nurses as they shock your heart with a defibrillator. There's no pain. A long, dark tunnel opens before you, with a bright light glowing at the end. As you move toward the light, you're filled with profound feelings of peace and love. You see people waiting for you—figures in long robes and some of your deceased loved ones. They smile and wave. Then a voice tells you to go back, that it's not your time.

You wake up in a hospital room. Perhaps you are filled with contentment—or maybe you are depressed at not having been able to complete the journey you started. You've just had a near-death experience (NDE), and you'll probably never be quite the same.

Each year, thousands of people report near-death experiences at the moment of clinical death, when their heart stops beating and their oxygen-starved brain shuts down. After survivors have been revived, they describe the vivid scenes and emotions they experienced while dead. The phenomenon has been described variously as supernatural, spiritual, psychological, or biological, but scientists have not yet come to a consensus about what actually occurs in these cases.

From the beginning of time, religions have attempted to define the soul and explain death, but serious-minded investigators have only recently taken on the challenge of discovering whether the human soul survives when physical life ends. One initiative, spearheaded by psychologist Kenneth Ring, now a professor emeritus at the University of Connecticut, has focused on gathering empirical data on types of NDEs. Using the ten most commonly reported sensations, Ring in 1980 created the Weighted Core Experience Index to study the physiology, phenomenology, and after-effects of NDEs. His work has been expanded by American psychiatrist Bruce Greyson, a professor at the University of Virginia, whose 16-point Near-Death Experience Scale was introduced in 1983 and has been widely used in documenting aspects of NDEs.

The Soul Hovering over the Body Reluctantly Parting with Life, by William Blake and Louis Schiavonetti.

POINT, COUNTERPOINT

A famous doctor maintained that there was life after life. Was he right?

In his 1975 bestseller, *Life After Life*, physician and psychologist Raymond Moody sparked a heated debate between those who attribute near-death experiences to biology and those who see more mysterious forces at work. Here are some of the arguments.

Point: Scientists say hallucinations are triggered when the heart stops and the part of the brain that controls vision malfunctions.

Counterpoint: People who believe in the paranormal say those who survive a near-death experience have specific, vivid memories, not disorienting hallucinations.

Point: The dying process changes brain chemistry, causing visions.

Counterpoint: Hallucinations occur once oxygen is not being delivered to the brain. But only 18 percent of people who have near-death experiences do so during this period, according to one study.

Point: Out-of-body experiences originate in specific regions of the brain and can be prompted by electrical stimulation.

Counterpoint: Just because there is activity in one part of the brain when an out-of-body experience occurs doesn't mean the activity caused the experience.

WHO KNEW?

Researchers estimate that at least 25 million people around the world have had a near-death experience in the past 50 years.

MORE THAN
ONE LIFE
TO LIVE

IT'S NOT JUST SHIRLEY MACLAINE. TODAY, MANY BELIEVE IN DISCOVERING PAST LIVES THROUGH HYPNOSIS.

WHO KNEW?

In the 1950s, psychiatrist Stanislav Grof, founder of the International Transpersonal Association, used LSD in clinical trials to access patients' past-life memories.

Remembering past lives can help people understand themselves better, cure them of their fears, and even improve their relationships. Or so say people who believe in reincarnation and a technique called past-life regression therapy that allows patients to delve into their former selves. There are even some psychiatrists and psychologists who rely on past-life regression, in tandem with other treatments, in their practices.

Meeting Other Selves

Sigmund Freud, a neurologist as well as the father of psychotherapy, is credited with elevating past-life regression from the universe of dark arts into the realm of science. He believed that people's personalities were shaped by their past experiences and that it made sense to attempt to get in touch with former lives.

Yet even with Freud's stamp of approval, experiments in past-life regression therapy were attempted only intermittently throughout the first half of the 20th century. The practice gained some notoriety in 1956 with the release of *The Search for Bridey Murphy*, a bestseller about a Colorado housewife who claimed that hypnosis helped her discover that she'd previously lived as a 19th-century Irishwoman. A number of other books on

the subject, such as *Reliving Past Lives* and *Many Lives, Many Masters*, also gave past-life regression more credibility with the public.

How It Works

According to some scientists, the key to accessing past-life memories lies in the alpha state, one of the five stages of brainwave activity during sleep, which include:

1. **BETA:** Subject is awake and alert.
2. **ALPHA:** Subject is not quite asleep and may experience hypnagogic hallucinations or "waking dreams." Hypnotherapy is performed in this stage.
3. **THETA:** Subject's subconscious, where emotional experiences are recorded, is fully active.
4. **DELTA:** Deep sleep.
5. **REM:** Most dreaming occurs in this stage.

During a past-life regression session, the therapist hypnotizes the patient, then asks a series of questions to reveal identities and events of alleged past lives, a method similar to recovered memory therapy. When administered properly, past-life regression can help eliminate certain psychosomatic illnesses by making the patient aware of relevant experiences, pains, and traumas from past lives, according to practitioners.

During the alpha-brain-wave state of sleep, so-called waking dreams may call forth memories of past lives.

In 2008, television personality Dr. Mehmet Oz brought Dr. Brian Weiss, author of the past-life regression classic *Many Lives, Many Masters,* to *The Oprah Show*. Before Oz and Oprah arrived, Weiss led the audience through a 45-minute exercise during which a number of people claimed to have been successfully hypnotized and were able to recall past lives.

The most dramatic moment came when Dr. Weiss hypnotized a funeral director named Leon. Under hypnosis, Leon, who was having a rocky relationship with his sister, recalled seeing a woman being raped, and being helpless to intervene. He expressed guilt over not acting. Then he revealed that the woman being raped was his sister. "I didn't see her face," he said, "it was an energy. It was just her."

Weiss went on to explain to the stunned audience that Leon's relationship with his sister was strained because of his feelings of guilt from the events in his past life. Later, Leon reported that he and his sister were getting along much better.

IN A FAMILY WAY

Actress Shirley MacLaine, a believer in reincarnation, says her daughter used to be her mother.

When Oscar-winning actress Shirley MacLaine was interviewed on *60 Minutes* by Mike Wallace in 1984, he scoffed at her claim that her daughter had been her mother in a past life. MacLaine accused him of being "cynical." Past-life regression therapy has helped MacLaine discover numerous past selves, she says, including:

- A Muslim gypsy girl living in the hills of Spain during the 1st century AD, who could cure impotence.
- A girl who seduced Charlemagne, who himself was reborn as Swedish prime minister Olaf Palme, one of MacLaine's lovers in her current life.
- An orphan raised by elephants.
- A Japanese geisha.
- An Egyptian princess.

What powers do modern witches claim? Some say they can conjure fire and light.

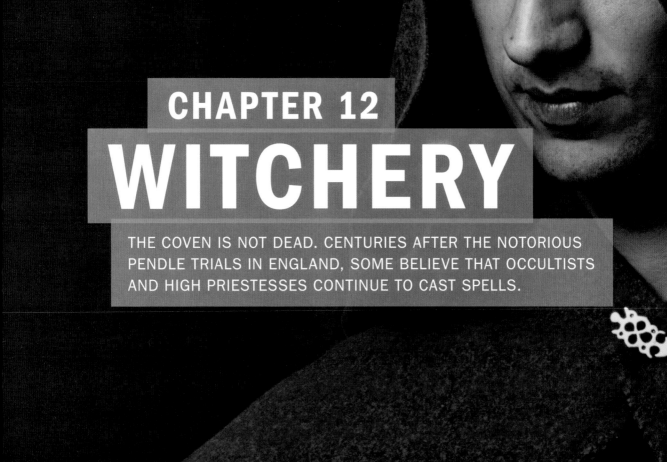

CHAPTER 12
WITCHERY

THE COVEN IS NOT DEAD. CENTURIES AFTER THE NOTORIOUS PENDLE TRIALS IN ENGLAND, SOME BELIEVE THAT OCCULTISTS AND HIGH PRIESTESSES CONTINUE TO CAST SPELLS.

Carney Bell, the distant grandson of John Bell, by the historic marker in Adams, Tennessee.

A SOUTHERN WITCH

As legend has it, a neighbor held a 19th-century Tennessee family spellbound.

In 1817, a mysterious entity began to haunt John Bell and his family in Adams, Tennessee. As local legend goes, for three years the invisible woman tormented the household. She sang, talked, quoted local sermons, and mocked and physically attacked the family. The entity said her spirit belonged to someone buried nearby whose bones had been exhumed without permission. She wanted John Bell dead.

Called "Kate," the entity became known as the Bell Witch and drew widespread attention. When John Bell died mysteriously in 1820, the voice of Kate took credit for poisoning him. Kate also is said to have insisted that Bell's daughter Betsy break off her engagement to her childhood sweetheart.

Who was Kate? Townspeople suspected she had been sent by a neighbor named Mary Catherine Batts. Batts was an odd woman whom the locals believed practiced black magic. But nothing was proven, and the Bell Witch mystery survives to this day, drawing visitors to Adams to see the Bells' home site—and perhaps to hear an unbidden voice.

RITUAL BEHAVIOR

ONE OF HISTORY'S MOST NOTORIOUS WITCH TRIALS TOOK PLACE IN ENGLAND, 80 YEARS BEFORE SALEM.

Long ago in pre-Christian England, before witches came to be associated with devils and darkness, witchcraft was a cultural tradition deeply connected with nature worship and folk medicine. But as Christianity spread in the Middle Ages, the Church denounced existing pagan practices. By the 16th century, when Christianity had split into the Roman Catholic and Protestant churches and religious tensions ran high, witchcraft had become synonymous with evil. Rooting out and destroying those who practiced it was a common practice, and a particularly handy way of dispatching one's enemies.

A Hostile Backdrop

In the early 17th century, King James I ruled an England where Catholics and Protestants were deeply suspicious of one another. The king himself, who had survived an assassination attempt by Catholics, was a staunch Protestant and an avowed witch hunter. In 1612, fears of witchcraft erupted in the Catholic-sympathizing borough of Pendle, in Lancashire. The area's lonely, forbidding moors were an ideal breeding ground for fear. Life in Pendle was hard, and when locals sought someone to blame for human and animal illnesses, they often turned to two unpopular families, the Demdikes and Chattoxes. Both clans were impoverished and headed by women, making them easy targets. It was whispered that some of their kinfolk practiced sorcery.

Terrorized Townspeople

After an incident involving a teenage member of the Demdike family, the suspicions escalated into accusations including murder. The teen, Alizon Device, was thought to have so-called special powers. Some townspeople even believed her dog could talk. When Alizon approached a peddler, John Law, to buy some pins, he refused to sell them to her. At that moment, Law fell to the ground, paralyzed and unable to speak.

While it is now believed that Law may have suffered a stroke, at the time, the peddler and the terrified townspeople believed that Alizon and her dog had cast a spell on Law. Alizon and her mother, brother, and others were accused of incapacitating Law and murdering 16 locals, as well as stealing holy bread to use in spells, bewitching a horse, and swiping the teeth of the dead.

Soon, trials were staged, unfolding during August 1612. The hearings were

Catherine Deshayes Monvoisin, a Parisian woman with connections to the royal court of King Louis XIV, was convicted of witchcraft and burned at the stake in 1680.

WHO KNEW?
Oddly shaped moles or warts were once believed to be a sign that someone was a witch.

filled with testimony of spellcasting, talking animals, and murder, according to a work by Thomas Potts, a court clerk, called *The Wonderfull Discoverie of Witches in the Countie of Lancaster.* Of the 12 who were prosecuted, ten were convicted and hanged, one died in prison, and one was found innocent.

Today, many see the trials as the result of social and political change and disorder.

POWERS THAT BE

MODERN-DAY WICCANS WORK PRACTICAL MAGIC THAT'S NEITHER WICKED NOR EVIL.

WATCHABLE WITCHES

"Enchanting" female characters have long been a television staple.

→ **Bewitched** (1964–1972) introduced viewers to Samantha Stevens. Although she continually promised her befuddled mortal husband, Darren, that she'd keep her powers on ice, she was forever succumbing to her witchier nature.

→ Willow Rosenberg in **Buffy the Vampire Slayer** (1997–2003), began as a meek geek but then blossomed into a power witch.

→ **Charmed** (1998–2006) featured three sisters who discover their bewitching ways and set out to battle evil.

Eight times a year, a coven in Chorley, England, gathers around a campfire to mark the passing seasons. As innocuous as the merry scene appears, the women are well aware of practicing just 30 miles from where Lancashire's so-called Pendle witches were arrested, imprisoned, tried, and hanged some 400 years earlier.

In New York City, high priestess Starr Ravenhawk founded the Temple Academy of Pagan Studies in 2007. "Studying to become a good witch is no different than studying to become a good Catholic," she told a *New York Times* reporter in 2013.

The age-old practice of witchcraft— some historians say it dates back 40,000 years—is embraced by contemporary practitioners of Wicca. While still not a part of mainstream culture, Wiccans have come a long way from the persecution to which their 14th- to 18th-century counterparts were subjected.

Modern witches worship not Satan but nature. They cultivate the art of holistic healing and the use of medicinal plants— as did many of the well-meaning women executed as witches in Renaissance and Reformation Europe.

Wiccan holy days and rituals are tied to the seasons and nature's cycles, with much activity occurring around the solstices. Spells addressing fertility, for example, are cast during a full moon. All Hallows' Eve—Halloween—celebrates the end of the growing season, when the god of hunting is in temporary ascendancy over the Mother Goddess of agriculture, two important Wiccan deities.

Witches often refer to their craft as the Old Religion, but they do not believe in heaven or hell. Rather, their focus is on doing good for others. One of the most dramatic examples of a spell cast to prevent evil occurred during World War II. British witches gathered and directed a single thought to a singular menace: "Don't come!" was their psychic command to the Adolf Hitler—who bombed but did not invade England.

By the Book

A *grimoire* (from the French word for "grammar"), or book of spells, is a commonplace journal used by many witches. These mysterious books tend to include rituals, dream logs, and personal musings related to the craft.

A well-known grimoire among witches, the 20th-century British occultist Gerald Gardner's *Book of Shadows*, is said to be

WHO KNEW?
Wiccans do not summon demons or sacrifice people or animals.

an inheritance from an earlier coven and includes many widely emulated spells.

"The smallness of the congregation and the intimacy of their rituals are advantages in harnessing the positive power of witchcraft," writes author Hans Holzer in *Witches: True Encounters with Wicca, Wizards, Covens, Cults, and Magick.*

Another high-profile contemporary Wiccan, Stacey Demarco, an Australian who once held corporate jobs, has said she is on a mission "to bring back honor to the word *witch*." Demarco, who founded the organization the Modern Witch, describes witchcraft as "a beautiful, spiritual practice" and hopes to bring practical magic to all. She professes to possess psychic abilities—not all witches do. In addition to being a prolific writer about modern witchcraft, Demarco sponsors the Pagan Prayer Project, a global initiative to gather and publish witchcraft prayers.

During the Middle Ages, as Europe adopted Christianity, the dragon became associated with the devil in art and literature. Here, an illustration of a dragon flying at night.

CHAPTER 13

CRYPTOZOOLOGY

AND

BOTANY

DRAGONS. FLESH-EATING PLANTS. MELON HEADS. WHILE SCIENTISTS DISMISS MANY STRANGER-THAN-FICTION FLORA AND FAUNA, A HANDFUL HAVE BEEN PROVEN QUITE REAL.

MONSTERS, MUTANTS, AND FREAKISH CREATURES

THE STRANGE BEINGS KNOWN AS CRYPTIDS CAN BE HYBRIDS OF MULTIPLE ANIMALS—OR RESEMBLE NOTHING AT ALL KNOWN IN NATURE.

Every corner of the world has its collection of stranger-than-fiction creatures, a few proven real, most as yet undocumented by science. Known as cryptids, these beasts may spring from the folklore of ancient peoples or can surface in reports from modern observers. In Australia, aboriginal mythology describes the *bunyip*, a swamp creature with the face of a dog, the head of a crocodile, the tail of a horse, the flippers of a seal, the tusks of a walrus, and dark fur. There have been reported sightings in Cameroon of the Olitiau, a giant vampire bat with a wingspan of 6 to 12 feet. Cryptids can even be plants: In Sudan, Kenya, and Egypt, some locals fear the Nubian tree, a man-eater whose limbs grasp its victims and whose leaves suck their blood.

When the line between myth and fact blurs, cryptozoologists and cryptobotanists step in to authenticate. To be worthy of inquiry, a cryptid must be "big, weird, dangerous, or significant in some way," writes author George M. Eberhart, who has cataloged more than 1,000 cryptids. It must also be legitimate. If someone observes a mysterious animal and someone else discredits the sighting, that doesn't count.

While some cryptids have been exposed as hoaxes, other strange animals are quite real. Within recent years, scientists have discovered the Yodabat, a fruit bat in Papua New Guinea that looks like a monkey, and the mysterious creature dubbed the cat-fox, a carnivorous mammal living in Borneo.

Cryptobiologists consider potential species worth researching when they meet one of a few criteria:

- They are convincingly described in local legend or anecdotal accounts from eyewitnesses.

- They have been declared extinct but have supposedly been seen alive.

- Their supposed remains—skulls, skeletons, hair, footprints, fossils—have been discovered but not identified.

- They resemble actual species but deviate from the norm, being either giant or sighted far outside their indigenous range.

- Their descriptions in stories or myths suggest they might be biologically authentic.

- They used to be classified as cryptids but have since been found to be real.

- They started as hoaxes that later seem to be fact-based.

A CONTINENT OF UNWORLDLY BEASTS

With jungles, deserts, and savannas, Africa, the second-largest continent, may be home to some of the most varied cryptids, from dinosaurs to killer trees.

Ngoubou: CAMEROON A triceratops-like creature with six horns. It reportedly fights elephants for food.

J'ba Fofi: CENTRAL AFRICA This alleged beast looks like a tarantula, but with a 4- to 6-foot leg span.

Nubian tree: SUDAN AND EGYPT Man-eating tree of lore with leaves that suck the blood of victims.

Agogwe: EAST AFRICA Reports of a humanoid creature with rust-colored hair and orange-ish skin date to the 1900s.

Olitiau: CAMEROON Giant vampire bat with a 12-foot wingspan and serrated 2-inch teeth.

Emela-ntouka: REPUBLIC OF THE CONGO An oversized aquatic rhinoceros of Congolese legend is known as elephant killer.

Mokele-mbembe: CONGO A digital rendering of this apatosaurus-like dinosaur, which swims in a swampy region.

Kraken: OCEANS WORLDWIDE Artist's rendition of this giant squid, 40–45 feet long.

Megalodon: OCEANS WORLDWIDE Artist's rendering of this huge prehistoric shark.

Umdhlebi: SOUTH AFRICA A toxic plant that reportedly poisons victims so bodies decay and enrich soil.

Madagascar tree: MADAGASCAR A man-eating tree of legend with hairy appendages that crush its prey.

THE
BIZARRE
BESTIARY

ZOOLOGISTS AND OTHER SCIENTISTS WEIGH IN ON THE OTHERWORLDLY DENIZENS OF CRYPTOZOOLOGY.

WHO KNEW?

In the 1920s, a Soviet scientist tried but failed to breed humans with apes to produce a hybrid cryptid called a humanzee, chuman, or manpanzee.

By definition, cryptids are organisms whose existence has been reported but not confirmed. Cryptozoologists take anecdotal reportage of cryptids very seriously, especially when they echo local folklore or mythology, or are accompanied by videos, footprint casts, "body parts," or other physical evidence. Most mainstream scientists, on the other hand, dismiss cryptids and nonscientific cryptid "evidence"—though a few of them have been willing to look deeper, hoping to discover the truth behind the reported sightings of mysterious beasts.

Occasionally, reliable scientists turn up hard physical proof of as-yet uncataloged creatures—fossils, specimens, verifiable photographs, and the like—that elevates a rumored cryptid to an established species. Time and again, though, scientists determine that accounts and evidence of cryptids are nothing more than hoaxes fueled by wishful thinking.

CRYPTIDS: ALL IN THE MIND?

There are many explanations of what is actually happening when people report seeing bizarre creatures. Some believe these sightings are psychologically based, resulting from human behavior or habits of thinking.

THE BEHAVIOR	THE EXPLANATION
Anticipation	Seeing what one wants or expects to see based on rumors and reports of other sightings, such as the Mothman of Point Pleasant, Ohio
Hoax	Fraud or pranks intentionally perpetrated by con artists or mischief-makers, such as the fur-bearing trout of North America and Iceland (tall tale, also faked taxidermy sample)
Illusion	Visual phenomena created by light, darkness, weather conditions, poor eyesight, etc., such as the Loch Ness monster (could be water patterns such as choppy waves or floating objects such as logs)
Misidentification	Mistaking a known animal for an unknown animal, such as mermaids (manatees of the Caribbean Sea, Gulf of Mexico, and coastal West Africa)
Tradition	Belief in local folklore or myths involving weird creatures, such as the Jersey Devil (originated in the 18th-century legend of Mother Leeds, in the New Jersey Pine Barrens)

LET THERE BE LIFE!

Here's another explanation for cryptids: They're real. On occasion, scientists discover species that have never before been cataloged.

Dingiso

While searching for the fabled bondegezou ("man of the forests") in 1994, researchers stumbled upon the dingiso, a boldly colored forest marsupial in western Indonesia. The local Moni people had long reported it as a small humanoid creature with black and white fur. The dingiso is rarely seen and has never been captured.

Giant squid

The sea monsters of yore were probably giant squid. These fearsome predators weren't seen alive in their underwater habitat until 2004, but 16th-century descriptions of kraken match up very well with images of the giant squid.

Komodo dragon

The world's largest lizard was discovered in 1926, during an expedition to Indonesia by researchers from the American Museum of Natural History. A species of venomous monitor lizard, the Komodo can grow to ten feet.

Okapi

In the 18th century, Europeans referred to this curious beast, which looks like a blend of giraffe, zebra, and donkey, as the African unicorn. The okapi was officially recognized in 1901, when a British official in Uganda brought specimens back to England.

Platypus

A venomous, egg-laying mammal from Australia with webbed feet, a duck's bill, and a beaver's tail sounded like a hoax. It wasn't.

Spot-bellied eagle owl

In Sri Lanka, folklore tells of the ulama, a seldom-seen horned bird that screams at night as if in terror. In 2001, it was identified as a new species of screeching horned owl.

HAIRY BIOLOGY
YETI, BIGFOOT, SASQUATCH

DESPITE GPS AND SATELLITES, UNEXPLORED AREAS OF THE EARTH REMAIN. WHO—OR WHAT—MIGHT LIVE IN THESE REMOTE PLACES?

NAZIS HUNT THE YETI

Some Nazis believed Tibet was the birthplace of the Aryan race and suspected that the yeti was the missing evolutionary link with humans. In 1938, German professor and SS member Ernst Schäfer was recruited by the Nazis to lead a research trip to Tibet, where he collected and analyzed more than 300 skulls. Yeti researcher Reinhold Messner later claimed Schäfer told him that the yeti was a Tibetan bear, not an early Aryan. "But if I had said this to the Nazis, they would have killed me," Schäfer told Messner.

The men had just crossed the Lhakpa-La Pass in Nepal in the early morning hours of September 22, 1921, when they came upon a set of strange tracks. British explorer Charles Howard-Bury, who was leading the first attempt to scale the north face of Mount Everest, the tallest mountain on Earth, kneeled down to inspect the prints in the moonlight. They looked as if they had been made by a barefoot man. But the Sherpas, the local Nepalese guides on the trek, said the impressions belonged to the *metoh-kangmi*, or man-bear snowman. A journalist writing about the trip mistranslated metoh as "abominable," thus introducing to the

A Tibetan priest portrays the Abominable Snowman.

west the Abominable Snowman, a creature the Nepalese had long called "yeti."

Howard-Bury was neither the first nor last adventurer to encounter evidence of the Abominable Snowman. Sightings of a tall, bipedal, ape-like creature had been reported as early as 1832, and in the 1950s yeti fever reached a fevered pitch, with a number of books and Hollywood films on the subject. The Nepalese government in 1957 even got in on the act, issuing yeti-hunting licenses at roughly US $650 each. Though most experts say the yeti is a hoax, sightings continue to this day: In 2013, a 12-year-old boy in Siberia took camera-phone footage of what looked like a large yeti carrying its infant.

Mystery Solved?

Theories and explanations ranging from melted tracks to rare ape breeds have floated around for decades—but modern science may hold the answer.

In 2013, Bryan Sykes, a human-genetics professor at Oxford University, conducted an extensive study of more than 30 supposed yeti hair and tissue samples. Two of them, collected about 800 miles apart in the Himalayas, revealed a 100 percent match with a polar bear jawbone found in Norway dating from between 40,000 to 120,000 years ago. This would support many scientists' belief that the yeti is simply a rare species of bear.

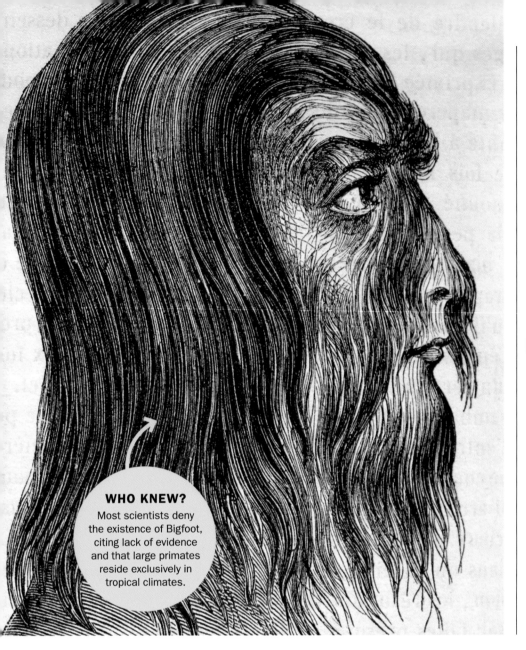

Gimlin, left, and Patterson, of Yakima, Washington, compare casts they made of footprints they claim were made by a Sasquatch, or Bigfoot, on October 27, 1967.

CAUGHT ON TAPE?

The most widely circulated photographic evidence of Bigfoot is a 16mm film shot on October 20, 1967, by Roger Patterson and Bob Gimlin at Bluff Creek, California. The brief clip depicts a large, hairy biped walking into the woods, occasionally looking back at the camera. Countless primatologists and Hollywood special-effects experts have examined the footage, some declaring it fake, others saying that if it is a hoax, it's an extremely well-executed one. A few people have said they appeared in the film in costume, but no such claims have been substantiated.

WHO KNEW?

Most scientists deny the existence of Bigfoot, citing lack of evidence and that large primates reside exclusively in tropical climates.

BIGFOOT: THE AMERICAN YETI

He is said to be almost eight feet tall, hairy, and smelly.

An illustration of Bigfoot kidnapping a woman, 1897.

For hundreds of years Native American tribes told tales of large, hairy wild-men that roamed the wilderness. In the 1920s, a Canadian journalist named the creature Sasquatch. Some 30 years later, large footprints were discovered in northwest California amid a rash of Sasquatch sightings, and the term *Bigfoot* was coined.

Accounts usually describe a bipedal humanoid primate, often almost eight feet tall, that is covered in hair. Sightings are often accompanied by a powerful stench, according to many reports. In Florida, where many of the spottings have occurred, Sasquatch is called Skunk Ape.

MOTHMAN
AND OTHER WINGED WONDERS

OUTSIZE, WINGED CREATURES HAVE BEEN KNOWN TO SWOOP DOWN ON UNSUSPECTING BYSTANDERS IN REMOTE PLACES.

A sandhill crane flying in front of the sun.

WHO—OR WHAT—WAS MOTHMAN?

If the giant winged creature with the smoldering red eyes was not a frightening crypto-creature, then what was Mothman?

→ **An oversize barn owl.** Witnesses describe stupendous dimensions, but other details fit. Sightings were often near a wildlife preserve, where owls would naturally congregate.

→ **A sandhill crane.** These birds are big and powerful, though they've never been known to live in the area of the Mothman sightings.

→ **A hoax.** Joe Nickell, the author of *The Mystery Chronicles: More Real Life X-Files*, says pranksters could have rigged helium balloons to impersonate Mothman, using red flashlights for the eyes.

On the night of November 15, 1966, two married couples, Steve and Mary Mallette and Roger and Linda Scarberry, were parked at a spot just outside Point Pleasant, West Virginia. They had come to enjoy the local lovers' lane, but then something alarming descended on them—a creature, large, white and forbidding, with a wingspan of ten feet.

The four friends said the beast seemed to have no separate head—just a pair of blood-red, smoldering eyes coming from its shoulders. As the couples sped back to Point Pleasant, the fiend pursued them to the city limits.

Angel, Butterfly, or Moth?

The Mallettes and Scarberrys were not first to relate such an encounter. One eyewitness identified the creature as an angel, another as a giant butterfly. By most accounts, the mysterious critter looked like a moth on steroids, and Mothman became its official moniker.

"All I could see were the eyes," said Faye DeWitt, who spotted Mothman shortly after the Mallettes and Scarberrys, "and red like you never saw red." As DeWitt told it, Mothman zoomed down close to the hood of her car, then opened its massive wings and soared away to the top of a five-story building.

Eventually, more than 100 Point Pleasant residents said they had encountered Mothman. It liked to frequent two places: One was the "TNT area," which during World War II was a hiding place for munitions but later became a wildlife preserve. The other was the suspension bridge connecting Point Pleasant to a neighboring town in Ohio. On December 15, 1967, the bridge collapsed, killing 46 people. Engineers were quick to identify structural problems that caused the Silver Bridge tragedy, but many in Point Pleasant wondered: Did Mothman have something to do with it?

Strange Calls

One theory was posed by John Keel, a writer on the paranormal. Keel was working on a story about UFOs for *Playboy* magazine in 1966 when he began looking into Mothman sightings at Point Pleasant. As Keel researched, he claimed he began receiving strange phone calls with tips on Mothman. One peculiar call suggested that when President Lyndon Johnson threw the switch to light the White House Christmas tree, the country would go dark.

As he watched the ceremony on television on December 15, 1967, Keel said he was on edge. While there was no national blackout, at that moment in Point Pleasant, the bridge on Highway 35 crumpled. Keel's subsequent book, *The Mothman Prophecies*, related the events and became the basis for a film starring Richard Gere and Laura Linney. No science has ever fully explained the episode, but Keel and many others believe that Mothman tries to warn people about disasters about to happen.

WHO KNEW?
Since 2001, the third weekend in September has been reserved for the annual Mothman Festival in Point Pleasant, West Virginia.

A still from the movie *The Mothman Prophecies*, about the strange phenomena in Point Pleasant, West Virginia.

THE OWLMAN OF ENGLAND

Does Mothman have a relative across the Atlantic?

British sisters Vicky and Jane Melling, ages 9 and 12, were the first to encounter the beast who would become known as Owlman. The girls were walking through the woods of Cornwall, England, on April 17, 1976, when a massive creature with tremendous wings and blood-red eyes appeared to them. Terrified, the youngsters ran to their father, who contacted a researcher of the paranormal to investigate. Three months later, in the same area, two other young girls reported hearing an ominous hissing from a monstrous "owl with pointed ears, as big as a man." Its feathers were gray, its claws and mouth black, and its eyes—red. Owlman sightings in Cornwall were reported three other times, once in 1995 by a marine biology student from the Field Museum in Chicago.

Could the owlman of England have been a barn owl like this one?

THE STRANGER SPECIES OF NORTH AMERICA

SCIENTISTS CAN'T CONFIRM THE EXISTENCE OF BIG-HEADED CANNIBALS AND VAMPIRIC HAIRLESS BEASTS. BUT EYEWITNESSES CLAIM OTHERWISE.

Many people have heard of the yeti, the Abominable Snowman of the Himalayas and the Loch Ness monster of Scotland. But not all mysterious creatures are found in faraway places. A slew of strange beings are said to lurk in the pockets of American wilderness. Devils on the land, monsters in the lakes, and a wild beast roaming the deserts: Who says there's no more to explore? Meet America's best-known cryptids, from the cannibalistic Melon Heads of Connecticut to the odiferous Skunk Ape of Florida.

Champ, the Creature of Lake Champlain

Dividing New York and Vermont is the sprawling 490-square-mile freshwater Lake Champlain. A rich fishery for bass and salmon, Lake Champlain is also said to be home to Champ, a slithery monster with silver-gray scales that has been compared to a great snake, a large dog, a yacht, a horse, a manatee, a periscope, a lizard, and a whale.

More than 300 Champ sightings have been reported in the media, starting with an article in the *Plattsburgh Republican* on July 24, 1819. In that story, a Captain Crum claimed the black monster was about 187-feet long, with a flat head rising more than 15 feet out of the water. After the Civil War there were a flood of such reports, and in the late 19th century, entrepreneur P.T. Barnum offered a big reward for the lake monster, dead or alive, but no hunter could deliver him.

The early 20th century brought another round of Champ spottings—so many that Port Henry, New York, on the west shore of Lake Champlain and the north end of Bulwagga Bay, erected a sign listing them all. Some believe the lake monster is a plesiosaur, a large marine reptile from the Jurassic period, but skeptics say it is a large sturgeon, an unusual fish called a gar, a row of otters, an enormous log, a peculiar piece of driftwood, or just a figment of the imagination.

In 1982 and 1983, state legislators in Vermont and New York, respectively, passed laws to protect Champ the sea serpent against death, injury, or harassment.

A rendering of Champ, the mysterious creature said to live in Lake Champlain.

The Jersey Devil is memorialized in the name of the state hockey team. The Colorado Rockies became the New Jersey Devils in 1982 when the franchise moved east.

The Jersey Devil

The story goes that Mrs. Leeds of Estellville, New Jersey, did not want another child; she already had 12 and soon there would be another mouth to feed. In sheer frustration, Mrs. Leeds cried out that she would rather have a devil than a baby. And so it happened that when the infant was born, it had a long forked tail, the face of a horse, bat-like wings, and horns. It flew out of the window and settled in a nearby swamp in the Pine Barrens of southern New Jersey.

The year was 1735, and according to some, the Jersey Devil still roams the Pine Barrens today, emerging from the mists of a desolate marsh to create havoc. Over the centuries, the Jersey Devil has supposedly raided chicken coops and farms, destroyed crops, and killed animals in at least 50 dif-

CHUPACABRA: THE DREADED GOAT SUCKER

With glowing red eyes and a hellish odor of sulfur, this monstrous animal shies away from bright light.

A hairless, vampiric creature with the skin of a lizard prowls the land, sucking the blood from goats, chickens, cattle, and horses. The drained victims are marked only with two, sometimes three, puncture wounds to the neck. From a mouth of fangs, the beast emits a savage growl.

This is the fabled chupacabra, the "goat sucker," whose Spanish name reflects its Latin American origins— or at least the origins of the legend. The bloodthirsty predator allegedly was first spotted in Puerto Rico in 1995 around the time some 150 farm animals and pets turned up dead near the town of Canóvanas, according to one witness, Madelyne Tolentino. Skeptics pointed out that Tolentino may have been influenced by the movie *Species*, which featured a startlingly similar creature. But Tolentino's story was enough to give birth to the belief in the chupacabra.

A NASA Experiment Gone Wrong?

Conspiracy theorists speculate that the chupacabra is a NASA experiment gone wrong or that the beast was left behind by space aliens who kept it as a pet. But wildlife biologists generally agree that the chupacabra is an ordinary animal—a coyote, dog, or raccoon—who has lost its hair because of sarcoptic mange or scabies.

Photographs that appear to show the beast seem to support the canine hypothesis, but it's also possible the animal is a raccoon, as many alleged sightings of chupacabras include descriptions of the animal sitting in a tree, eating with its hands. It should be noted that neither raccoons nor coyotes are anatomically capable of sucking the blood from their prey.

In 2007, Phylis Canion, a nutritionist in Cuero, Texas, found an animal she identified as a chupacabra. Here, Canion holds the beast's head.

A Baby Chupacabra

In 2014, scientists missed a chance to examine what might have been a living chupacabra. A couple in Ratcliffe, Texas, captured what they claimed was a baby chupacabra and kept it in a pen, feeding it corn and baby food. But before any examination could take place, the couple said it had the critter euthanized.

ferent towns. In one week in January 1909, the Devil terrorized thousands in New Jersey and Pennsylvania; later, hunting parties were organized to catch the Devil, but it proved elusive. A $10,000 reward for the beast's capture was offered in 1960 by a group of merchants in Camden. The prize remains unclaimed.

In 1939, the Jersey Devil was declared the Official State Demon of New Jersey; it is the only state to have such a designation.

Melon Heads

In the 1997 American cult-film classic *The Hills Have Eyes*, a family stranded in the Nevada desert is hunted by a clan of deformed cannibals in the surrounding hills. The plot echoes Connecticut lore, which describes big-headed, human-like creatures that emerge from hiding to attack and eat people. According to one story, the Melon Heads descended from a family accused of witchcraft in colonial times that was forced to live in the wilderness. The notable head size was supposedly caused by mutations from centuries of inbreeding.

The Skunk Ape

Far to the south, thousands of Floridians have reported encounters with a terribly smelly ape-like creature that runs upright on two legs, known as the Skunk Ape. In 1977, the Florida state legislature debated a bill to protect the smelly man-ape. The bill proposed making it a misdemeanor for "Any person taking, possessing, harming, or molesting any anthropoid or humanoid animal which is native to Florida, popularly known as the Skunk Ape." Despite some discussion, the bill never passed into law.

Purported Wendigo spirit in the Rouge National Urban Park, Ontario, Canada.

THE WENDIGO

A Native American hunting party once lost its way in the forest in winter and ran out of food. Fearing starvation, one hunter was driven to cannibalism, a taboo in Algonquin culture with serious consequences: The violator would be possessed by evil spirits and transformed into a horrible half-beast.

Thus was born the story of the Wendigo, a violent creature fated to forever roam the northeastern United States and Canada—anywhere winters were long and hard, food was limited, and survival difficult. Described as tall and incredibly thin, with bones pushing out against its skin, the Wendigo was believed to be obsessed with feasting on human flesh. This unending hunger could never be satisfied, so a Wendigo must search constantly for new victims.

The Florida state legislature debated a bill to protect the Skunk Ape.

A SEA MONSTER CALLED KRAKEN

TALES OF SEA MONSTERS HAVE TERRIFIED SAILORS FOR CENTURIES. ONE BEAST IS REAL.

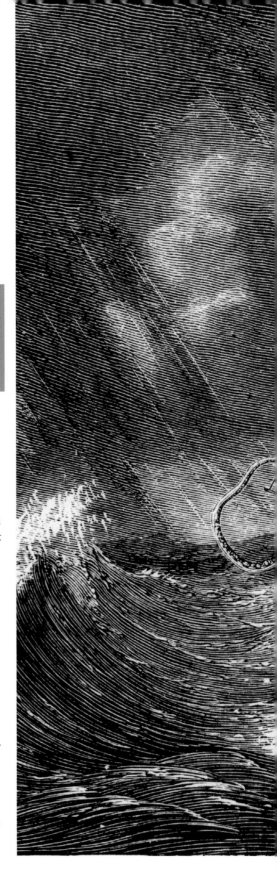

> "[W]e now gazed at the most wondrous phenomenon which the secret seas have hitherto revealed to mankind. A vast pulpy mass, furlongs in length and breadth, of a glancing cream-color, lay floating on the water, innumerable long arms radiating from its centre, and curling and twisting like a nest of anacondas…"
>
> —From *Moby Dick*, by Herman Melville, 1851

For centuries, sailors were haunted by fear of the mighty kraken—a tentacled sea monster measuring more than a mile long. Rising from the ocean, the beast was believed to be able to topple even the tallest sailing ship, sending the crew to a watery death or devouring them.

The first reports of the kraken date to 12th-century Norway, and it has remained an object of fascinated speculation ever since. The question persists: Are the fantastic tales of the kraken merely the ultimate fish stories, products of the fevered minds of isolated sailors, or does this fabled creature actually exist? The famous 16th-century taxonomist Carl Linnaeus was just one scientist who maintained that the kraken was real. In his work *Systema Naturae* (1735), he gave the monster the scientific name *Microcosmus marinus*.

More concrete evidence emerged in the 1870s, when several giant squid washed up on the beaches of Newfoundland,

This engraving from 1870 shows a larger-than-life giant squid attacking a sailing vessel.

> "Below the thunders
> of the upper deep;
> Far, far beneath in
> the abysmal sea, His
> ancient, dreamless,
> uninvaded sleep The
> Kraken sleepeth…"

—From "The Kraken," a sonnet
by Alfred, Lord Tennyson, 1830

Canada. Many scientists suspected that the giant squid were in fact the "monsters" long feared by sailors. Today it is known that the giant squid can measure up to about 50 feet long, about the size of a four-story building.

They are enormous, but not as treacherous as the fabled kraken: Although giant squid are widespread, inhabiting all of the world's oceans, they dwell in waters ranging from at least 1,000 to more than 3,000 feet deep. They are generally seen on the surface only when they have become entangled in fishing nets or stranded on beaches. These giants of the deep feed not

on ships and sailors, but rather on deep-sea fish and smaller squid species. Giant squid are sometimes even preyed upon themselves, by one of the few creatures large enough to tangle with them—the sperm whale.

Until recently, no one had seen a living giant squid in its natural habitat. The first sighting came in 2004, when a Japanese team dropped a camera hooked to 3,000 feet of fishing line into the Pacific. When one of the creatures attacked the line, it triggered the camera, which took more than five hundred pictures. More recently, in 2012, American marine biologist Edie

This engraving of the kraken as a sea serpent is based on earlier depictions going back to the 17th century.

Widder, also working off the coast of Japan, went in search of what she called "the Holy Grail of natural history film-making"—video footage of the giant squid in its natural habitat. Widder's account of what the recording revealed echoed tales of the kraken of old: "It is this alien creature that's got eight arms and two slashing tentacles writhing around and a parrot beak that rips flesh and an eye that's as big as your head."

In fact, Widder's video corroborated almost every detail of the fantastical description in Jules Verne's 1870 novel, *Twenty Thousand Leagues under the Sea*: "Before my eyes was a horrible monster...watching us with its enormous staring green eyes. Its eight arms, or rather feet, fixed to its head...were twice as long as its body, and were twisted like the furies' hair....The monster's mouth, a horned beak like a parrot's, opened and shut vertically. Its tongue, a horned substance...furnished with several rows of point teeth, came out quivering from this veritable pair of shears."

Modern science may have solved the mystery of the kraken. But only an estimated 5 percent of the ocean has been explored. No one knows what other equally bizarre creatures might be lurking deep in the sea.

Dr. Edie Widder, left, prepares for a dive in the Johnson Sea llnk, which is one of the submersibles she uses for deep-sea exploration.

BY THE NUMBERS

Widder's expedition racked up some impressive statistics.

→ **Weeks at sea:** 8

→ **Number of hours undersea:** 285

→ **Submersibles used:** 3

→ **Sub dives taken:** 55

→ **Depths reached:** more than 3,000 feet

→ **Length of the giant squid filmed:** 26 feet

IN AN OCTOPUS'S GARDEN

Ancestors of giant squid may have had an artistic bent.

On a family vacation in Nevada, paleontologist Mark McMenamin became intrigued by fossils of nine ichthyosaurs, prehistoric marine reptiles that grew to the size of a city bus. Scientists have long been puzzled by what killed these massive beasts. In 2011 McMenamin came up with his own guess—an ancient and enormous octopus much like the creature in legends of the kraken.

McMenamin theorized from the markings on the fossils that this kraken snapped the necks of its ichthyosaur victims and carried the bodies back to its lair. Based on the behavior of modern octopuses, he believed that, after eating its prey, the kraken purposefully arranged the bones that were left. The vertebral discs of the ichthyosaurs were placed in double lines, a pattern that eerily resembles the sucker discs of the kraken's tentacles. McMenamin went as far as to suggest that the bone arrangement was an early version of a self-portrait.

McMenamin has not convinced many of his peers of the existence of this artistic ancient kraken. "It's fun to think about, but I think it's very implausible," paleontologist Ryosuke Motani has said.

Paleontologist Mark McMenamin believes some ichthyosaur fossils may reveal the dining habits of prehistoric kraken who lived in the age of dinosaurs.

THE LAKE BEAST

THE LOCH NESS MONSTER HAS LURKED IN THE IMAGINATION FOR GENERATIONS.

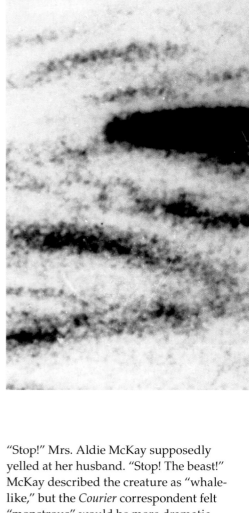

MONSTERS, INC.

From Japan to the Congo, mysterious water beasts are said to lurk in lakes around the world.

Lake Tianchi Monster, Japan.
→ Nessie-like animals have been spotted in Japan's Lake Tianchi since 1903. Scientists are dubious, since the lake is too cold for such a beast to live there.

Gryttie, Sweden.
→ Sonar and robotics have been used to search Sweden's Lake Gryttjen for a creature that could be a strange sea serpent or just a rogue sea cow.

Mokele-mbembe, Congo.
→ The Mokele-mbembe ("one who stops the flow of rivers") is a sauropod dinosaur rumored to live in the Congo river basin. Sightings date back over two hundred years.

Deep under the surface of Loch Ness, a prehistoric, 23-mile lake in the Scottish Highlands, lies a mysterious 1,400-year-old legend. Tales of the so-called Loch Ness monster, a cryptid thought to be an ancient dinosaur, has haunted the area for centuries. But in spite of millions of dollars and thousands of man-hours invested to prove the existence of "Nessie," no one has ever produced concrete evidence of the monster.

There have been reported sightings of an unidentified animal in the loch as far back as 565 AD, when an Irish monk was said to have stopped a "sea beast" from killing a swimmer in the River Ness. But it wasn't until the 20th century that the concept of a Loch Ness monster entered the mainstream. On May 2, 1933, Scotland's *Inverness Courier* published an article detailing the sighting of a "monstrous" creature by a local woman. According to the account, a local hotel manager had been driving with her husband when she looked out over the Loch and saw something "black and wet" rolling in the water.

"Stop!" Mrs. Aldie McKay supposedly yelled at her husband. "Stop! The beast!" McKay described the creature as "whale-like," but the *Courier* correspondent felt "monstrous" would be more dramatic.

The international press soon latched on to the story, and the Loch Ness monster was born. Sightings of "Nessie" soon poured in.

Fact or Fiction?

There have been close to a thousand Nessie sightings recorded over the years, many by café and hotel proprietors seeking to boost

This grainy black-and-white image, which appeared in the April 21, 1934, *Daily Mail*, is the first photo published of the purported Loch Ness monster.

Loch Ness, Scotland.

IF NESSIE EXISTS, WHAT IS SHE?

The Loch Ness monster has been called an alien, a ghost, and even an elephant. She also might be one of the following:

A PLESIOSAUR
A plesiosaur was a type of dinosaur that could swim. It had a small head, long neck, and broad, turtle-like body, and conceivably could survive the waters of Loch Ness, but it has long been extinct.

A LONG-NECKED SEAL
In 1934, Sir Edward Mountain financed an expedition to uncover the truth about the Loch Ness monster. Photographs and film from the trip revealed a long-necked seal, a creature that has been known to visit area waterways.

AN OPTICAL ILLUSION
In April 2014, a satellite image of the Loch taken by Apple Maps created a stir when it revealed what looked like the silhouette of a large creature with flippers. Debunkers soon revealed "the beast" to be a boat's wake.

their business, according to a recent report by the BBC Scotland. In 2012, for example, Loch Ness cruise boat operator George Edwards circulated a photograph of the monster, which depicted the beast's hump rising from the middle of the lake. The following year, Edwards admitted he had photographed a fiberglass Nessie in order to lure tourists.

The best-known image of Nessie, dubbed the Surgeon's Photograph, was supposedly taken by Dr. Robert Wilson in 1934. The picture depicts what looks like the head and neck of a plesiosaur, a prehistoric marine mammal, emerging from the water. While fans embraced the image as proof of Nessie's existence, critics dismissed it as suspicious, citing the strange ripples around the monster's neck. The matter was put to rest in 1975 when a man named Ian Wetherell revealed to the Sunday *Times* newspaper that his father, a movie director, and an accomplice had staged and shot the photo for Dr. Wilson. The men used a toy submarine to help create the illusion of a beast. Wilson had the image developed in Inverness before selling it to the *Daily Mail*.

PLANTS
THAT EAT FLESH

THESE BLOODTHIRSTY FLOWERS LURE THEIR PREY WITH SCENTS, ENTRAP THEM WITH GOO, AND THEN . . . *SNAP*!

European explorers and scientists who first investigated Indonesian jungles in the 17th, 18th, and 19th centuries were astonished to find that some of the strange plants there actually ate animals. What they discovered were Nepenthes, a genus of plants commonly known as pitchers. Just like the pitchers that hold margaritas or iced tea or water, the Nepenthes hold liquid, too. But oh, to what a deadly end for a thirsty insect or mouse.

Jaws of the Plant World

All pitcher plants are ingeniously designed to lure insects and small rodents into their inner chamber. Stiff hairs near the opening point downward, so once the prey starts its descent, it's trapped and can't turn back. From there, the creatures fall into a small pool of water and drown, and their bodies are broken down into a meal by the plant's enzymes. Break open some Nepenthes and you might even find fragments of mouse bones.

Southeast Asia and Australia are home to more than 90 species of Nepenthes. A *Nepenthes spathulata*, native to Java and Sumatra, can grow as large as 17 feet from stem to lip. The king-sized *Nepenthes rajah*, found in Borneo, eats not only insects but also small birds, frogs, lizards, and mice. The stem of its sister plant, *Nepenthes attenboroughii*, a native of the Philippines, can reach 12 inches in diameter.

Red Death in the Deep Sea

The biblical book of Exodus describes ten plagues in Egypt: in one, the Nile turns to blood. Could there be any science to such apocalyptic visions? Marine biologists say when the blue sea turns red, beware: It may be the deadly red algal blooms, known today as red tide. It occurs when algae in the water multiply, starving the water of oxygen and releasing toxins. Water temperature may also trigger a bloom, which can be transported long distances by storms and ships.

Shellfish can survive exposure to red tide, but humans who eat the contaminated creatures don't fare so well. Bivalves infected by red algal blooms can be packed with enough poison to paralyze or kill people who eat them. Even cooking doesn't neutralize the toxin.

Nepenthes attenboroughii is named for the British broadcaster and scientist Sir David Attenborough.

Actress Sheridan Smith played Audrey in a 2007 stage production in London.

PITCHER PLANT "BIOPIC"

The star of the 1982 musical *Little Shop of Horrors* was a man-eating plant.

A mild-mannered florist raises a human-eating plant and names it for his unrequited love; chaos ensues. That's the unlikely plot of *Little Shop of Horrors*, a 1982 musical spoof based on a low-budget 1960 film. (There is also a 1986 movie musical starring Steve Martin and Rick Moranis.) The giant *Nepenthes spathulata* puppet with the booming basso—Audrey II—steals the show. Could a plant really devour a human? As far as we know, only on stage and screen.

FIRE FROM THE SKY

IN MYTHS OF OLD, LIZARD-LIKE FLYING MONSTERS EMERGED FROM ISOLATED PLACES TO SPEW FLAMES.

A LEGEND IS BORN

Dragons have played key roles in myth, religion, and literature since ancient times.

Anzu
In ancient Mesopotamian texts, Anzu was a servant of the powerful sky god Enlil. Anzu stole the Tablet of Destinies, and with it, the power to rule the universe.

The giant red dragon of the Apocalypse
In the biblical book of Revelations, this dragon is described as "the Devil and Satan, the deceiver of the whole world."

Yamata no Orochi
An enormous eight-headed and eight-tailed Japanese dragon with red eyes appears in the *Kojiki*, Japan's oldest book (c. 680 AD).

Drogon, Viserion, and Rhaegal
This trio of dragons appears in *A Song of Ice and Fire*, a series of novels by George R.R. Martin that was adapted into the popular television series *Game of Thrones*.

Hanging at the entrance of Poland's famous Wawel Cathedral is a jumble of bones, said to be the remains of Smok Waweleski, the local dragon. Legend has it that the skeleton parts date to a time before the city of Krakow was founded, when Smok lived in a cave under a rolling hill. He terrorized the locals for years, subsisting on a diet of livestock and young women, until a local hero fed Smok a lamb spiked with sulfur. The dish made the dragon so thirsty, he drank gallons of water from the Vistula River and exploded.

While nonbelievers say that the church display is just fossilized whale or mammoth bones, even skeptics credit the

Wawel Dragon gargoyle at Wawel Cathedral.

remains with magical powers. The Wawel site is considered holy and has attracted many pilgrims over the centuries.

Winged Menace

Flying, fire-breathing beasts with incendiary tempers to match are a fixture in the myths of cultures around the world. No matter where they appear or in what period, dragons are depicted with certain characteristics: They tend to be enormous, their bodies are elongated and covered with scales like a crocodile, and they have huge webbed wings and massive legs with claws like a lizard. They tend to live in isolated places such as swamps, forests, mountains, deserts, ruined castles, and caves.

Dragons take on other attributes depending on geography. European dragons are usually depicted as evil—or at least downright mean—and often trace their origins to Greece. The word *dragon* comes from the Greek word *draconta,* meaning "to watch," because dragons were often tasked with guarding valuables such as piles of gold coins or a beautiful young woman. Sometimes, the treasure was the designated reward for any brave soul who could vanquish the beast. In many European

Detail of *St. George and the Princess*, late 15th century, attributed to Antonio Cicognara.

stories, a dragon terrorizes the land until he is fed a human sacrifice.

Dragon as Satan

During the Middle Ages, as Europe adopted Christianity, the dragon became associated with the devil in art and literature. Slaying a dragon was considered the most heroic act imaginable, and legends grew up around those who were said to have done so. The image of St. George, the patron saint of soldiers and archers, is familiar even today. Astride a stallion and wearing a white tunic emblazoned with a red cross, St. George skewers a dragon as he saves a fair maiden. This legend is told in many versions and is depicted variously in art, but it nearly always involved a mighty sword and a princess in distress.

The eastern Asian dragon can be fierce as well, but unlike its European counterpart, it is almost always helpful to human beings. The Asian dragon loves jewels, especially jade; it hates centipedes and anything made from iron. In China, the dragon is the highest-ranking animal in the cosmology; it was associated with the power and majesty of the Chinese emperor, and is still linked to fertility and prosperity.

An artist's rendering of the lights, textures, and fractal elements of the night sky.

CHAPTER 14

UNNATURAL SCIENCE

THE HUM FROM NOWHERE. STRANGE ORBS ON THE HORIZONS, AND BUZZING RODS. SUCH SOUNDS AND SIGHTS CAN BE PROFOUNDLY DISTURBING. WHERE DO THEY COME FROM?

GET THE LEAD OUT

ALCHEMISTS BELIEVED MAGIC COULD HELP THEM TURN LESSER METALS INTO GOLD.

It may seem silly that anyone would think they could magically turn lead into gold or discover the secret to immortality. But in the Middle Ages and the Renaissance, spiritually minded apothecaries dedicated themselves to creating a host of mystical potions and objects, including an elixir of life and a Philosopher's Stone, a chemical substance with the power to change one thing into something better. This enigmatic protoscience, with its symbolic connection to personal transformation, was called alchemy.

Alchemy was based on the theory that all matter was interconnected and evolved from four classical elements—fire, air, water, and earth. Matter could also be described according to qualities such as combustibility. Alchemists believed that the tendency of nature, whether inanimate, animal, or human, was to improve itself to become its ideal form. Because gold was the most perfect of metals, lesser metals wanted to be gold and would eventually become gold over time. The goal of turning lead into gold was presented as an analogy for personal improvement.

Though alchemists used protoscientific techniques, such as combining chemical ingredients and heating them, theirs was not a true science. Instead, alchemists incorporated spirituality, mythology, and magical thinking into their quest to perfect the natural world and achieve spiritual enlightenment. They thought that if they could discover the key to immortality, they could live long enough to find absolution for their sins and be purified.

The Philosopher's Stone

No alchemist of the era, and no one since, has discovered the elixir of life. The question of the Philosopher's Stone is a little more complicated. In the literature of alchemy, there doesn't seem to be much agreement as to what the stone is, how to make one, or if the process is even possible. Sometimes it is described as an actual stone, usually red in color. But it was also described as a powder or some other physical substance. Creating it supposedly started with a primary ingredient, such as copper or gold or even urine. Then the alchemist would treat it with different processes, heating, distilling, or submerging it in sand. There was little agreement on the steps.

Spiritual Transformation

The concept at the heart of alchemy was transfiguration, the evolution of a substance from imperfection to perfection. Modern scholars often interpret alchemy in a metaphorical way, and some alchemists themselves looked at alchemy allegorically. In the 20th

The Alchemist (c. 1645), by David Teniers the Younger, shows an alchemist at work on the left, attended by a young apprentice.

LITERARY GOLD

Alchemy, whether real or spiritual, is certainly popular with novelists.

→ *The Alchemist* (1987). Paul Coelho's self-help allegory of a shepherd boy seeking treasure in Egypt includes a character who possesses the elixir of life and the Philosopher's Stone.

→ *Harry Potter and the Sorcerer's Stone* (2007). J.K. Rowling's blockbuster was originally titled *Harry Potter and the Philosopher's Stone*; Harry's mentor, Albus Dumbledore, claims to have been a friend of real-life alchemist Nicholas Flamel.

→ *A Discovery of Witches* (2011). In the first novel of a trilogy, historian Diana Bishop accidently calls forth the long-lost text of a 17th-century alchemist, sparking the interest of every supernatural creature in the world.

century, the psychologist Carl Jung proposed that alchemists had been seeking spiritual transformation through self-discovery.

Alchemy fell out of fashion as the Enlightenment dawned and the principles and practices of modern science developed in the 17th and 18th centuries. By the 19th century, alchemists were dismissed as charlatans. But the alchemists of earlier eras have, in recent years, gotten more respect. Their experimentation led to legitimate scientific discoveries and processes.

PSEUDOSCIENCE? MAYBE, BUT...

These celebrated Renaissance men dabbled in alchemy, and in doing so stumbled on legitimate scientific discoveries.

The Alchemist	The Claim	The Legacy
Albertus Magnus, German philosopher and theologian	Said he witnessed the creation of gold by transmutation	Discovered arsenic, experimented with photosensitive chemicals
Paracelsus, Swiss physician	Proposed that the Roman god of fire, Vulcan, should be the patron god of alchemy	The father of modern medical research; pioneered the use of chemicals in medicine
Isaac Newton, English physicist and mathematician	Supposedly created a recipe for the Philosopher's Stone	Discovered the laws of motion and gravity

THE SKY IS FALLING!

WHEN FISH POURED DOWN ON AN AUSTRALIAN TOWN, RESIDENTS WERE SHOCKED. SCIENTISTS, NOT SO MUCH.

WHO KNEW?

The expression "It's raining cats and dogs" used to refer to a heavy downpour. It is not clear where the saying came from, but many languages have similar sayings for a very heavy rain.

The day it rained fish on Lajamanu, Australia, residents described the scene as biblical, or like a made-for-TV movie. Hundreds and hundreds of fish descended from the sky on the remote desert outback town in Northern Territory. "They were all alive when they hit the ground, so they would have been alive when they were up there flying around the sky," marveled one local.

The precipitation may have been unusual for Lajamanu, but it was just one of many recorded cases of animal downpours that have included frogs, fish, worms, and snakes. Some scientists explain the phenomenon in meteorological terms. They claim that these animals—small, light, and usually aquatic—are picked up in a waterspout, tornado, or strong wind, carried to a height of 40,000 feet, then dropped many miles away.

Believers in the paranormal, however, suggest the events are the work of aliens, or caused by shifts in time and space. They point to several holes in the waterspout theories:

1. Waterspouts, which are composed of water droplets formed by condensation from the surrounding air, cannot lift anything more than light surface debris, and cannot transport it any distance.

2. Likewise, tornadoes do not "carry" items hundreds of miles and do not really lift anything into their column of moving air. Instead, they simply pick up debris and hurl it outward. Typically, such matter is destroyed by the time it lands.

3. Creatures that fall from the sky are often isolated into specific groups: only frogs, or only fish, or only worms fall in one location. If the waterspout/tornado hypothesis were correct, wouldn't people experience a variety of pond or ocean organisms raining down on them?

4. Although many people have reported incidents of "raining animals," no one has ever witnessed a waterspout or tornado picking up a pond's worth of living creatures and carrying them all thousands of feet through the air.

5. The waterspout/tornado hypothesis depends on an actual storm, or at least strong winds. Yet, many cases of animal rainfall have reportedly occurred in fair weather.

An artist's rendering of a fish storm.

FISH KEEP FALLING ON MY HEAD

For more than two hundred years, countries around the world have reported storms of various creatures.

FISH

→ In June 1901, hundreds of **small fish** fell during a heavy rain in Tiller's Ferry, South Carolina. Afterward, they were found swimming in pools of water that had accumulated between cotton rows.

→ In October 1947, **fish fell** on the town of Marksville, Louisiana. It was not raining at the time, and the weather was described as calm.

→ Residents of Kandanassery, India, were stunned in February 2008 when **small fish** began raining down at the end of a sudden downpour.

FROGS

→ In September 1953, a downpour of **frogs and toads** fell in Leicester, Massachusetts, choking rain gutters.

→ In June 2009, officials and scientists were baffled by the **downpour of tadpoles** in Ishikawa, Japan.

→ Horrified shoppers thought they had gone crazy when a **shower of frogs** fell on them in a thunderstorm in Rákóczifalva, Hungary, in June 2010.

WORMS AND SPIDERS

→ *Scientific American* from February 1891 reported that **worms fell** from the sky in Randolph County, West Virginia.

→ Large, tangled **clumps of worms** fell from the sky over Jennings, Louisiana, in July 2007.

→ In April 2007, **spiders** were reported falling from the heavens in Salta, Argentina.

BRIGHT LIGHTS
SMALL TOWN

FOR OVER 100 YEARS, A STRANGE SIGHT IN THE WEST TEXAS
SKY HAS AWED WITNESSES AND STUMPED SCIENTISTS.

Dusk has fallen. A dozen cars have pulled to the side of a desert highway, their passengers expectant. Nine miles east of the tiny town of Marfa, Texas, they've come to watch the mystery lights.

No one disputes that these strange lights exist. But what are they, and where are they from?

Back in 1883, a rancher reported seeing the lights from a spot in the desert, and they still appear to this day. Observers describe them as luminous spheres usually about a foot across. Sometimes, though, they grow from basketball-size to up to ten feet in diameter. They range in color from reddish-orange to yellow to blue and vary in brightness from a pale glow to a spotlight glare. They appear singly or in clusters, sometimes splitting to form more lights. They fly around the sky at high speeds, moving up and down unpredictably. Sometimes the lights pursue people, but if you chase them, they retreat or fade away.

By far the most popular theory about the Marfa mystery lights is that they emanate from UFOs. Another is that the lights are evidence of top-secret government experiments. Some identify the lights as supernatural beings.

Scientists, of course, brush such notions aside, preferring to call the lights "anomalous luminous phenomena" (ALPs). They propose that the lights result from natural causes or are optical illusions. But they have found no definitive answer so far.

Glow-in-the-Dark Bunnies

One of the weirder explanations for the Marfa mystery lights is that they're jack-rabbits that have come into contact with phosphorescent dust or have eaten plants growing near phosphorescent gas deposits. Radioactivity remains a common thread in many theories. The nearby Marfa Army Airfield, a shut-down World War II training base, is said to be a secret chemical dumping ground. Even some scientists suggest that the lights are radioactive bursts.

Ghosts or supernatural beings are another popular theory. Perhaps the lights are the spirits of Apache Indians who roam the desert. Or the lights are what remains of a rancher whose family was tortured and murdered: The rancher haunts the area, carrying a lantern to search for them.

Natural phenomena such as solar storms or ball lightning have also been suggested as sources, as have man-made phenomena, including high-powered ranch lights. Many scientists favor a combination theory: The mystery lights are the distorted glare of car headlights. A 2004 study by the Society of Physics Students found conclusively that the lights appear to observers at the Marfa Lights Viewing Area, a special roadside structure from which to see the spectacle, exactly when vehicles are passing through the main area of light activity, up to 30 miles away.

The apparently floating and erratic movement of the lights arises from a phenomenon called temperature inversion.

That sounds about right, except for one thing: How to account for sightings before the invention of the automobile. Maybe they're radioactive rabbits after all.

The town of Marfa is proud of its unusual phenomenon.

MARFA'S MYSTERY LIGHTS
VIEWING AREA
1 MILE

WHO KNEW?

The Marfa Lights Viewing Area, built in 2003, was designed by students at Marfa High School.

Mystery lights have been spotted on every continent. Are they natural or supernatural?

Naga Fireballs, Thailand
Each October, hundreds of mystery lights appear along a 60-mile stretch of the Mekong River. Locals believe they are the breath of the *Naga*, a mythical river serpent who awakens once a year. Earthly explanations include army tracer rounds fired from over the Laos border and methane gas released by the river.

Hessdalen Light, Norway
Two hundred miles north of Oslo, a bright light appears on the horizon several times a year, often hovering for an hour or more. UFO believers say it's a spaceship, while scientists say the light emanates from quartz crystals under tectonic pressure, or is radioactive dust.

Min-Min Lights, Australia
These Queensland mystery lights vary in color and shape and reportedly follow and approach observers. Aborigine folklore tells of ghost lights believed to be ancestors, gods, or demons. Scientists say they are car headlights.

233

STRANGE SOUNDS AND STRANGER SILENCE

MYSTERIOUS HUMMING, EERIE RADIO SILENCE...
IN CERTAIN AREAS, THE LAWS OF SOUND TRAVEL
JUST DON'T APPLY.

WHO KNEW?
According to the *Guinness Book of World Records*, the quietest place on earth is a soundproof room, called an anechoic chamber, at Orfield Laboratories in Minneapolis, Minnesota.

Zona del Silencio landscape, North Mexico.

The story of the Mapimí Silent Zone goes like this: Back in 1970, the United States launched a test missile from the Green River military base in Utah toward the White Sands Missile Range in New Mexico. They missed. The rocket went awry, landing 400 miles south in the Mapimí desert in the northwestern Mexican state of Durango. The U.S. military eventually found the rocket, dug it out of the sand, and built a road to transport it back home. But soon the story began to spread that there was something special about Mapimí. According to local lore, it was the site of a magnetic vortex that pulled things out of the sky—missiles, meteorites, and even radio waves. Supposedly, the magnetic energy in the area made radio transmission impossible.

In the years since, the zone, located within the Mapimí Biosphere Reserve, has become a destination for tourists who like to take home rocks and other natural souvenirs, not to mention leaving behind trash. Their visits have upset conservationists seeking to maintain the reserve, a fragile desert environment protected by the United Nations Educational, Scientific, and Cultural Organization (UNESCO).

The Sound and the Fury

A thousand miles to the north, at the opposite end of the noise spectrum, there's the Hum, a weird vibration with seemingly no source, which only certain people can hear. Reports of the maddening phenomenon, often described as similar to the distant idling of a truck engine, began to surface in the early 1990s in Taos, New Mexico.

Eventually, at the behest of local officials, a team of scientists came to Taos to investigate but could come up with no logical explanation for the Hum: It wasn't seismic, it wasn't electromagnetic, and it wasn't in the ears of those who heard it, caused by a medical condition such as tinnitus. Microphones didn't even detect it.

To protect the Robert C. Byrd Green Bank Telescope in Green Bank, West Virginia, from radio interference, the FCC designated a 13,000 square mile National Radio Quiet Zone around it.

Highway lights can shut off mysteriously.

RUNNING INTERFERENCE

Lots of places on and above Earth seem to be strangely affected by electromagnetic disturbances.

PHENOMENON **Street Lamp Interference**

WHAT HAPPENS Some people, who call themselves SLIders, claim that public streetlights routinely turn off when they are near.

WHY Believers say it's telekinesis; skeptics say it's just coincidence.

PHENOMENON **The South Atlantic Anomaly**

WHAT HAPPENS When satellites and spacecraft pass through a particular area about 125 miles above the Atlantic Ocean off the coast of Brazil, their systems can malfunction; some astronauts report seeing hallucinations.

WHY The area has a high level of natural radiation.

PHENOMENON **I-4 Dead Zone**

WHAT HAPPENS Drivers on this "haunted" highway across a bridge near Orlando, Florida, say there's no cell reception, or that their phones pick up unearthly voices.

WHY Some people posit interference from nearby power plants.

The source of the Hum, which has also been reported in other areas of the U.S. and in the U.K. and elsewhere, remains elusive. One theory is that those who can hear it are delusional, or just especially conscious of plain old background noise. But some people insist that the Taos Hum is caused by aliens or secret military activity.

SORRY, NO SERVICE

When you enter the zone of silence in West Virginia, don't bother trying to use your cell.

If you've ever longed to escape your smartphone, there is a perfect destination for you. The National Radio Quiet Zone is a designated 13,000-square-mile area in West Virginia that encompasses much of the Monongahela and George Washington National Forests, the town of Harrisonburg, and a swath of Interstate 81. Within the Zone, there is no Wi-Fi service and only the barest, low-frequency radio transmission. Don't bother to check your cell; you won't see any bars.

It's a seemingly bizarre phenomenon with a very simple explanation: The government established the Quiet Zone in the late 1950s to protect the nearby Robert C. Byrd Green Bank Telescope. This huge, supersensitive piece of equipment measures energy waves from far out in space, but it will also pick up any hint of electromagnetic interference nearby. Those who live in the area communicate the old-fashioned way, using dial-up phones, ham radios, and face-to-face conversation.

TARGET EARTH

AN EXPLOSION IN SIBERIA MORE POWERFUL THAN AN ATOMIC BOMB: WAS IT A COMET, ASTEROID, OR ALIEN ATTACK?

Nikola Tesla in his Colorado laboratory with his "magnifying transmitter" in 1899.

On June 30, 1908, at about 7:40 AM, an enormous fiery explosion lit up the sky at 15,000 to 30,000 feet over central Siberia in Russia, near the Podkamennaya Tunguska River. The blast charred more than 38 square miles of forest and flattened some 500,000 acres. Local people of the Evenk culture believed the event was a curse visited on them by a god.

Terrified eyewitnesses nearby reported seeing a fiery ball on the horizon, followed by a cloud of smoke; they heard a thunderous boom and several deafening bangs. The ground trembled violently and hot winds rushed across the region. People as far away as northern Europe and Central Asia saw brilliant-colored sunsets, luminescent night skies, and huge silvery clouds. Seismic waves were recorded in Western Europe.

Investigations Inconclusive

For more than a century, scientists have debated the cause of the Tunguska event. Accepted wisdom is that a cosmic body exploded above Siberia, but no fragments have ever been found and no impact craters have been discovered. Some scientists, citing the luminous, multicolored cloud formations in European skies afterward, concluded that the rapid vaporization of an exploding comet caused a sudden influx of ice crystals into the upper atmosphere. Other scientists theorized that a 150- to 300-foot stony or carbonaceous asteroid exploded in the atmosphere, creating the massive fireball.

The Russian scientist Leonid Alekseyevich Kulik first investigated the site between 1927 and 1930. Members of his expedition came upon a marshy bog below the epicenter of the explosion, surrounded by scorched devastation and little evidence of regrowth. Felled, splintered trees lay in a ten- to 20-mile radius with their tips pointing away. Although other groups of scientists visited the site between 1958 and 1961, with an additional Italian-Russian expedition in 1999, no one has come up with an explanation for the blast.

The Tesla Connection and UFO Theories

Some people believe that the Tunguska explosion was the result of the activities of Nikola Tesla (1856–1943), the Serbian-American who discovered the rotating magnetic field, developed the three-phase electric-power-transmission system,

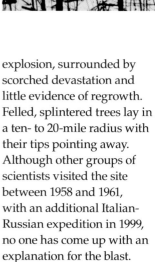

Tunguska damage in Siberia, Russia.

WHO KNEW?

NASA's @Asteroidwatch Twitter feed has more than a million followers.

and invented the Tesla coil. The Tesla electric car is named for him. Rumors of his other discoveries and their possible uses have circulated for years. Some theorized that an unknown government was experimenting with Tesla's theories and test-firing an energy weapon.

An alternative thesis: Earth was a target from beyond. Some paranormal theorists said the event might have been the result of a crashed UFO or a deliberate warning attack by malicious extraterrestrials. Others speculated that a UFO deliberately collided with an approaching cosmic body in an attempt by benign extraterrestrials to save Earth from disaster.

COSMIC MATTERS

Watch out for a basketball-size object from outer space.

The impact of a large comet or asteroid 65 million years ago may have caused the extinction of the dinosaurs. The Tunguska event, if it was in fact caused by a cosmic collision, was the largest such occurrence in modern human history and stands as a grim foreboding of the ongoing threat from outer space. If the explosion had occurred over a large metropolis, hundreds of thousands of people would have died instantly.

At NASA's Jet Propulsion Laboratory, managed by the California Institute of Technology, scientists watch for asteroids, comets, and other space rocks orbiting near earth. According to researchers there, our planet is bombarded daily by more than 100 tons of cosmic matter, mostly dust and tiny particles. We sometimes see these as meteors, or shooting stars, when they burn up on entering earth's atmosphere.

- About once daily, a basketball-size object makes its way into our airspace.
- A few times a year, a fragment the size of a small car enters earth's atmosphere, creating a dazzling fireball.
- On rare occasions, sizable fragments impact the earth's surface, becoming meteorites.

HOLE-Y TERROR

Craters around the world bear testimony to the powerful effects of meteorite strikes.

Vredefort Crater, Free State, South Africa
→ Estimated formation: 2 billion years ago
→ Estimated radius: 118 miles
→ Declared UNESCO World Heritage Site, 2005

Popigai Crater, Siberia, Russia
→ Estimated formation: 35.7 million years ago
→ Russian scientists say it contains trillions of carats of diamonds

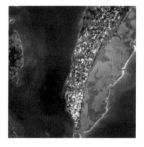

Chesapeake Bay Crater, Virginia, United States
→ Estimated formation: 35 million years ago
→ Estimated radius: 53 miles wide
→ Created the Chesapeake Bay

SELF REFLECTION

HOW TO EXPLAIN MYSTERIOUS HUMAN AND RELIGIOUS IMAGERY THAT MATERIALIZES IN UNEXPECTED PLACES?

WHO KNEW?

The Galle crater on Mars is known as the "happy face crater" because of the illusion of a smiley face created by the mountain ranges that form it.

Many people look up at the night sky and see the man in the moon; others identify strange faces in ceiling cracks or familiar ones in cloud formations. The visions are not the product of overly active imaginations. Humans are actually hardwired to see faces in random visual patterns, whether in nature or in man-made objects such as the grille of a car. The scientific term for the phenomenon is *pareidolia*.

Most explanations of pareidolia are centered on innate survival tactics. One of the first things a newborn baby can recognize is a human face, so it is hypothesized that humans' keen ability to detect faces, even when they aren't there, may be embedded in our DNA. Perhaps our ancient ancestors needed to differentiate friends from foes with split-second accuracy and this facility for "pattern recognition" helped them stay alive.

The flipside of the brain's pattern-recognition machinery is that people sometimes see faces where there are none, as scientist and author Carl Sagan has pointed out. The phenomenon could play a role in humans' tendency to see the face of significant religious figures such as Jesus or the Virgin Mary in unexpected places.

The Shroud of Turin

The Shroud of Turin, the ancient linen cloth bearing a faint image of what some perceive as Jesus's face and body in reddish-brown blood stains, is one of the most studied objects in human history.

Housed in a the Cathedral of St. John the Baptist in Turin, Italy, the shroud, with its ghostly skeletal imagery of a naked man, has been controversial since it was first observed in 1898. Believers have argued that the shroud was used as Jesus's burial cloth because what seem like wound impressions are consistent with those of a crucifixion. Skeptics have been equally ardent, countering that the supposed relic is a forgery.

In 1978, scientists from the U.S. government's Los Alamos National Laboratory and Jet Propulsion Laboratory sought to put the debate to rest when they initiated the Shroud of Turin Research Project (STURP). The test results, released in 1981, were less than definitive. While the scientists determined that the stains were real blood and the impressions those of a crucified man, they also cautioned that "there are no chemical or physical methods known which can account for the totality of the image." The identity of the man could not be determined.

Subsequent testing dated the cloth to the medieval period, disqualifying it as Jesus's shroud—results that were rejected by the faithful, who say the test was unreliable and the sample may have been damaged by fungus or smoke. Today, there is no general consensus on how the skeletal image came to be fixed on the cloth.

Floor Plans

In 1971, María Gómez Cámara recoiled when a terrifying face appeared in the concrete floor of her family's home in Andalusia, Spain. The image became known as La Pava and was the first and most famous of the "Bélmez faces," a series of human images said to have formed and disappeared in the house without human intervention. Considered by some parapsychologists as the 20th century's best-documented and most important paranormal phenomenon, the faces have drawn large numbers of sightseers to the town.

Witnesses say that even after a new concrete floor was poured, La Pava reappeared. "Wherever you stood, the face watched you," said Gómez Cámara, who died in 2004. "Only God knows why the faces appeared to me."

Some investigators believe the faces were a "thoughtographic" phenomenon, that Gómez Cámara psychically "burned" images from her mind onto the concrete. Other skeptics maintain that the faces were simple forgeries, formed by human hands. Ramos Perera, president of the Spanish Society of Parapsychology, has stated that tests found properties of La Pava's coloration indicating that it was in fact hand-painted.

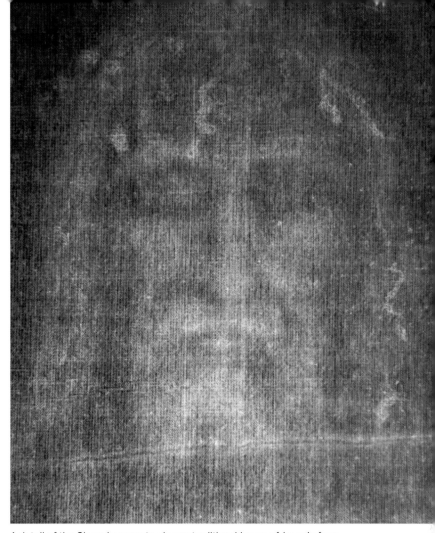

A detail of the Shroud seems to show a traditional image of Jesus's face.

HOLY VISIONS

The devout may turn their gifts for pattern recognition into miraculous sightings.

Jesus's face in a pancake.

For centuries people have said they've seen Jesus's face in everyday objects, including food. Some more recent sightings include one by a North Carolina woman who discovered what she believed to be the face of Jesus in her grilled cheese sandwich.

A Glendale, Arizona, woman saw the face of the Virgin Mary in a pancake she was making for breakfast; others have seen Jesus in pancakes.

A Splendora, Texas, woman claimed to see the head, hair, and cloak of Jesus in bathroom mold. "People say my house is blessed," she told ABC News.

While cleaning her toilet, a Las Vegas woman noticed Jesus's likeness in an "I Love Vegas" bumper sticker plastered on the lid.

FACES ON THE BRAIN

Brain dysfunction can affect our perceptions in ways we don't always realize.

The fusiform gyrus is the area of the brain that governs facial recognition. It enables humans to identify the emotions being expressed by particular facial expressions. Damage to this area may result in a disorder known as *prosopagnosia*, the loss of ability to recognize faces.

THE ROD SQUAD

BIZARRE, STICK-LIKE CREATURES WHIZ ACROSS THE SKY AT LIGHTNING SPEED. WHAT COULD THEY BE?

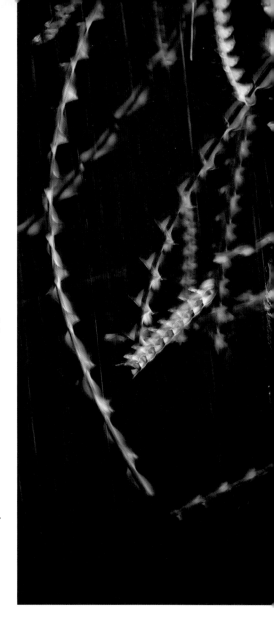

SKY HIGH

When some fast-moving creatures gave Indiana a scare.

Did the residents of Crawsfordsville, Indiana, behold a mysterious flying rod back in 1891? On two separate occasions that year, townspeople reported seeing a finned, serpentine creature, about 18 feet long and eight feet wide, hovering hundreds of feet above them. According to the local newspaper, "There was no tail or head visible, but there was one great flaming eye, and a sort of a wheezing plaintive sound was emitted from a mouth which was invisible." The paper went on to report that two eyewitnesses followed the creature around town and eventually discovered that it was a flock of birds, most likely disoriented by the area's newly installed electric lights.

In 1994, a Roswell, New Mexico, filmmaker named Jose Escamilla was researching UFOs with his wife in the nearby town of Midway. While reviewing footage, he noticed something strange: a cylindrical streak through the frame. Escamilla assumed at first that his camera had caught a fast-moving insect or bird, but when he examined the footage, he ruled those things out. Thus began his journey into the mystery of "rods," named by his wife for their shape.

Escamilla, who has since filmed other examples of his discovery, describes rods as barely visible "cigar- or cylindrical-shaped objects" that "travel at extremely high velocities." He says they range from a few inches to 100 or more feet in length. He has identified three different types: white and ribbonlike; thin, ultrafast, and spearlike; and rods that have what look like multiple blurry fins or wings along their length.

Caught on Tape

Escamilla is not the only person to make note of rods, which are also sometimes referred to as skyfish, solar entities, or flying rods. In the 1950s, the UFO writer

Trevor James Constable used infrared film to record what he called "critters." A professional videographer named Mark Lichtle inadvertently captured one of the most famous examples of the phenomenon in 1996, while shooting the extreme sport BASE jumping in Mexico. Escamilla saw Lichtle's footage on television and noticed something strange in the background. Sure enough, when he analyzed the video, he saw what looked liked hundreds of rods swimming through the air. They were darting around the jumpers so quickly they couldn't be seen without video equipment.

Moths attracted by a floodlight appear as rods.

A mass of flying gnats. As they change speed, they appear as flying rods with rotating wings.

Escamilla established a website about rods and started lecturing on the topic. Since then, people from around the world have reported sightings and have come forward with more video and photographs. Some people believe rods are a type of extraterrestrial life; others think they may be military weapons or UFOs. Still others suspect that they're time-traveling beings from another dimension.

The Truth About Rods

Skepticism about rods abounds in the scientific and even pseudoscientific communities. The writer Cecil Adams, a noted debunker, maintains in his syndicated question-and-answer newspaper column, "The Straight Dope," that rods are simply insects. Each video or film frame captures several beats of the insect's wings, making the insect look like an elongated creature with blurred bulges along its length. In 2008, the cable television series *MonsterQuest* devoted an episode to rods, spotlighting several videos believed to contain evidence of them. The show's verdict: The rods were simply distorted images of ordinary bugs.

PRAIRIE PREDATORS

WHAT KIND OF MONSTER—HUMAN OR OTHERWISE— WOULD MUTILATE GRAZING LIVESTOCK?

THEY'VE GOT A BEEF

Natural causes? No way, say doubters. Here are some common alternative theories about the mutilations.

→ They're the work of various sick, twisted individuals who kill for fun.

→ They're ritual sacrifices carried out by organized groups or Satanic cults.

→ The U.S. government kills the livestock while conducting covert research on Mad Cow disease. This theory has been fueled by helicopter sightings near mutilation sites.

→ Aliens mutilate the cattle to gather genetic material, harvest hormones, and/or perform experiments on mammals.

→ It's the work of bloodthirsty supernatural creatures called chupacabras.

Some of the bodies had been seemingly drained of blood. In some cases, organs had been removed. And there were no tracks or footprints to provide clues to the perpetrators.

One thing people were sure of: The livestock had not been mutilated by wolves, coyotes, or other natural scavengers or predators. As a Colorado sheriff told a United Press International reporter in 1976, "My staff was all raised on farms and ranches. We know what a predator will do. We've seen these mutilated critters, and there's just no way."

For decades, beginning in the late 1960s, farms and ranches in the United States and Canada have been plagued by the random, gruesome, and mysterious mutilation of cattle and sometimes horses and sheep. The phenomenon peaked in the 1970s, when shocked and baffled residents of more than a dozen states, including Mon-

SPREADING RUMORS

When it comes to propagating theories about the paranormal, the news media can be a gossip machine.

Though cattle mutilation was big news in the 1970s, there are still unexplained instances of it today—at least, that's what news reports would have us believe. Between 2011 and 2013, for example, a Missouri rancher found three of her Black Angus cattle dead and seemingly mutilated. Organs had been removed with "surgical precision," various news outlets reported, and there was no blood near the carcasses, nor any sign of attack by animals. The rancher said the sheriff's department and a veterinarian had investigated the deaths, but since they couldn't provide a definitive answer, she wasn't ruling out something more out of the ordinary. The media was quick to report that she suspected cults or extraterrestrials—though that may be the reporters' conclusion, not the rancher's.

Cattle graze near Crested Butte, Colorado.

tana, Colorado, Minnesota, and Kansas, discovered previously healthy livestock lying dead in pastures. And the animals weren't just dead: They had wounds that seemed bizarrely surgical and precise. Locals began to worry: Was this the work of a Satanic cult—or even of aliens?

To add fuel to the fire, the Colorado owner of a mutilated horse nicknamed "Snippy" had reported strange markings on the ground nearby, as if extraterrestrials had landed there.

Calling in the Authorities

In 1975, Floyd Haskell, a Colorado senator, asked the FBI for help. There had been 130 instances of livestock mutilation in his state alone, he wrote, and "the ranchers and rural residents of Colorado are concerned and frightened by these incidents." Although the FBI did not have jurisdiction to investigate, a few years later, in 1979,

the state of New Mexico launched Operation Animal Mutilation, an investigation led by a former FBI agent named Kenneth Rommel.

His conclusion: The supposedly mutilated livestock had, in fact, died of natural causes and had been consumed by garden-variety scavengers. Scavenger animals tend to first consume the softest parts of a carcass (as in the organs). As for the seeming lack of blood: It had simply dried up and coagulated inside the carcass. "In short," Rommel wrote, "during my investigation of the 117 mutilations that have been reported in New Mexico since 1975, I have not found one single case which, after careful scrutiny of available evidence, could be confirmed as a 'classic mutilation.'"

Not surprisingly, his conclusions were met with skepticism by those who believed that the livestock deaths had a more sinister, possibly supernatural, cause.

An illustration of a UFO in the upper atmosphere.

CHAPTER 15
ALIENS AND UFOS

"THE UNIVERSE IS A PRETTY BIG PLACE," ASTRONOMER AND ASTROPHYSICIST CARL SAGAN ONCE SAID. "IF IT'S JUST US, THAT SEEMS LIKE AN AWFUL WASTE OF SPACE."

CLOSE ENCOUNTERS

ACCORDING TO EYEWITNESS ACCOUNTS, THE SKIES ARE FULL
EXOTIC EMISSARIES FROM WORLDS FAR BEYOND OUR OWN.

By definition, anything spotted in the sky that can't be explained as an astrological phenomenon or a man-made device is a UFO, an Unidentified Flying Object. Most reported sightings are explained away by experts as planets, meteors, clouds, mirages, aircraft, or satellites, but an estimated 5 to 20 percent of reported UFOs remain a mystery.

Typically the objects appear to be metallic flying discs or saucers, bright lights, or flying triangles. They tend to move irregularly—hovering, climbing steeply, and/or flying rapidly—and sometimes they seem to be following human vehicles.

Interplanetary Paranoia

UFOs are popularly assumed to be alien spacecraft controlled by extraterrestrials who sometimes abduct humans in order to study them. Witnesses have claimed to have seen nonhumans piloting UFOs or busying themselves around craft that have landed. Government agencies in the U.S. and around the world have investigated UFOs,

ALIENS IN THE SKY

Alleged UFO sightings and encounters with aliens have cropped up regularly across the United States since the turn of the 20th century. Here are some of the numerous reported but unproven sightings.

Helmer, Indiana, 1903
A glowing cigar-shaped object with two rows of windows hovers in the sky before rapidly zigzagging away.

San Francisco, California, 1904 Three huge, bright-red flying objects are spotted by crew of the U.S.S. *Supply*.

Lewes, Delaware, 1908
A radiant, metallic cloud envelopes and magnetizes a ship, causing the vessel to glow; the ship's compass spins and the crew's hair stands on end.

Youngstown, Pennsylvania, 1917 A boy sees a lighted, domed, saucer-shaped object in a field and watches it take off with a high-pitched sound.

Salt Lake City, Utah, 1926
An airmail pilot is forced to land by a gigantic cylindrical craft.

Roswell, New Mexico, 1947
A flying saucer crashes; the U.S. military allegedly recovers the UFO and its alien crew, but denies the incident.

Washington, D.C., 1952
Local airports report several sightings of and radar contacts with UFOs.

Levelland, Texas, 1957
There are numerous reports of glowing, egg- and cigar-shaped objects that shut down the engines of cars and trucks.

Lancaster, New Hampshire, 1961 Betty and Barney Hill claim to have been abducted by small beings in a huge flying disk; the Hills say they were examined before being returned to earth.

Leary, Georgia, 1969 Future president Jimmy Carter sees a UFO.

at various times concluding that there is indeed a possibility that they are of alien origins. In recent decades, though, a number of nations, including the U.S., have shut down their UFO-related agencies and defunded most official research. Government officials claim that, for all of the effort and money that has gone into research, the existence of extra-terrestrial life has never been proven.

In response, UFOlogists—those dedicated to studying the phenomena—have developed various conspiracy theories suggesting that governments are engaged in a massive cover-up. American UFO advocates have even petitioned the government to admit as much, though no such admission seems to be forthcoming. In November 2011, the White House released a statement that there is "no credible information to suggest that any evidence is being hidden from the public's eye," and that "the odds of us making contact with [extraterrestrials]—especially any intelligent ones—are extremely small, given the distances involved.

This composite image depicts a UFO flying over the desert, where many such sightings have been reported.

Eglin Air Force Base, Florida, 1973 Military radar tracks four UFOs flying in formation along a highway; numerous witnesses report glowing balls of light.

New Caney, Texas, 1980 A diamond-shaped UFO accompanied by U.S. military helicopters is seen by Betty Cash and Vickie Landrum, who are later treated for radiation poisoning.

Copely Woods, Indiana, 1983 Strange marks are found on the scene after numerous witnesses see hundreds of glowing, basketball-size objects.

Anchorage, Alaska, 1986 Japan Airlines flight 1628 is followed by three UFOs for 50 minutes; one object is seen on military radar.

Bovina, Texas, 1995 America West Airlines flight 564 is followed by a gigantic cigar-shaped UFO equipped with strobe light.

Phoenix, Arizona, 1997 Witnesses including Governor Fife Symington report seeing UFOs of various sizes and shapes during the so-called Phoenix Lights incident.

Highland, Illinois, 2000 Police officers and civilian witnesses in five locations see an immense, wedge-shaped UFO hovering silently and flying at high velocity.

Tinley Park, Illinois, 2004–2006 A triangular array of red lights is seen by hundreds of witnesses, on three separate dates, over Chicago's O'Hare International Airport.

Chicago, Illinois, 2006 United Airlines employees report seeing a UFO hovering above gate C-17 at O'Hare International Airport.

Stephenville, Texas, 2008 A large UFO is spotted by 30 residents, headed toward the Crawford, Texas, ranch of President George W. Bush.

New York, New York, 2010 White, cylindrical UFOs are seen flying over the city by hundreds of witnesses.

Loganville, Georgia, 2013 A woman and two girls see three enormous glowing orbs hovering and moving slowly.

INVENTING ALIENS

NOTIONS OF HOW EXTRATERRESTRIALS LOOK AND ACT HAVE EVOLVED OVER TIME TO REFLECT HUMAN CULTURE.

It isn't hard to imagine ancient stargazers looking up and wondering whether others like them were somewhere out there. But it wasn't until the publication of *The War of the Worlds* in 1898 that Americans got their first exhaustive popular-culture description of what these creatures might look like. The invading Martians in H.G. Wells's science-fiction classic resembled octopi, with large heads, tentacles, and a single ear. They were smart and they were nasty, hoping to take over Earth for their own use. When CBS famously broadcast a radio adaptation of the novel in 1938, the story tapped into the fears of a nation already made anxious by the growing threat from Nazi Germany.

The scientific advancements of the 1950s, as well as the Cold War, brought widespread interest in space travel and exploration. Alien invaders began to pop up in movies looking decidedly human. From *Earth vs. the Flying Saucers* (1956) to *Invasion of the Body Snatchers* (1956) in which aliens took over the bodies of the people in a small town, the plots were metaphors for our fear of nuclear war. In *The Day the Earth Stood Still* (1951), aliens come to give Earthlings a warning: Either surrender your nuclear weapons or face destruction by other planets.

Star Trek and Star Wars

In the 1960s, aliens got more cuddly. *Star Trek*'s U.S.S. *Enterprise* had multicultural characters, women crewmembers, and a pointy-eared Vulcan–human hybrid, Dr. Spock. The group worked together to navigate conflicts with other alien races on an altruistic mission that encapsulated the progressive, civil rights–minded spirit of the era.

The kinder, gentler alien life form continued through the *Star Wars* films (1977–2005), with their interplanetary cast of thinking, feeling aliens and robots. Notably, the most sinister characters, Darth Vader and his Stormtroopers, were humans—as was also the case with *E.T.* In Steven Spielberg's 1982 drama, the cute, stranded alien who only wanted to go home was relentlessly pursued by humans obsessed with

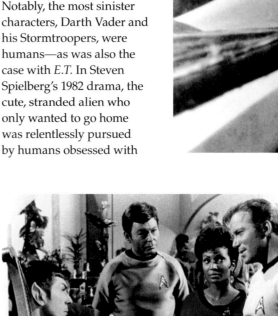

Leonard Nimoy, Deforest Kelley, Nichelle Nichols, and William Shatner in a scene from *Star Trek* (1969).

Klatu, Patricia Neal, and Michael Rennie in *The Day The Earth Stood Still* (1951).

The bar scene from *Star Wars*.

OBI-WAN, MEET HAN

Has there ever been a more memorable group of aliens assembled in one place than the cantina sequence of the 1977 *Star Wars* film?

Luke Skywalker and Obi-Wan Kenobi first meet Han Solo and his Wookie companion, Chewbacca, at a dive bar on the desolate planet of Tatooine. But they also encounter a number of other drinking, dancing, fighting and canoodling creatures of the reptilian, one-eyed, arachnid, and wolfish varieties:

→ **Greedo**, the green bounty hunter from Rodia

→ **Ponda Baba**, the walrus-like Aqualish smuggler from Ando

→ The hammerheaded Ithorian **Momaw Nadon**

→ The all-Bith cantina band the **Modal Nodes**

→ **Jawas, Lutrillians**, and sundry other life forms

studying him. There was no ambiguity as to who the bad guys were. That trend has continued with the benevolent blue-skinned Na'vi of 2009's *Avatar*.

It's not surprising that we often imagine aliens looking and acting human. In the absence of any concrete evidence of extraterrestrial life, we look to ourselves as frames of reference. It seems that in popular culture, at least, intelligent life forms have come a long way.

MORE ICONIC ALIENS

These fictional extraterrestrials continue to live long and prosper in our collective imagination.

Superman (1938–present)
Make that Super*alien*: This Marvel Comics character is a native of the planet Krypton.

Marvin the Martian (1948–1991)
The *Looney Tunes* extraterrestrial is clever, cunning, hilarious, and out to destroy Earth.

Dr. Who (1963–present)
A time-traveling, shape-shifting humanoid scientist from planet Gallifrey, he battles evil adversaries on TV.

The *Alien* aliens (1979)
The grotesque parasites in this horror movie gestate in human bodies.

The *Men In Black* extraterrestrials (1997–2012) In these comedies, the world is full of bug-like, slug-esque, furry, multi-armed, and just plain creepy aliens.

The *District 9* prawns (2009)
Massive and lobster-shaped, they're detained in a militarized zone in South Africa.

INCIDENT AT
ROSWELL

DID THE U.S. GOVERNMENT COVER UP AN ALIEN VISIT TO
EARTH? FOR DECADES, RUMORS HAVE SWIRLED.

In 1947, near Roswell, New
Mexico…something hap-
pened. And the more the
U.S. government denied it,
the more convinced people
were that "something" was
the crash of an extra-terrestrial craft. The incident,
and the ensuing activity
at a nearby Air Force base
known as Area 51, contin-
ues to fascinate, with new
witnesses coming forward
in recent years to describe
what they saw.

The Discovery
On July 7, 1947, rancher
William Brazel was making
the rounds on his 8,000-acre
property about 70 miles
north of Roswell, New
Mexico. There had been
a terrible lightning storm
three nights earlier, and Brazel was checking his land
and cattle.

As the rancher moved
his herd, he came upon a
strange debris field about "a
quarter mile long and several hundred feet wide," according to his son, Bill. The
area was littered with foil-
like metal pieces covered

in a rubber-like substance
on one side. They were
inscribed with undecipher-
able lettering like Japanese
or Chinese figures, according to Bill. There was also
string, plastic sticks, and
odd light material strewn
across the field.

Brazel contacted the local
sheriff, who in turn contacted an intelligence officer at
Roswell Army Airfield.

The Cleanup
Meanwhile, Glenn Dennis,
an assistant at Ballard Mor-
tuary in Roswell, claimed he
received a strange request
from the Roswell Army
Airfield. The caller wanted
to know if Ballard coffins
could be hermetically sealed
and if the company had
child-sized ones in stock,
according to Dennis. The
funeral home worker said
Ballard did have small coffins, but not the number the
army was requesting.

Later that day, Dennis
said, he saw a number of
military ambulances parked
in the area with their back
doors open, and inside

them, metallic wreckage
and a canoe-shaped object
with strange markings. At
the hospital, Dennis found
things unusually hectic and
asked a nurse what was going on. She told him to leave.
According to Dennis, he
was then confronted by two
military officials who told
him to forget what he'd seen
and that there had been no
aircraft incident. The nurse
who had spoken to him was
transferred to England and
then disappeared, he said.

The Cover-Up
Initially, a U.S. govern-
ment spokesman called the
wreckage a "flying disc," but

This image combines a shot of the New Mexico landscape with an imaginative digital reconstruction to show what eyewitnesses claim to have seen.

officials quickly recanted and said it was a weather balloon. In ensuing decades, numerous ex-military officials came forward with details of an alleged government conspiracy.

Brigadier General Thomas DuBose of the 8th Air Force said, "[It] was a cover story, the whole balloon part of it. That was the story we were told to give to the public and news."

The most popular theory has been that the extraterrestrial wreckage and bodies were transported to Area 51 for study and storage. Supposedly even retired army and air force person-nel have corroborated this, including a retired Army colonel.

In 2013, the Central Intelligence Agency declassified information about Area 51, saying that the base had been used to test a U-2 reconnaissance aircraft. The spy plane, which flew at 70,000 feet, was misidentified by witnesses, according to the documents.

The new information has not silenced the many conspiracy theorists who believe there's much more to Roswell than Americans have been led to believe. Area 51 is still off limits to visitors.

ALIEN OR MUTANT?

Were the supposed space invaders actually a Cold War plot?

Area 51: An Uncensored History of America's Top Secret Military Base, was published in 2011. The book, by journalist Annie Jacobsen, presented an unusual Cold War theory about the Roswell incident. According to Jacobsen, the downed aircraft was the handiwork of Joseph Stalin, in 1947, the leader of the Soviet Union. Stalin had allegedly commissioned Nazi doctor Josef Mengele to genetically engineer child-size pilots to fly an aircraft to the United States via remote control. The plan was to land the plane and create a *War of the Worlds*–like panic, but a storm intervened, causing the New Mexico crash.

FEAR OF FLYING SAUCERS

THE SPECTER OF UFOS BEARING ALIEN VISITORS FUELED COLD WAR PARANOIA—AND VICE VERSA.

According to the Central Intelligence Agency (CIA), nine out of ten Americans have heard of Unidentified Flying Objects (UFOs), and more than half of them believe that they are real, possibly extraterrestrial in origin. Perhaps it's mere coincidence that the first reported sighting of a UFO happened in 1947, shortly after the advent of the Cold War—or perhaps not.

Americans had long been wary of the Russians, even as the two nations fought side by side in World War II. In the post-war years, when the U.S.S.R. began to expand its sphere of influence, a new ideological fight between democracy and Communism flourished. During this period, dubbed the Cold War, both countries raced to advance atomic weapons and space and military technology. When

one nation scored a victory, such as the Soviet launch of the first artificial Earth satellite, *Sputnik,* in 1957, the other worried it was being outstripped in the battle for supremacy.

The Cold War definitely affected how Americans viewed UFOs. The idea that super-powered aliens might threaten Earth mirrored Americans' fears of the "other"—the Communists. Some suspected UFOs were real visitors from alien civilizations, covered up by the American government, while others thought they were a government fabrication, used to divert the public's attention from military exercises taking place.

Governments and UFOs

There are a number of unverified theories about how governments and UFOs have intersected since the Cold War began.

THEORY 1: The Russian military deliberately attracted UFOs. In 2013, a former top-level defense minister in Russia, Alexey Savin, announced that the Russians had collected information on the appearance of UFOs and attempted to draw UFOs to its base in Vladimirovka, in the hope of harnessing alien brainpower.

THEORY 2: Aliens were acting as peacekeepers during the Cold War, intentionally sabotaging nuclear weapons on both sides to prevent a "hot" war. Nuclear weapons were reported to malfunction inexplicably when a UFO had been sighted nearby. In 1967, for example, a U.S. Air Force captain at the Malmstrom Air Force Base in Montana witnessed a "pulsating red oval-shaped object" hovering near the base's Minuteman missiles. The missiles then mysteriously shut down.

THEORY 3: UFOs weren't real—but the fear of them was used by the CIA. According to David Clarke and Andy Roberts, the authors of *Out of the Shadows,* the CIA "looked at ways of using the public panic over UFOs as a psychological weapon against the Russians."

THEORY 4: UFOs were real—but their existence was covered up by the U.S. and Soviet governments. These authors maintain that since the government officials were unable to explain the UFO sightings, they felt it was better to dismiss them as natural phenomena than to cause panic. A U.S. Air Force report of the 1940s tried to deflect the public's fears, saying UFOs were solar reflections, meteors, or aircraft. In 2013, the Russian

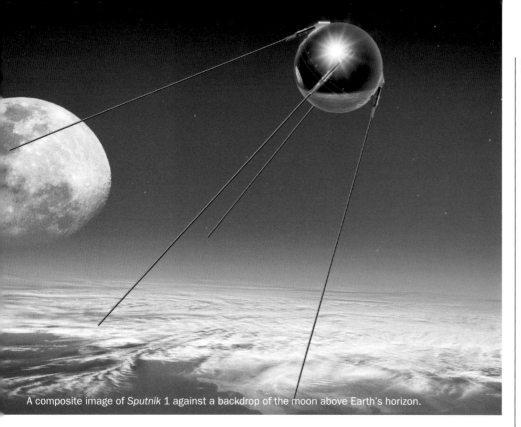

A composite image of *Sputnik* 1 against a backdrop of the moon above Earth's horizon.

navy declassified its records of encounters with UFOs that had been kept since the Cold War. The decades-old documents included reports of suboceanic UFOs, which often appeared where NATO and Soviet fleets were located.

THEORY 5: Rumors of UFO sightings were used by the U.S. government to deflect attention from evidence of covert missions. British journalist Mark Pilkington, author of *Mirage Men: An Adventure into Paranoia, Espionage, Psychological Warfare, and UFOs,* believes that UFO sightings in the early 1950s were radar blips from planned Defense Department missions. That would explain why they so often occurred near military installations.

THE FIRST EYEWITNESS

Like "a saucer if you skip it across water."

On June 24, 1947, private pilot Kenneth Arnold was flying near Mount Rainier in Washington when he spotted a series of nine large objects emanating a bright, blue-white glow. He thought they were military aircraft, especially because he observed that they flew like geese, in "a rather diagonal chain-like line as if they were linked together," as he stated to Army Air Force intelligence. But the military later said there had been no test flights there that day. A prospector working at Mount Adams at the same time, approximately 31 miles away, reported witnessing the same thing. The sighting gave rise to a furor of publicity and has never been explained.

Telegram from Kenneth Arnold.

Kenneth Arnold.

STOLEN AWAY

BETTY AND BARNEY HILL'S EXPERIENCE MAY BE THE MOST FAMOUS REPORTED ABDUCTION IN THE HISTORY OF UFO TALES.

DO YOU KNOW SOMEONE WHO HAS BEEN ABDUCTED BY ALIENS?

Many people who claim to have been abducted by aliens share five traits, according to *Psychology Today* magazine.

→ They regularly experience sleep paralysis and hallucinations as they wake up.

→ They have a tendency to recall false memories.

→ They are highly susceptible to hypnosis and suggestion.

→ They tend to believe in New Age practices such as astrology.

→ They are often familiar with the cultural narrative of alien abduction, as found in folklore and popular culture.

On the night of September 19, 1961, on a deserted road in the White Mountains of New Hampshire, a middle-aged couple was abducted against their will by aliens—or so they insisted. Betty and Barney Hill described the creatures who took them as four to five feet tall and bald, with large eyes, no ears, and small noses. The couple claimed they were taken aboard a pancake-shaped spacecraft and subjected to painful physical and psychological examinations.

According to the Hills' account, they had been returning by car from a vacation in Montreal, Canada, and Niagara Falls, New York. Initially, Betty, a social worker, and Barney, a postal employee, said they had no clear memories of the incident. They arrived home together that evening with two-hour gaps in their memory. Betty's dress was torn and stained; Barney's shoe was scraped. They saw strange marks on their car. A few days later, Betty began

to have excruciating nightmares. She began to research the subject of UFOs, and two years later, the couple began speaking about the incident to others in their Unitarian congregation.

Eventually, such discussions prompted the couple to seek the help of Boston psychiatrist Benjamin Simon. He treated them with hypnotherapy in private sessions separate from one another, during which they each recalled details of the incident.

Dr. Simon taped the sessions, during which Betty can be heard sobbing and Barney screaming in terror. Both husband and wife described being followed by a white, lighted object as they drove. Barney related being especially afraid when he spotted several figures standing at the windows of what appeared to be a circular craft. Betty recalled the aliens inserting a giant needle into her belly button.

Although Dr. Simon treated the Hills for several

months, he remained skeptical that their symptoms were caused by an encounter with extraterrestrials. Instead, he believed the Hills' recall of the events were a fantasy sparked by Betty's dreams. Dr. Simon's tapes of the hypnosis treatments are now stored with other documentation in the Betty and Barney Hill Collection at the University of New Hampshire.

For the rest of her life, Betty Hill researched UFOs and became well known in the field. In 1966, the Hills' story became a best-selling book, *The Interrupted Journey*; in 1975 it was made into a television movie starring James Earl Jones as Barney Hill and Estelle Parsons as Betty.

The tale continues to spark interest among believers and skeptics alike, years after the Hills' passing; Barney died in 1969 and Betty in 2004. Today there is a marker on Route 3 in Lincoln, New Hampshire, at the spot where the alleged encounter occurred.

BETTY AND BARNEY HILL INCIDENT

On the night of September 19-20, 1961, Portsmouth, NH couple Betty and Barney Hill experienced a close encounter with an unidentified flying object and two hours of "lost" time while driving south on Rte 3 near Lincoln. They filed an official Air Force Project Blue Book report of a brightly-lit cigar-shaped craft the next day, but were not public with their story until it was leaked in the Boston Traveler in 1965. This was the first widely-reported UFO abduction report in the United States.

2011

The state marker in Franconia, New Hampshire, where Betty and Barney Hill saw a large, flying disc-shaped object.

Betty and Barney Hill.

RECOVERED MEMORY SYNDROME

Were the Hills' memories real or imagined? Even their hypnotherapist can't say for sure.

While the Hills believed they had experienced a terrifying event, they were unable to recount details until they underwent hypnotherapy. Psychologists refer to such recollections as recovered memories.

Many professionals are skeptical about memories that arise during hypnosis. Research shows that memory itself is highly unreliable and can consist of pure fantasy, and some experiments have demonstrated that memories can be implanted while subjects are in a suggestible hypnotic state.

MOVIE STAR ALIENS

Martians, are you ready for your close-ups? A look at some of Hollywood's unlikeliest scene-stealers.

→ *Communion* **(1989):** Bug-eyed, large-headed extraterrestrials abduct author Whitley Strieber from his remote vacation cabin.

→ *Mars Attacks!* **(1996):** The Martians who invade Earth in this 1996 comedy breathe nitrogen supplied through their life vests or, in the case of the Martian girl infiltrator, through special gum.

→ *Independence Day* **(1996):** Arriving in biomechanical suits that give them superstrength, the aliens in this action adventure thriller have two legs, two arms, a head…and tentacles.

UFO
AT GATE C17

O'HARE INTERNATIONAL AIRPORT IN CHICAGO SERVES MORE THAN 60,000 PASSENGERS A MONTH. IN 2006, IT MAY HAVE HOSTED A UFO AS WELL.

A low-flying unidentified object.

ANCIENT ALIENS?

UFO sightings date to the earliest recorded history.

Location: Rome, Italy
Source: Titus Livius Patavinus
Year: 214 BC

The Roman historian known as Livy wrote about the city from its earliest legends through the reign of Augustus. In his work *Books From the Foundation of the City*, he wrote, "Phantom ships had been seen gleaming in the sky."

Location: Phrygia (now in Turkey)
Source: Plutarch
Year: 74 BC

The Greek historian Plutarch wrote of the sky bursting and a "flame-like body" falling as a Roman army was preparing to engage in battle. The object, the color of molten silver, was reportedly witnessed by the Romans and their enemies.

On the afternoon of November 7, 2006, an employee working on a ramp at Gate C17 at O'Hare, one of the busiest, most heavily trafficked airports in the United States, spotted a mysterious object hovering silently over the terminal. Concerned about safety, the worker reported the object to air traffic control, describing it as dark gray, metallic, and without lights. He estimated the craft to be 6 to 24 feet in diameter and elliptical in shape. Though airport radar detected nothing unusual and no air-traffic controllers observed any alien aircraft, the ramp worker's alert alarmed some employees. Pilots, supervisors, and others raced out to the runway to catch a glimpse.

Jon Hilkevitch, a reporter at the *Chicago Tribune*, broke the story with a January 1, 2007, article reporting that at least 12 reliable United Airlines employees, including senior managers and pilots, substantiated the details of a dark gray, saucer-shaped object above the airport.

The witnesses agreed that the UFO hovered motionlessly for several minutes and then shot off at amazing speed, bursting through the clouds that hovered in the dark, overcast sky. They described it as slicing through the atmosphere, leaving a cylindrical hole through which a brilliant blue sky was visible for several minutes, until the clouds closed up. It was unlikely the craft was a commercial liner, since airplanes do not take off or land in such a manner, the observers said.

The Federal Aviation Administration (FAA), which is mandated to investigate potential security breaches, declined to investigate the reported UFO sighting at O'Hare. Five years later, in February 2011, additional reports of possible UFOs at O'Hare arose, but none of the later sightings were corroborated by such numbers of witnesses.

An illustration of a UFO in the upper atmosphere.

IT'S A BIRD, IT'S A... REFLECTION?

Two sides to every sighting.

Below is a list of arguments and reports from United Airlines employees, the Federal Aviation Administration, and others, both for and against claims that the O'Hare Airport incident involved a UFO.

A UFO!	NOT A UFO!
United Airlines supervisor phoned an FAA manager in the control tower to report a mysterious flying object.	The FAA manager denied receiving the phone call. Following filing of a Freedom of Information Act (FOIA) request by the *Chicago Tribune,* a recording of the call was uncovered.
Twelve United Airlines employees observed the object hovering over the terminal and bursting through the clouds as it sped away.	No air-traffic controllers detected the object on radar or witnessed the event.
Air traffic control must have overlooked the object, as it hovered outside their viewing height.	Air traffic control would have witnessed the object at its reported height.
A cylindrical, gray metallic UFO hovered over the United Airlines terminal for several minutes.	The "object" and its motion were a trick of the eye caused by a reflection of the United Airlines terminal's lights against the overcast sky.

PATROLLING FOR
ALIENS

OUR SEARCH FOR INTELLIGENT LIFE IN THE UNIVERSE
USES PROBES, TELESCOPES, AND CHUCK BERRY TUNES.

Is there anyone else out there? Scientists think so. "The universe is a pretty big place," Carl Sagan once said. "If it's just us, that seems like an awful waste of space."

With that in mind, humans have been doing their best to find and make definitive contact with extraterrestrials. So far, people have done neither. But just in case we run across anybody in our space travels, we're prepared.

We Will Rock You

Take Voyager 1, an unmanned NASA space probe launched in 1977 to study the planets of the outer solar system: Jupiter, Saturn, Uranus, and Neptune, and their various moons. After almost four decades of returning data to us, the spacecraft went on to its next assignment and left the solar system in 2013, becoming the first machine to do so. Now it's way, way out there—11.8 billion miles from Earth, to be exact— and still transmitting data to us. But there's of course a possibility that it may encounter intelligent life on its journey. So just in case, it carries some information about our own planet as well. The spacecraft has a gold-plated phonograph record (remember, it was launched before the DVD age) with greetings in 55 languages, photographs of Earth, and music by artists ranging from Mozart to Chuck Berry.

While Voyager 1 may have a chance encounter with other life forms, NASA's Kepler Mission is actively searching. This space observatory was launched on March 7, 2009, with the sole mission of discovering Earth-like planets. The spacecraft orbits the sun every 371 days, monitoring the brightness of 100,000 stars and looking for dips in intensity that could signify that a star is a sun with orbiting planets.

On April, 17, 2014, Kepler's telescope discovered a planet 500 light years away that could possibly sustain life. Named Kepler-186f, the planet orbits a star within what scientists call the "habitable zone"—neither too far from nor too close to its sun for life to exist. Kepler-186f is roughly the size of our planet and appears, like ours, to have a rocky surface. NASA hopes to find other comparable planets close enough to us that we can study their atmospheres.

Inviting Trouble

The search for extraterrestrial intelligence isn't without its critics. Making our presence known to other life forms would be "foolhardy," Stephen Hawking writes in *A Brief History of Time*. After all, human history has shown definitively that technologically superior civilizations are dangerous to less-advanced ones. If aliens landed on Earth, "The outcome would be much as when Christopher Columbus first landed in America," the renowned physicist said in 2010 on his cable series *Stephen Hawking's Universe*, "which didn't turn out very well for the Native Americans."

The Hat Creek Radio Observatory in Mountain View, California, is home to the Alien Telescope Array.

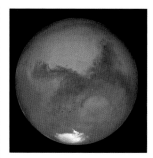

A clear view of Mars, taken from NASA's Hubble Space Telescope.

EARTHLINGS INVADE PLANET MARS!

The space-travel world is sure humans will end up on the Red Planet. The question is, how soon will we get there?

Depending on whom you believe, travel to Mars will be a reality two or three decades from now. A company called SpaceX claims that by 2026, it will be able to take volunteers to our neighboring planet to establish a permanent colony there. Many consider this plan optimistic—including NASA, which hopes to send humans to Mars about a decade later, by 2035. Another difference: NASA says its travelers will come back to Earth. Though eventually there would be "a sustained human presence on Mars," NASA chief scientist Ellen Stofan said in 2014, "We want it to be possible for those people to come back if they want to." Officials estimate that a trip to and from Mars, including time spent exploring, would take about 10 months.

SPYING ON OTHER BEINGS

A proposed mega-telescope could detect faraway civilizations without them detecting us.

Hey, aliens: We can see you.
Rather, maybe we could if we had a proposed 250-foot, $1 billion, massive mega-telescope that might be able to detect signs of life on planets up to 70 light years from Earth. Called Colossus, the scope would detect heat generated by alien civilizations. (This "alien heat" would be different from that of volcanoes and other natural sources, with a slightly higher radiation level.)

The best part:
Colossus could search for extraterrestrials without alerting them to our presence. The technology would have its limitations; the telescope would have a tough time detecting civilizations on cloud-covered planets, or on planets on which alien life is widely dispersed, as opposed to clustered in cities. But so far, this is all moot: Colossus has not been funded.

WHO KNEW?

Planets with seemingly habitable conditions are called "Goldilocks planets" because they are neither too hot nor too cold, but just right.

INDEX

A

abductions, alien, 254–255
Abominable Snowman, 208
Akashic Records, 17
Aksakov, Alexander, 28–29
Alcatraz, 168
alchemy, 228–229
Alexander the Great, 118–119
aliens
    abductions by, 254–255
    in Norse mythology, 106
    in popular culture, 248–249
    search for extraterrestrial
        intelligence, 258–259
Amityville, New York, 176–177
Ammons, Latoya, 175
Ancient Ram Inn, 164
Anderson, William R., 32–33
angels, 184–185
animal downpours, 230–231
animal intuitives, 20
animals, 20, 225. See also
    cryptozoology
anomalous luminous
        phenomena (ALPs),
        232–233
Area 51, 250–251
*Area 51: An Uncensored History
    of America's Top Secret
    Military Base* (Annie
    Jacobsen), 251
armies, disappearances of, 121
Arnold, Kenneth, 253
Arthur, King, 50–51
asteroid monitoring, 237
astrologers, 66–67
Atlantis, 16, 17, 92–93
augury, 48

B

Bambino, curse of the, 76–79
baseball, curses in, 76–79
Beck, Frank, 120
Bell Witch, 198
Bélmez faces, 239
Bermuda Triangle, 126–127
Bible, 2–3, 42–43, 63
Bigfoot, 208–209
Black Orlov (gem), 75

Bodhisattva, 184
Boleyn, Anne, 154, 158, 164, 165
books. *See* literature and books
Borely Rectory, 170–171
Boston Red Sox, 76–78
Bower, Doug, 111
Bowers, William H., 32, 33
Buddhism
    angels in, 184
    levitation in, 42
    reincarnation in, 190

C

Cadbury Castle, 51
calendar, Mayan, 63, 97
Carter, Howard, 72–73
castles, haunted, 164–165
cattle mutilation, 242–243
Cayce, Edgar, 16–17, 92
    Basic Cayce Diet, 16
Central Intelligence Agency
        (CIA), 252
Chambers mansion, 163
Champ (creature), 212–213
Chappaquiddick incident, 80
Chattox family, 198–199
Chicago Cubs, 79
Chichen Itza, 96–97
chiromancy, 56–57
Chorley, Dave, 111
Christianity
    angels in, 184
    levitation in, 42–43
    predictions of end of the
        world in, 3
    reincarnation in, 190
chupacabra, 214
CIA (Central Intelligence
        Agency), 252
clairvoyance, 25, 26, 31
Cold War
    fear of UFOs in, 251–253
    psychic weapons in, 30–31
Colossus mega-telescope, 259
covert missions, 252, 253
Crandon, Mina "Margery," 12
craters, 237
Crawfordsville, Indiana, 240
crop circles, 110–111

"Crossroad Blues," 82–83
Crowley, Aleister, 136, 137,
        182–183
cryptids, 204–207
cryptozoology, 204–225
    Bigfoot, 208–209
    dragons, 224–225
    kraken, 216–219
    Loch Ness monster, 220–221
    Mothman, 210–211
    in North America, 212–215
    yeti, 208–209
crystal balls, 64–65
crystals, 65
curse(s), 72–83
    Hope Diamond, 74–75
    Kennedy family, 80–81
    on movie casts, 173
    on musicians/songs, 82–83
    in sports, 76–79
    on tombs, 72–73

D

Dalai Lama (Tenzin Gyatso),
        191
Dare Stones, 117
death
    life after, 192–193
    predictions of one's own, 61
Death Valley, 108–109
decapitation, 98–99
déjà rêve, 60–61
déjà vu, 68–69
Demdike family, 198–199
demonolatry, 182
demonology, 182
demons
    deals with, 180–181
    exorcism of, 174–177
    Jersey Devil, 214–215
    Zozo, 15
dice, rolling, 48
dingiso, 207
divination. *See* predicting the
        future
dragons, 224–225
dreams, visions in, 60–61
dybbuks, 187

E

Earhart, Amelia, 122–125
Easter Island moai, 100–103
Eastern European folklore,
        141–143
electromagnetic interference,
        235
end of the world, 3, 62–63
energy grid, psychic, 104–107
enlightenment, 42–43
epilepsy, 68, 174
ESP (extra-sensory perception),
        25–27
exorcisms, 174–177
extraterrestrial intelligence,
        258–259
Eye of Brahma Diamond, 75
eyewitnesses, UFO, 246–247

F

false prophets, 2–3
Fata Morgana, 129
Federal Aviation
        Administration,
        256–257
female werewolf characters, 151
feng shui, 58–59
financial astrologers, 66–67
firestarters, 44–45
fish, raining, 230–231
flesh-eating plants, 222–223
flights, disappearances of,
        124–125
Flying Dutchman, 129
flying rods, 240–241
football, curses in, 78
Forer Effect, 57
Fox, Maggie and Kate, 6–7
Franklin Castle, 160–161
Freemasons, 136
Freud, Sigmund, 35

G

Gallipoli, Turkey, 120–121
Geller, Uri, 38–39
George, Saint, 225
ghost hunting, 170–171, 176–177

ghosts, 156–177
    in China, 166–167
    cultural beliefs about,
        156–157
    and exorcisms, 174–175
    getting rid of, 161
    historical perspectives on,
        158–159
    in India, 167
    in Japan, 166–167
    poltergeists, 172–173
    types of, 170
ghost ships, 128–129
ghost stories, 159
giant squid, 207, 216–219
Glastonbury Tor, 106–107
golems, 186–187
Great Beast, 182–183
Great Pyramids, 86–87
Great Sphinx, 88–89
Greece, ancient, 118–119, 182
Grimoire, 200–201
Grotto of Massabielle, 94–95
Gyatso, Tenzin (Dalai Lama),
        191

H

haruspices, 48–49
haunted houses, 160–163
hauntings
    in parapsychology, 25
    in public places, 162,
        168–169
    in U.K., 164–165
    in U.S., 160–163
Hawes, Jason, 171
healing
    by Edgar Cayce, 16–17
    psychic surgery, 36–37
    by water at Lourdes, 94–95
Hill, Betty and Barney, 254–255
Hindu astrology, 67
Hinduism
    angels in, 184
    levitation in, 42
    reincarnation in, 190
holistic medicine, 16–17
Holy Grail, 51
Hongyi Qiu, 40–41
Hope Diamond, 74–75
hotels, haunted, 169
Houck, Jack, 38
Houdini, Harry, 10–13
Hum, 234–235

human images, on objects,
        238–239
hypertrichosis, 153
hypnosis, 28, 194–195, 254–255

I

Iceman, curse of, 73
I Ching, 52–53
ideomotor effect, 14
India, 67, 167
inns, haunted, 164–165
INSCOM (United States
        Army Intelligence and
        Security Command), 39
internet, zombie stories on,
        148–149
intuitives, 20, 66–67
Isla de Las Munecas, 169
Islam, 184
Island of the Dolls, 169

J

Jack the Ripper, 18
Jainism, 42
Japan
    cursed song in, 82
    ghosts in, 166–167
Jersey Devil, 214–215
Jesus, 43, 180, 238–239
jinns, 166
Judaism
    angels in, 184
    golems in, 186–187
    pulsa denura in, 73
Julia Set, 111
Jung, Carl, 34–35

K

Kazhinsky, Bernard, 32
Kennedy family curse, 80–81
Kinnitty Castle, 165
Komodo dragon, 207, 225
Kopechne, Mary Jo, 80
kraken, 216–219
Kübler-Ross, Elisabeth, 192
Kukulkan, 96–97
Kulagina, Nina, 29

L

Lajamanu, Australia, 230–231
Lake Champlain creature
        (Champ), 212–213
Lalaurie, Louis and Delphine,
        162–163
La Pava, 239
levitation, 42–43
ley lines, 105–107
life after death, 192–193
Lincoln, Mary Todd, 7
literature and books
    alchemy in, 229
    déjà vu in, 69
    dragons in, 224
    vampires in, 144–145
    werewolves in, 151
Little Shop of Horrors, 223
livestock mutilations, 242–243
Loch Ness monster, 220–221
Lorenz, Ralph, 109
lots, casting, 48, 52–53
Lourdes, France, 94–95
Lugosi, Bela, 145, 150
lumokinesis, 40

M

MacLaine, Shirley, 195
Madden, John, 78
Mapimí Silent Zone, 234
Marfa mystery lights, 232–233
Mars, travel to, 259
Mary, Virgin, shrine to, 94–95
Mary Celeste, 128–129
mass hysteria, 180
Mayan calendar, 63, 97
Mayan pyramids, 96–97
McLean, Evalyn Walsh, 75
McMenamin, Mark, 219
mediums
    Harry Houdini's debunking
        of, 10–13
    19th century, 6–7
    Ouija boards for, 14–15
    in parapsychology, 25
Melon Heads, 215
memories, recovered, 255
memory, errors in, 68–69
meteorite strikes, 237
Michel, Anneliese, 174–175
Middle Ages, 152, 158, 241
mind control, 31
moai, 100–103
Moody, Raymond, 193

Mothman, 210–211
movies
    aliens in, 248–249, 255
    Ouija boards in, 15
    Roswell incident in, 250
    vampires in, 144–145
    werewolves in, 150–151
    zombies in, 149
Moya, Alfred, 148
mummies, 87
musicians, 83, 183
Myrtles Plantation, 161
mythology
    aliens in, 106
    angels and flying deities
        in, 185
    dragons in, 224
    werewolves in, 150
"My Way," 82

N

Narcisse, Clairvius, 147
National Radio Quiet Zone,
        235
Nautilus, U.S.S., 32–33
Navy of Alexander the Great,
        118–119
navies, disappearance of,
        118-119
Nazca heads, 98–99
Nazis, yeti hunting by, 208
near-death experiences
        (NDEs), 190–195
    belief in reincarnation,
        190–191
    in parapsychology, 25
    past life regression, 194–195
    and proof of life after death,
        192–193
Nepenthes, 222–223
Nessie, 220–221
New Age movement, 35
Newgrange, 90–91
new moon ritual, 201
New Orleans, Louisiana,
        162–163
New York Giants, 79
New York Yankees, 77–78
Nicholas II, Tsar of Russia, 28
Noonan, Fred, 123–125
Norfolk Island, 168–169
North America, cryptozoology
        in, 212–215
Nostradamus, 4–5, 64

O

O'Hare International Airport,
226–257
okapi, 207
Old New Synagogue, 187
ooscopy, 48, 49
Opus Dei, 136, 137
Ordo Templi Orientis, 136–137
Ötzi, curse of, 73
Ouija boards, 14–15
out-of-body experiences, 25
Owlman, 211

P

palmistry, 56–57
parapsychology, 24–45
    Carl Jung's interest in, 34–35
    and Cold War, 30–31
    firestarters, 44–45
    history of, 24–25
    J.B. Rhine's interest in, 26–27
    psychic surgery, 36–37
    qigong, 40–41
    Russian interest in, 28–29
    spoonbending, 38–39
    superpowers in religious
        texts, 42–43
    telepathy with U.S.S.
        Nautilus, 32–33
pareidolia, 238–239
past lives, 190, 194–195
Pattinson, Robert, 145
Pearce, Hubert, 26
Pendle witch trials, 198–199
Perron, Carolyn and Roger, 176
Peru, 98–99
Philadelphia Phillies, 79
Philosopher's Stone, 228–229
physicians, psychic, 36–37
pitcher plants, 222–223
plants, flesh-eating, 222–223
platypus, 207
Point Pleasant, West Virginia,
    210–211
Poltergeist (film), 173
Poltergeists, 172–173
popular culture
    alchemy in, 229
    aliens in, 248–249, 255
    déjà vu in, 69
    dragons in, 224
    Ouija boards in, 15
    Roswell incident in, 250
    vampires in, 144–145

werewolves in, 150–151
witches in, 200
zombies in, 148–149
Poveglia Island, 169
precognition, 25, 26
precognitive dreaming, 60–61
predicting the future, 48–69.
    See also psychics
    about end of the world,
        62–63
    ancient Rome, 48–49
    chiromancy, 56–57
    déjà vu, 68–69
    in dreams, 60–61
    feng shui, 58–59
    I Ching, 52–53
    intuitives and astrologers,
        66–67
    King Arthur, 50–51
    scrying, 64–65
    tarot cards, 54–55
Price, Harry, 170–171
prophesies, 2, 4–5
prophets, 2–5
Psi, 25, 26
psychic detectives, 18–19
psychic energy grid, 104–107
psychics
    Biblical seers, 2–3
    corporate, 66–67
    Edgar Cayce, 16–17
    modern, 8–9
    Nostradamus, 4–5
    pet, 20–21
psychic surgery, 36–37
psychic warfare, 30–31
psychokinesis, 25, 26, 38–39
public spaces, hauntings in,
    168–169
Pulsa denura, 73
pyramids, ,
    Egyptian 86–87, 106
    Mayan, 96–97
pyrokinesis, 40, 44–45

Q

Qigong, 40–41
Quetzalcoatl, 96

R

rabies, 143
Racetrack Playa, 109
Ramsey, Bill, 177
Rapa Nui, 102, 103
Rapture, 3
Rasputin, 28, 29
recessions, 66–67
recovered memory syndrome,
    255
red tide, 223
reincarnation, 25, 69, 190–191
religions. See also specific
        religions
    dragons in, 224
    reincarnation in, 190–191
    superpowers in, 42–43
religious beings, 180–187
    angels, 184–185
    demons, 180–181
    golems, 186–187
    Great Beast, 182–183
religious figures, images of,
    238–239
remote viewing, 31
Rhine, J.B., 26–27
Roanoke Island colony, 114–117
Rome, ancient, 48–49
Rosicrucians, 135, 136
Roswell, New Mexico, 250–251
Russia. See also Soviet Union
    telekinesis and ESP in,
        28–29
    Tunguska event, 236–237
    UFOs in, 252
Ruth, Babe, 76–78

S

sailing stones, 108–109
Sandringham Company,
    120–121
Sasquatch, 208–209
Satan, 180–181, 225
scientific discoveries, by
        alchemists, 229
scrying, 64–65
secret societies, 132–137
    Freemasons, 136
    Opus Dei, 135–137
    Ordo Templi Orientis,
        136–137
    Rosicrucians, 135, 136
Sedona, Arizona, 104–105
seers, 2–3, 48–49

Shakespeare, William, 159
SHC (spontaneous human
        combustion), 44–45
ships, ghost, 128–129
Shroud of Turin, 238–239
Siddhasana, 43
Skirrid Mountain Inn, 164–165
Skunk Ape, 215
Smurl, Jack and Janet, 172
songs, cursed, 82–83
sortilege, 48
Soubirous, Bernadette, 94–95
sound travel, anomalous,
    234–235
Soviet Union. See also Russia
    parapsychology in Cold
        War effort, 30–31
    psychic weapons research,
        33
    UFO sightings in, 252–253
spell casting, 201
Sphinx, Great, 88–89
spirit photography, 7
spiritualism
    Carl Jung's belief in, 34–35
    Harry Houdini's debunking
        of, 11–12
    in 19th century, 6–7
    Russian interest in, 28–29
spontaneous human
        combustion (SHC),
        44–45
spoonbending, 38–39
sports, curses in, 76–79
spot-bellied eagle owl, 207
Stargate Project, 31
Star Trek (television series), 248
Star Wars (film), 248–249
superpowers, 42–43
    Russian, 28–29
Surgery, psychic, 36–37

T

Tabitha (cat), 20
tarot cards, 54–55
telekinesis, 25, 28–29
telepathy
    with animals, 20
    in parapsychology, 25, 26
    with U.S.S. Nautilus, 32–33
television series
    aliens in, 248, 249
    werewolves in, 151
    witches in, 200

Tesla, Nikola, 236–237
Thelema, 136182–183
tombs, cursed, 72–73
tourism, for haunted places, 164
Tower of London, 164–165
Transfiguration, 228–229
triremes, 119
Triskele, 90
true prophets, 3
Tuen Mun Road, 168
Tulloch Castle Hotel, 165
Tunguska event, 236–237
Tutankhamen, 72–73
27 Club, 83

U

UFOs (Unidentified Flying
    Objects)
    eyewitnesses of, 246–247
    fears during Cold War
        about, 252–253
    incident in Roswell, New
        Mexico, 250–251
    at O'Hare International
        Airport, 256–257
United Airlines, 257

United Kingdom
    haunted inns and castles of,
        164–165
    Owlman in, 211
    Pendle witch trials, 198–199
United States
    haunted houses in, 160–163
    parapsychology in Cold
        War effort, 30–31
    UFO sightings in, 246–247,
        250–251, 252–253
United States Army
    Intelligence and
    Security Command
    (INSCOM), 39
Universities, haunted, 163

V

vampire bats, 141
vampires
    historical basis for, 141–143
    in popular culture, 144–145
vanishings, 114–129
    Alexander the Great's navy,
        118–119

Amelia Earhart, 122–125
    in Bermuda Triangle,
        126–127
    ghost ships, 128–129
    Roanoke Island colony,
        114–117
    Sandringham Company at
        Gallipoli, 120–121
Van Tilburg, Jo Anne, 102
Vedic astrology, 67
Vikings, 106
Virgin Mary, shrine to, 94–95
virus, zombie, 148
Visconti tarot deck, 55
visions, in dreams, 60–61
voodoo, 146–147

W

Warren, Edward and Lorraine,
    176–177
water beasts, 216-221
water with healing powers,
    94–95
Watkins, Albert, 105, 106
Weiss, Brian, 195
Wendigo, 215

werewolves
    female werewolf
        characters, 151
    in myths and popular
        culture, 150–151
    persecution of, 152
Wiccans, 200–201
Wilson, Grant, 171
witches, 198–201
    modern Wiccans, 200–201
    Pendle witch trials, 198–199
world, end of the, 3, 62–63

Y

Yeti, 208–209
yin and yang, 40, 52

Z

Zener Cards, 27
Zhou Ting-Jue, 40
zombies, 146–149
zombie virus, 148
Zozo, 15

PHOTO CREDITS

TIME HOME ENTERTAINMENT

Publisher Jim Childs
Vice President and Associate Publisher Margot Schupf
Vice President, Finance Vandana Patel
Executive Director, Marketing Services Carol Pittard
Executive Director, Business Development Suzanne Albert
Executive Director, Marketing Susan Hettleman
Publishing Director Megan Pearlman
Associate Director of Publicity Courtney Greenhalgh
Assistant General Counsel Simone Procas
Assistant Director, Special Sales Ilene Schreider
Senior Marketing Manager, Sales Marketing Danielle Costa
Associate Production Manager Kimberly Marshall
Associate Prepress Manager Alex Voznesenskiy
Associate Project Manager Stephanie Braga

Editorial Director Stephen Koepp
Senior Editor Roe D'Angelo
Project Editors Eileen Daspin, Lauren Lipton
Editors Jonathan White, Katie McHugh Malm
Copy Chief Rina Bander
Design Manager Anne-Michelle Gallero
Editorial Operations Gina Scauzillo
Editorial Assistant Courtney Mifsud

Special thanks: Katherine Barnet, Brad Beatson, Jeremy Biloon, Susan Chodakiewicz, Rose Cirrincione, Assu Etsubneh, Mariana Evans, Christine Font, Hillary Hirsch, David Kahn, Jean Kennedy, Amy Mangus, Nina Mistry, Dave Rozzelle, Matthew Ryan, Ricardo Santiago, Divyam Shrivastava, Adriana Tierno

Produced by The Stonesong Press, LLC
Project Director Ellen Scordato
Project Editorial Director Laura Ross
Writers Kerry Acker, Walter Bonner, Bree Burns, Jennifer Foley, Constance Jones, Lauren Lipton, Nancy Shore, Jon Sterngass
Photo Researchers Jane Martin, The Photo Editor, Inc., Washington D.C.
Designed by Vertigo Design NYC
Art Director Alison Lew
Designers Gary Philo, Lisa Story